Searching for Yellowstone

Ecology and Wonder in the Last Wilderness

Paul Schullery

MONTANA HISTORICAL SOCIETY PRESS

Helena, Montana

AUTHOR'S NOTE

I have been an employee of the National Park Service for about twelve of the past twenty-five years, but I must make clear that in this book I do not represent the park service either formally or informally. In January 1996, after working full time at Yellowstone for several years, I became a part-time employee so that I could pursue my own writing projects. In researching this book I have used no information that is not available to any other writer; my sources are given in the notes. Interested researchers should know that the informational resources of Yellowstone are as great as its natural resources; I especially recommend the great wealth of material in the Yellowstone Library, Archives, and Museum Collection at park headquarters in Mammoth Hot Springs.

Printed by Edwards Brothers, Ann Arbor, Michigan

For information about permission to reproduce selections from this book, write to Permissions, Montana Historical Society Press, P.O. Box 201201, Helena, Montana 59620-1201

Distributed by the Globe Pequot Press, 246 Goose Lane, Guilford, Connecticut 06437, (800) 243-0495

      07 08 09 10   11 10 9 8 7 6 5 4 3 2

ISBN 0-9721522-1-0

Library of Congress Cataloging-in-Publication Data
Schullery, Paul.
    Searching for Yellowstone : ecology and wonder in the last wilderness / Paul Schullery.
      p. cm.
    Previous ed.: Boston : Houghton Mifflin, 1997.
    Includes index.

    ISBN 0-9721522-1-0 (pbk. : alk. paper)

    1. Yellowstone National Park—History. 2. Yellowstone National Park—Description and travel. 3. Natural history—Yellowstone National Park. 4. Yellowstone National Park—Environmental conditions. 5. Ecology—Yellowstone National Park. I. Title.

F722.S378 2004
978.7'52—dc22

                  2003027806

For Starker, Graeme, and Mollie:
the search is not the same without you.

CONTENTS

Illustrations

The outstanding scientific discovery of the twentieth century is not television, or radio, but rather the complexity of the land organism.

— Aldo Leopold, *Round River*, 1953

The earth is a gambler. She has a real lust for rolling the evolutionary dice. Too, whatever gods there are have a keen and rather slapstick sense of humor.

— Harry Middleton, *The Earth Is Enough*, 1989

I am now ready for the Yellowstone Park, and look forward to the trip with intense pleasure.

— General William Strong, *A Trip to the Yellowstone National Park*, 1876

SEARCHING FOR YELLOWSTONE

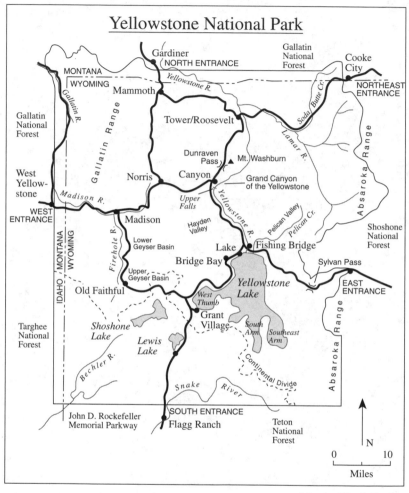

Yellowstone National Park

MONTANA
WYOMING

Gallatin
National
Forest

West
Yellow-
stone

Gallatin
National
Forest

Gallatin R.

Gallatin Range

Madison R.

WEST
ENTRANCE

IDAHO | MONTANA
WYOMING

Firehole R.

Gardiner
NORTH ENTRANCE

Yellowstone R.

Mammoth

Tower/Roosevelt

Norris

Madison

Canyon

Dunraven
Pass

▲ Mt. Washburn

Upper
Falls

Hayden
Valley

Lower
Geyser Basin

Upper
Geyser Basin

Old Faithful

Shoshone
Lake

Lewis
Lake

Bechler R.

Targhee
National
Forest

Gallatin
National
Forest

Cooke
City

**NORTHEAST
ENTRANCE**

Soda Butte Cr.

Lamar R.

Grand Canyon
of the Yellowstone

Yellowstone R.

Pelican Valley

Pelican Cr.

Lake

Fishing Bridge

Bridge Bay

West
Thumb

Grant
Village

Yellowstone
Lake

South
Arm

Southeast
Arm

Continental Divide

Snake River

Absaroka Range

Shoshone
National
Forest

Sylvan Pass

EAST
ENTRANCE

Absaroka Range

John D. Rockefeller
Memorial Parkway

SOUTH ENTRANCE
Flagg Ranch

Teton
National
Forest

N

0   10

Miles

Map by Wendy Baylor

PREFACE TO
THE NEW EDITION

I AM DELIGHTED and honored that the Montana Historical Society is publishing this new edition of *Searching for Yellowstone*, and I welcome the opportunity to make some additions and corrections. In the few years since the book was first published, the search for the park's history has advanced in interesting ways.

First, new interpretations and research have modified our understanding of some historical points mentioned in the first edition.

Yellowstone's famous and rapidly deteriorating wickiups, remnants of Native American shelters that I said were attributed to the work of Crow Indians (p. 26), have more recently been credited to the Sheepeater Shoshone instead.[1] These structures were once widely scattered through what is now the park and surrounding area, and though I readily defer to the experts on these new interpretations, it should remain open to question if all these mysterious structures were made by the same group of people.

My consideration of the folklore of Yellowstone's "creation myth" (pp. 56–63) has been improved upon in a detailed study just completed by Yellowstone's Park Historian Lee Whittlesey and me, titled *Myth and History in the Creation of Yellowstone National Park*.[2] The man most responsible for originating the myth, Nathaniel Langford, and the man who most energetically promoted it among the conservation community and the public, Horace Albright, both need considerably more attention from historians.

---

1. Peter Nabokov and Lawrence Loendorf, *American Indians and Yellowstone National Park: A Documentary Overview* (Yellowstone National Park: Yellowstone Center for Resources, 2002), 146–47. This thoroughly documented review of archeological and ethnographic information on Yellowstone's Indians is by far the most complete such work ever attempted for the park; it is fascinating, and required reading for park historians. The authors are preparing a book based on it.
2. Paul Schullery and Lee Whittlesey, *Myth and History in the Creation of Yellowstone National Park* (Lincoln: University of Nebraska Press, 2003).

The overview of the reported elk slaughter of 1875 (pp. 72–73) confused a couple friends I know to be careful readers, so I should clarify one detail. I pointed out that contemporary reports seem to give a total of at least 8,000 elk killed that year (p. 72), but in the following paragraphs I intended to make it clear that such a high number was not only impossible to confirm but also unlikely. Lots of elk were killed—thousands, I assume—but 8,000 seems mighty high, just given the ecological realities of how many elk the area could even support.

The history of aspen on the park's northern range (pp. 228–29) can be reconsidered in light of additional tree-ring studies. This new work suggests that what seemed to be a brief period of aspen escapement from browsing in the late 1800s may not have been so distinctively short-term a feature of the landscape. In their 2002 review of the research on northern range topics, the National Academy of Sciences Committee on Ungulate Management in Yellowstone National Park were persuaded by new studies that suggest that in fact aspen may have been thriving throughout the nineteenth century and earlier.[3]

My discussion of the well-known twentieth-century decline of willow on the northern range (pp. 229–30) has had a new and vastly stimulating chapter added to it. Not long after the first edition of this book was published, several stands of willow in the Lamar Valley, though seemingly as vulnerable to elk browsing as ever, have returned to much higher stature, something that critics of park policy long maintained was impossible in the presence of so many elk.[4]

Among the theories for this change is that the new wolves are

3. David R. Klein, Dale R. McCullough, Barbara Allen-Diaz, Norman Cheville, Russell W. Graham, John E. Gross, James McMahon, Nancy E. Mathews, Duncan T. Patten, Katherine Ralls, Monica G. Turner, and Elizabeth S. Williams, *Ecological Dynamics on Yellowstone's Northern Range* (Washington, D.C.: National Academy Press, 2002), 58–59. We are a long way from understanding the historical nuances of Yellowstone aspen history. The relationships among late nineteenth-century elk slaughters, human-caused fluctuations in beaver populations in the nineteenth and early twentieth centuries, climatic variation (including the end of the Little Ice Age in the late nineteenth century and the famous drought of the 1930s), fire management practices by Native Americans and whites, predator destruction in the late nineteenth and early twentieth centuries, and probably other factors are extremely complex. I realize that quite a few people consider the aspen a straightforward historical story, but they are wrong. There is a lot of work to do here.

4. D. W. Smith, R. O. Peterson, and D. B. Houston, "Yellowstone after Wolves," *BioScience* 53, no. 4 (April 2003): 330–40.

influencing how elk occupy and use the valley, and limiting their access to the willow.[5] As comforting as that theory may be to pro-wolf advocates (and I am one), it sounds a little too easy a theoretical fix to me, as if we have gone from one overconfidence to another. Some really smart people think that wolves are at least a factor in the changes in willow, though, and the idea does have a satisfying plausibility.

I am also pleased to update some information I gave about the discovery of new waterfalls in Yellowstone (p. 248). At the time I completed the manuscript of *Searching for Yellowstone*, Paul Rubinstein, Lee Whittlesey, and Mike Stevens were nearing completion of the manuscript of their own book on the park's waterfalls and had identified about 130 waterfalls. But by the time their book was published, they were able to report not 130 but about 290 waterfalls. That 200 of these were essentially unreported in the previous (and enormous) literature of Yellowstone travel and science is a remarkable testament to the ability of Yellowstone to keep its obscure corners to itself, and to the ability of adventurous individuals to seek out and celebrate those corners.[6]

UPDATES

Yellowstone's joys and controversies roll on. Among the joys, many millions of visitors have come here since my book was published, and they seem to be having as big a time as ever.

---

5. W. J. Ripple and E. J. Larsen, "Historic Aspen Recruitment, Elk, and Wolves in Northern Yellowstone National Park," *Biological Conservation* 95, no. 3 (2000): 361–70; W. J. Ripple, E. J. Larsen, R. A. Renkin, and D. W. Smith, "Trophic Cascades among Wolves, Elk and Aspen on Yellowstone National Park's Northern Range," *Biological Conservation* 102 (2001): 227–34.

6. Paul Rubinstein, Lee H. Whittlesey, and Mike Stevens, *The Guide to Yellowstone Waterfalls and Their Discovery* (Englewood, Colo.; Westcliffe Publishers, 2000). Though this book is in fact about waterfalls, and is a beautiful celebration of them, it is also, perhaps more than any other natural-resource guidebook ever published about Yellowstone, a serious work of history. The authors have spent many years tracing the discovery, mapping, literary careers, and name origins of the waterfalls, and their accounts of the individual waterfalls are rich in local history and lore.

The book also initiated an especially interesting debate—a heated little example of the complexities of the ongoing search for Yellowstone—over whether or not such "secret" wonders should be exposed and chronicled so precisely. Some critics of the book have objected, angrily and even eloquently, that it's better to leave such things unpublicized so that future visitors can make their own discoveries. The authors address this question with considerable sympathy and thoughtfulness on pages 23–24; their views have occasionally been attacked (and misrepresented), so if you are curious about this matter, or have strong feelings on the subject, you ought to start by reading and understanding the intentions of the authors.

Among the controversies, the perennial favorites—such as man-agement of bison and grizzly bears, winter use planning, bio-prospecting, fire management, and wolf recovery—are occasionally joined by this or that other hot topic, including the abrupt reversals of national conservation policy direction initiated by the Bush Administration since 2001. A preface lacks space to deal with all these matters, but wolf recovery might serve as representative of the excite-ment that continues over Yellowstone management issues.

The wolves have thrived, not only making plenty of new wolves but also making large numbers of friends for themselves and the park.[7] The unfortunate cutting off of funding for additional translo-cation of Canadian wolves to Yellowstone after the first two seasons failed in its apparent attempt to cause wolf recovery to fail. Wolves are now abundant in appropriate habitats in the park and nearby, and, though some people in the region still oppose their presence, the wolves have become a well-loved and, for many people, essential ele-ment of the wild Yellowstone landscape.

Wolf recovery has had a profound effect on another perennial Yellowstone controversy, over the condition of Yellowstone's northern range. As I discussed at considerable length in the first edi-tion, a supposed overpopulation of elk was long thought to be caus-ing grave harm to the park's vegetation communities. The major review of northern range research completed by the National Acad-emy of Sciences in 2002, mentioned earlier, greatly advanced the scholarly conversation in this controversy. In a remarkable break from the widespread scientific opinion of only two decades ago. the NAS committee pronounced the park's grasslands to be healthy. They continued to uphold more traditional views as far as woody vegetation, seeing those species as sometime victims of overintensive use by elk, but withheld any final judgments on that matter because wolf recovery needed time to play out its effects on the whole wild system before anybody dared decide that something had gone irreparably wrong (not that there is even yet much agreement over what "wrong" might mean).[8] In a less than ringing endorsement of

---

7. Smith, Peterson, and Houston, "Yellowstone after Wolves."
8. Klein et al., *Ecological Dynamics on Yellowstone's Northern Range*, 134.

any management approach, the NAS committee concluded that the park's famous and often-attacked "natural regulation" policy was as likely as any other approach to work.[9]

The apparent effects of this NAS report, particularly the revelation that hard-line livestock grazing standards really didn't work for evaluating Yellowstone's wildlands, were impressive. It wasn't just that the more or less constant cries and complaints of "overgrazing" in the park have almost disappeared from most public dialogues. It is what replaced that outcry that makes the change so entertaining. As wolf recovery has proceeded since 1995, there has appeared a new view of what is wrong with Yellowstone. As predicted in many scientific works and management documents leading up to 1995 (and as was intuitively obvious), the wolves like to eat elk, and elk numbers have declined. Almost overnight, attacks on National Park Service management policy literally reversed themselves. The perpetual claims of "too many elk" were replaced by perhaps even more shrill cries of "too few elk."[10]

It was an amazing change, demonstrating the rhetorical agility of park critics, the swiftness with which new constituencies can form and express themselves, and the perpetual viability of park policy as a moving target. As for the ultimate rightness or wrongness of judging any single wildlife population as too large or too small in Yellowstone, it does seem that most people still see the park's ecological system in such quantifiable terms, rather than in the broader

9. Their wording, on page 134 of *Ecological Dynamics on Yellowstone's Northern Range*, was: "YNP's practice of intervening as little as possible is as likely to lead to the maintenance of the northern range ecosystem and its major components as any other practice. If the park decides that it needs to intervene to enhance declining species like aspen, the smaller the intervention, the less likely it is to do unintended damage." The committee, though clearly rejecting some specific scientific interpretations favored by park leadership (such as those related to climate and aspen), seemed to favor keeping human manipulation of the setting to a minimum whenever possible, certainly a departure from management approaches favored by many park critics, who continued to call for wholesale reductions of the elk and possibly other species.

10. For two popularly written reports on this new controversy, see Jim Robbins, "More Wolves, and New Questions, in Rockies," *New York Times*, Dec. 17, 2002; and B. A. Christianson, "Rebuttal Offered to Fanning's 'Yellowstone's Dying,'" *Gardiner Howler*, Aug. 7, 2002. A Gardiner, Montana, resident tells me that one of the local businesses that takes an active role in these public debates illlustrated this abrupt change in local sentiment. He says that one day there was a petition on the sales counter asking for signatures objecting to the elk overpopulation, and the next day there was a petition objecting to the disappearance of the elk population.

terms of a system in which variability itself is the central ingredient of survival.

OMISSIONS

The reviews of *Searching for Yellowstone* were kind, even generous, and I was grateful for the approval, and for the confirmation that the book's ideas had some value in understanding where the park fits in our world. Actually, I think that I might have had a longer list of criticisms of my book than did any of the reviewers. There were some topics that I have always felt weren't adequately covered.

The book is subtitled "ecology and wonder in the last wilderness," but I think I gave much more attention to the ecology than to the wonder. For practical reasons, I tended to concentrate on the factual end of things, rather than on emotional, spiritual, and aesthetic elements of the story. With an additional fifty or so pages interspersed here and there in the text, it would have been satisfying to consider more deeply how Yellowstone does work on our aesthetic sensitivity and spirituality; how religious values are reflected or affected by the experience of Yellowstone; and how a variety of scholars have attempted to make sense of important questions about human response to wild nature and the shared experience of it.[11]

Also, like too many historians I have tended, if inadvertently, to treat Native Americans as a group of people whose experience and opinions of Yellowstone rather ceased to matter when white people took over the land. There is no doubt about it; in many ways that is precisely what happened. But what that takeover meant to Native American society, and what lingered in the way of an important Native American presence in Yellowstone, has always deserved much more of our attention than we have given it. In this, my approach to

---

11. For more on this topic, especially as it applied to visitor responses to Yellowstone National Park's wonders before 1930, I recommend Judith Meyer's *The Spirit of Yellowstone* (Lanham, Md.: Rowman & Littlefield, 1996) as a stimulating organization of the types of responses to the various types of park features. When I reread this book in preparation for using it in a course on Yellowstone history that I taught at Montana State University in early 2003, I was newly impressed with its insights, and puzzled why I didn't make much more use of it in *Searching for Yellowstone*. Of course the activation of public interest in Native American roles in Yellowstone has likewise enriched the conversation over Yellowstone's spiritual values.

writing *Searching for Yellowstone* was too much that of the administrative historian rather than the cultural historian. As I have emphasized in other forums, the disenfranchisement of the Native American from Yellowstone was never as complete as most people may have imagined, and the reenfranchisement of them into modern management dialogues has been one of the healthiest signs of the park's vitality as an institution.[12]

ADDITIONS

Last, I am pleasantly surprised by the steady stream of fine new books on the history of Yellowstone. I realize that books are only the beginning of any such study; Yellowstone inspires and requires a steady flood of periodical publication in many disciplines as well. But these new books are a good start, and their reference lists and notes will lead you to vast amounts of other material.

For a penetrating account of the development of natural resource policy in Yellowstone, read James Pritchard's *Preserving Yellowstone's Natural Conditions*, a scholarly milestone that chronicles the mix of politics, emotion, aesthetics, and economics that have shaped those policies. For a terrific study of comparative photographs that show the often striking ecological changes in Yellowstone's landscape in the historical period, see Mary Meagher and Douglas Houston's handsomely produced *Yellowstone and the Biology of Time*. The commentary following the photographic analysis in this book would have been worth publication as a book by itself. Mary Meagher and Douglas Houston were conducting ecological history and environmental history studies in Yellowstone before those two disciplines fairly even had named themselves. For a fresh view of southern Yellowstone and northern Jackson Hole, see Kenneth and Lenore Diem's *A Community of Scalawags, Renegades, Discharged Soldiers and Predestined Stinkers?: A History of Northern Jackson Hole and Yellowstone's Influence, 1872–1929*. For a lively and lavishly illustrated history of artistic interpretations of Yellowstone,

---

12. For a conversational and, we hope, entertaining inquiry into the dilemmas faced by modern society in determining the place of Native Americans in national parks, see John D. Varley and Paul Schullery, "The Yellowstone Genetic Reservoir," *The George Wright Forum* 17, no. 2 (2000): 4–12.

see Peter Hassrick's *Drawn to Yellowstone: Artists in America's First National Park*.[13]

Those few titles are barely representative of the recent historical work that has been done. I could happily name many other favorite recent Yellowstone books, and I have even read a few that I think are less good (there are only a couple that I think are real dogs). But all of them make the point that historians have discovered, as never before, the exciting research opportunities in the search for Yellowstone.[14] Readers seem more eager than ever before to share in that wonderful journey of discovery.

PAUL SCHULLERY
Yellowstone

13. The titles I mention in this paragraph are as follows: James Pritchard, *Preserving Yellowstone's Natural Conditions* (Lincoln: University of Nebraska Press, 1999); Mary Meagher and Douglas Houston, *Yellowstone and the Biology of Time: Photographs across a Century of Time* (Norman: University of Oklahoma Press, 1998); Kenneth Diem and Lenore Diem, *A Community of Scalawags, Renegades, Discharged Soldiers and Predestined Stinkers?: A History of Northern Jackson Hole and Yellowstone's Influence, 1872–1929.*(Moose, Wyo.: Grand Teton Natural History Association and the University of Wyoming Research Center, 1998); and Peter Hassrick, *Drawn to Yellowstone: Artists in America's First National Park* (Los Angeles: Autry Museum of Western Heritage and University of Washington Press, 2002).

14. Whatever your field of interest, you should also be aware of the proceedings of the series of conferences sponsored by the National Park Service since 1991 on the Greater Yellowstone Ecosystem. These proceedings, along with the more than ten-year run of *Yellowstone Science*, the park's quarterly natural and cultural resources magazine, constitute a kind of mother lode of current information on park studies.

INTRODUCTION:
ESTABLISHING YELLOWSTONE

IN 1965 MICROBIOLOGIST Thomas Brock identified a new organism, a microscopic bacterium that lived in the 160-degree-plus waters of Mushroom Pool, a little-known thermal feature in the Lower Geyser Basin of Yellowstone National Park. From *Thermus aquaticus*, or Taq for short, other biologists extracted an enzyme known as Taq polymerase, which California biochemist Kary Mullis used to develop a gene-replicating procedure known as polymerase chain reaction, or PCR.

If this sounds a trifle off the subject for a book of history, consider that in 1993 Mullis was awarded the Nobel Prize for his work, and that PCR, which one biologist has called the "Swiss army knife of molecular biology," has changed our world.[1] Consider that because of PCR, we now have the entire discipline known as DNA fingerprinting, which has revolutionized not only medicine but also criminology. Consider that spectacular advances in microbiology have opened new avenues in our search for the origins of life itself and that hot-water organisms like Taq polymerase hold vast promise for a host of other revelations and applications. Last, consider that the scientific consensus is that less than one percent of the organisms in Yellowstone's 10,000 thermal features have even been identified, much less studied or put to work. Yellowstone's fabulous reach seems only to grow longer as time passes and as we learn more about what the creation of the park may yet mean.

We say that Yellowstone National Park was established on March 1, 1872, but in fact we have never stopped establishing Yellowstone. Whether as first-time visitors or as world-famous biologists we continue to discover and explore it, and we also continue to create it. That is why I have called this book *Searching for Yellowstone*. Our continuing attempt to understand the park and fit it into our national and international life is the most important and certainly the most exciting thing we do here. We had no idea in 1872 where this search might lead us, and sometimes we seem not to have any better idea now. Caring for Yellowstone National Park brings to mind all the metaphors of growth and change; it is a process more organic than political; a crucible of ideas, ambitions, dreams, and belief systems; a cultural, intellectual, and spiritual crossroads at which we are forever debating which way to turn.

Historically, the educational metaphor most commonly applied to Yellowstone has been that of a great outdoor laboratory in which the workings of nature are exposed for our study and edification. In fact Yellowstone has become a sort of university, where we are the students and the landscape is the faculty and where an amazing array of human interests is tested.

There is a remarkable contrast in the search for Yellowstone. Unless you live close to the park or are among the relatively few people directly or professionally involved in its issues, you will most often hear about it, even in today's media-intense world, as a place of great goodness. Television nature shows, travel magazines, and visitors extol this wonderful vacation destination with its unearthly geysers and almost unbelievable wildlife show. Even the fires of 1988, once they were smothered by a winter's snow, led mostly to a reinforcement of the view of the park as a place of great wonder. Yellowstone is almost always depicted as a pristine wilderness, a place of beauty where nature is preserved. Our search, then, is for a glimpse of this place, a chance to embrace its wonder.

But there is another Yellowstone, one that may be just as important to the world even if it has little immediate reach among most people or even among most park visitors. Just as the visitors conduct their search through the time-honored traditions of tourism and wilderness adventure, other people are conducting other searches. Hundreds of scientists are pursuing their disciplines, extracting this or that new tidbit or theory or microbiological miracle. At the same time various entrepreneurs seek to encourage and satisfy appetites for the commerce generated by all this searching. Advocates of alternative management approaches grow progressively more shrill as they compete for attention in the park's saga of legal and philosophical definition. And generations of land managers in and around the park struggle with the pressures exerted by all of these forces. This more complex Yellowstone is also, at least when viewed from a distance, a place of great goodness, but on any given day it may seem a place of overwhelming contention, nastiness, and even hate.

In the 1990s the discovery of PCR led inevitably to an explosion in "bioprospecting" in Yellowstone by high-tech companies interested in developing, patenting, and marketing other useful new organisms. This led to a public debate over whether or not such "mining" of unique geothermal life forms was an appropriate use of the park, which led to calls for royalties paid to the public coffers, which led to conferences and proposed protocols, which will lead to some sort of legal resolution of this particular issue and to a new aspect of Yellowstone's role in our society.[2] The search goes on. Dozens of issues, with thousands of competing interested parties, career through such processes in the park. Few are unique to Yellowstone; most are paralleled in other parks or areas with similarly special resources, though quite often Yellowstone, because of its singular eminence, takes a leadership role.

I find myself thinking of the search for Yellowstone in the first person, not merely because I take it so personally but because all of us participate in the search. Even those who have never given the place a serious thought are participants, through apathy, ignorance, or innocent inattention; in natural resource issues, as in most other political issues, nonvotes are often as significant as negative or positive votes. So when I invite you to join me in following this search, I am inviting you to consider your part in it as well. When I say "we" in this book, I am not speaking of some small group, like the employees of the park or the members of the conservation community or even the members of all the respective interest groups that surround and demand things from Yellowstone. I am speaking of all of us, nearby or distant, detached or immersed, who share responsibility for the fate of the park. I say "we" a lot, because at every stage Yellowstone's course has been largely a reflection of or reaction to public attitudes.

That is not to say that the park is a democratic institution whose direction has always mirrored some majority opinion, but that public opinions and perceptions have driven the process by which it grew and changed. It is a subtle and diffuse process, not especially comforting to those who prefer to see history as a fairly simple chain of events in which good people and ideas emerge and triumph. In this book I spend a fair amount of time in conversation with past historians, professional and amateur, who have attempted to draw certain lessons from the park's story but have had to simplify that story in order to do so. Yellowstone, like life, is not simple.

Two great scholarly monuments of Yellowstone's administrative history already exist, written by Aubrey Haines and Richard Bartlett. In the notes at the back of the book I happily and repeatedly acknowledge their pioneering work. They provided the chronological and thematic foundation for practically all later historical work. But in the quarter-century since Yellowstone's one hundredth birthday, its history has been battered about by dozens of ecologists, social scientists, politicians, conservationists, anticonservationists, advocates of every stripe, a few other historians, and thousands of journalists. The 125th anniversary of the park seems a fitting time to reconsider our understanding of Yellowstone's history. The work of Haines and Bartlett has to some extent freed me from exhaustively covering every administrative development; here I will consider not only our ongoing search for the real meaning of Yellowstone but also the ways in which that search sometimes goes astray. Interestingly, it has gone as far astray in our consideration of the place's history as in any other way. This is a history of the park's most dynamic ideas and issues rather than of its bureaucracy or physical plant. I believe that even the newcomer to Yellowstone history will find it a useful and entertaining approach.

After a century or so of poking along in whatever seemed like the right direction at the time, our search for Yellowstone has become substantially more self-aware. While a lot of people still view it as a place where certain things are right to do and others are not, a growing number of people recognize that the park is the site of something much more dynamic in human culture, a kind of perceptual experiment that will never end. We are embarked on a great journey of discovery in Yellowstone, one of the most exciting and instructive adventures we have undertaken in our quest to understand this exasperatingly elusive thing we call nature. Being only human, we diminish the journey through our incessant bickering, but we are learning to celebrate the greater wisdoms to which we are exposed along the way.

In 1972 Yellowstone National Park welcomed its fifty millionth visitor. It took a century to reach that remarkable total but only another twenty years to double it. The pressures on this place mount continually, and long ago it began to show the wear. The search for Yellowstone has taken on an urgency it did not always have, mostly because there are now so many searchers, and we have so many hopes, ambitions, and dreams for what we may find. Like our predecessors, we often find things we weren't even looking for. And, like our predecessors, we did not know until we found them that they were what we needed in the first place.

1 | ANCIENT YELLOWSTONE

A FEW YEARS AGO I was scanning the hills above a meadow near Mammoth Hot Springs. I was looking for grizzly bears, but along a low slope on one side of a small drainage that emptied out into the meadow, two parallel rows of boulders caught my eye. Ranging in size from one to several feet across, the boulders ran downhill in lines so straight and perfect that there could be no doubt they were put there by humans. They had clearly been there a very long time, but nobody, not even the archeologists and other historians I later asked, had noticed them. I took an archeologist to see them, just to confirm my suspicion, but the purpose of the boulder lines was pretty obvious to me. Crouching behind them, a hunter would have been well concealed from elk, deer, or bison as they descended through the narrow draw and out onto the meadow on their way to the nearest standing water.

I started spending time in that meadow in 1972, and I glassed those slopes countless times looking for bears, but it took me eighteen years to notice those rocks.

As I consider the long story of humans in Yellowstone country, I find myself in agreement with historians and archeologists who are uncomfortable with the term "prehistoric" when applied to American Indians.[1] It is a European concept of North America, indeed a European concept of what matters most about the passage of time. To say that all those thousands of years of human activity, all those lives and thoughts and accomplishments, came before "real" history is to imply that nothing meaningful happened here until Europeans (Euramericans, as they are now called) arrived and started writing things down. It is narrow enough to consider recent history the only history because it's the only kind we can read, but it's far worse to ignore all manner of history that was recorded in many ways earlier. The intellectual, cultural, and spiritual history of many North Americans was recorded in architecture, craft, art, oral tradition, and, in some cases in Mexico and Central America, something very like our written language.

An example of the power of these non-European expressions was provided by a recent analysis of petroglyph sites in the Yellowstone Valley north and east of the park. In 1985 a Montana researcher wrote about a Crow acquaintance who knew of unstudied petroglyphs but would not reveal them "because they are still used."[2] "Use" certainly involved ceremonial visits and related activities, suggesting that patterns our culture would casually have considered little more than doodles were an important and extraordinarily durable presence in the lives of another people. What Native Americans did in their elaborate and compelling belief systems in terms of maintaining knowledge and tradition was for generations dismissed by most whites as superstition or folklore, even though it carried much of what history should carry — the weight of accumulated knowledge and wisdom that allows a culture to sustain itself and thrive.

In 1959, during the construction of the post office in Gardiner, Montana (a few hundred yards from the park's north entrance), a fragment of a Clovis projectile point, apparently made of local obsidian, turned up. Yellowstone's historian at the time, Aubrey Haines, wrote of this small artifact: "The Gardiner locality of 11,000 years ago can be pictured as a wrack of postglacial debris, the silt and boulders thinly veiled by transitional vegetation consisting mainly of grass and willows. There our Early Hunter probably camped, sitting by his fire to replace a projectile point broken in an unsuccessful cast."[3]

Though "early" was a formal archeological designation, it is especially appropriate for this hunter, who lived during a time when the Yellowstone Plateau was being recolonized by life forms after thousands of years of deep glaciation. A Folsom point, made of obsidian from Yellowstone's Obsidian Cliff and dated to more than 10,200 years ago, was later found in the Bridger-Teton National Forest south of Yellowstone.[4] Humans followed the retreating ice as soon as enough plant and animal life had become reestablished to support their presence.

The American West was strikingly different when the ice first retreated from the Yellowstone Plateau. Along with many of the mammals we would readily recognize today, there were mammoths, bighorn bison, and other herbivores, pursued by dire wolves, Pleistocene lions, saber-toothed cats, short-faced bears, and other carnivores.[5]

The recolonization of the area progressed at the pace the still-cold climate would allow. From about 14,000 to 12,800 years ago, tundra probably dominated, gradually replaced by Engelmann spruce, then by whitebark pine, subalpine fir, and lodgepole pine, the latter coming to dominate much of the area during a dry period from about 9,000 to 6,000 years ago. The dryness was so extreme at the end of that period that Yellowstone Lake did not even have an outlet.[6] By then the mammoths and many other giant fauna had long disappeared from North America (for reasons still being debated, but possibly including overhunting by humans), and the modern western fauna was all that remained.

By that time, 6,000 years ago, humans were very familiar with the highest country of the Yellowstone, perhaps living here even in preference to the drier prairies between the Rockies and the Mississippi Valley. These people, lacking the abundant protein provided by the great post–Ice Age herds of mammals, were generalists; they gathered plants, hunted both large and small mammals, and developed systematic migration patterns that put them in the most hospitable places at the most hospitable seasons. They were by all evidence incredibly adaptable.[7]

Their versatility was suggested in a recent analysis of stone tools collected by archeologists in Yellowstone. Seventy-eight tools, including a variety of points, scrapers, and other devices, found during excavations along the shore of Yellowstone Lake, were tested for blood residue. Recent developments in forensic science have made it possible to analyze such residues even if they are thousands of years old. Identifiable blood was found on twenty-three of the tools. A 9,000-year-old chert knife had bison blood on it. An obsidian point 8,500 to 9,000 years old showed bear blood. Another obsidian point, 9,000 to 10,000 years old, had rabbit blood, and various tools, 2,500, 4,500, 5,000, and 7,000 years old, had deer blood. Bison, deer, elk, sheep, rabbit, bear, cat, and canid were all included in the sample (the technique cannot yet distinguish different species of bear, cat, or canid; canids, for example, could include wolf, coyote, fox, or Indian dog).[8] The procedure does not tell how the blood got there, of course; a strip of fresh rabbit skin might have been used to attach a point to a wooden shaft, thus smearing rabbit blood on a point intended for other prey. The researchers were surprised to discover elk blood on a sandstone metate, or grinding stone. These stones were usually used only to grind plant matter, but this one may have been used to make pemmican, which contains meat.

The diversity of species in such a small number of blood samples (the sample size dictates caution in all interpretations) was another surprise, indicating that these people hunted many animals. The high percentage of predators was both interesting and puzzling; one would expect most of the points to be used to kill favored food species, such as bison, deer, and elk. But for all its puzzles and potential shortcomings, this study offers revealing evidence that hunters in the Yellowstone area were successful generalists, more inclined to hunt a variety of species than were the Plains tribes, which focused on bison.

The climate of Yellowstone has been subject to many kinds of change on many scales. As good as our paleoecological techniques are these days, they give us only general, long-term trends, but the closer we get to the present, the more kinds of evidence are available for correlation. For example, Yellowstone has few trees that live even 500 years, so tree-ring data — often a very good indicator of growing conditions over the tree's lifetime — come into play very late in the story. But through studies of pond sediment (the rich pollen record reveals the vegetation of the pond's basin over time, and the charcoal layers in the sediment reveal fire frequency, an excellent indicator of the climate's dryness), combined with analysis of bone fragments found in the strata of natural trap caves (of which Yellowstone has many), the charcoal record in mudflows, and other climatic indicators, scientists are piecing together the ancient biography of Yellowstone to an extent that would have seemed unimaginable just thirty years ago.

We know now, for example, that between 1,500 and 1,000 years ago the climate of Yellowstone's northern range — the lower-elevation grazing lands that would have provided the best hunting opportunities for humans — became wetter, entirely displacing at least two small mammals, the prairie vole and the western jumping mouse.[9] Since then the climate has become slightly wetter again (the vole and the mouse haven't come back yet; perhaps greenhouse warming will invite them).

This last 1,500 years was also a period of increased human presence in Yellowstone. Among the many possible reasons for the increase may be the growth in human populations in North America generally, but it also seems that there was more meat to be had. Though the archeological and paleontological records don't provide a detailed picture, at least some large mammal species, such as elk, seem to have increased significantly after about 500 B.C., which would not have gone unnoticed by the humans in the area.

Our understanding of human history in Yellowstone prior to the arrival of whites is further complicated by the Little Ice Age, which was a general cooling of the Northern Hemisphere in the last three or four centuries before 1850.[10] It seems that Yellowstone was just coming out of this cooler era in 1872, when the park was established. The effects of the cold temperatures — deeper snow, longer winters, more moisture — on human activity in the area can be imagined but have not yet been fully demonstrated.

Several thousand years of human occupation certainly had effects on the Yellowstone setting, but so far we have little concrete evidence of just what those effects were. Less than five percent of the park has been surveyed for archeological sites, but more than five hundred sites have been mapped, ranging from tiny campsites identified only by a few obsidian chips to a well-known burial site near

Fishing Bridge and a recently discovered bison-kill site along the shore of Yellowstone Lake. There are any number of hearth sites, stone circles, wickiups, and other cultural alterations of the landscape.[11]

American Indians, so long popularly viewed as a few primitive innocents who "lived off the land" with no technology to influence their environment, were in fact very aggressive land managers. They also were a lot more numerous than most people realize. In the past twenty years historians have published dramatic and persuasive reconsiderations of the pre-Columbian human population of North America. Fifty years ago estimates of the number of humans living north of Mexico in 1492 were as low as 1 million. Now, though debate continues and intensifies, estimates have grown to 7 million, with some arguing that there were even more (and a conviction that the total population of North, Central, and South America may have exceeded 100 million, more than the population of Europe at the time).[12]

These early Americans exerted many influences on their landscapes. They used fire to manipulate vegetation or to force the movements of animals; many North American landscapes were shaped and then maintained quite differently from those that had previously been free of human activities.[13] Besides the effects of burning on wildlife habitats, human hunting also affected herd numbers, distribution, and behavior.

Exactly how Native Americans affected wildlife in Yellowstone is unknown. The traditional majority view has been that humans had at most a modest effect on the numbers and distribution of animals in the area before the coming of whites.[14] However, the opposite extreme position, that American Indians were so abundant that they, in concert with predation by wolves and other predators, actually suppressed the populations of large mammals in Yellowstone to nearly zero, has recently joined the chorus of viewpoints.[15] We have a lot to learn about pre-Columbian humans as managers of the landscape.

What is abundantly obvious, even without much digging around in the known archeological sites, is that people found many ways to make a living here. The sheer number of sites is significant. In 1880 Philetus Norris, the park's second superintendent and a self-taught amateur archeologist, described numerous structures and "countless driveways and coverts in every stage of decay" from which hunters killed large mammals.[16] Of course, Norris was seeing remnants of a long human past, and the many structures he reported could represent many generations of activity.

Norris concluded, however, that "these Indians have left fewer enduring evidences of their occupancy than the beaver, badger, and other animals on which they subsisted."[17] In a sense, he was right. Though archeologists now regard the park area as a rich location, with many interesting sites, the peoples of the northern Rockies did not build the sorts of lasting structures that would impress a nineteenth-century white man like Norris, unlike the Mound Builders of the Mississippi Valley or the Anasazi of the Southwest.

As is true of many archeological sites, much of this evidence is simply fading away. The rows of boulders I described earlier are settling into the soil and will be harder and harder to notice in the future. I've relocated a number of "tipi ring" sites (if that's what they really are — all we know for sure is that they're human-created stone circles) mapped by archeologists only thirty years ago, and it's easy to see that they are blending back into the landscape. In the rocky terrain of the park, with so many natural forces working on the surface features, a human structure has to be tough to last, and the people who built these weren't necessarily concerned about that sort of durability.

Take a tipi ring, say a twenty-foot-wide double circle of rocks in a field full of similar rocks. These human-placed rocks, like all the others, are energetically pushed and lifted by frost and roots, rolled and rerolled and rolled again by many generations of passing bears looking for goodies underneath, inadvertently kicked by the occasional elk or bison while digging in or walking through snow, perhaps peeled by lichen or abruptly split by fire, so they tend to float around pretty easily on the soil's most active and fluid layer. Other rocks simply sink into the ground. Although their sinking may ensure that they stay more or less in place, it also ensures they will be even harder to see, especially under the cover of the monochromatic and remarkably camouflaging combination of lichens, mosses, dried vegetation, and weathering animal feces that adorn most of the park's grasslands.

DESPITE OUR limited knowledge of these early Yellowstone residents and visitors, we know that they had a significant impact on many other early Native Americans, because Yellowstone was the site of one of North America's first nationally influential industries. Yellowstone's volcanic activity provided large sources of superb obsidian, a popular stone for working into surgically sharp blades, weapon points, and ornamental finery. An archeologist I know held up a grapefruit-size chunk of obsidian in the field one day, looked at it with admiration, and said, "This was primo stuff." Obsidian points and other elegantly carved artifacts found in Hopewell gravesites as far away as Ohio and Ontario were made from Yellowstone rock (those same sites also contained material from the Gulf Coast, suggesting the truly continental scope of trading in pre-Columbian America).[18]

In the Ohio Valley, because of its rarity and because of the great cost of moving it so far, Yellowstone obsidian was made into ceremonial points and blades for burial with important people. The curator at Hopewell Culture National Historical Park, in southern Ohio, described this as "the first example of conspicuous consumption in North America."[19]

Because freshly exposed obsidian surfaces (such as those created when a new point is made) absorb moisture at a known and measurable rate, it is possible to determine how long ago a point was made. And because each obsidian formation has its own unique chemical "signature," it is also possible to track these far-flung artifacts back to their sources. As these analysis technologies have improved in the past thirty years, Yellowstone's most intriguing and instructive detective story has unfolded.[20]

Archeologists once proposed that the Yellowstone obsidian found in eastern North America came from one large shipment, but it is now clear that obsidian from many western sites was carried

Elegant spear blades (the largest about eight inches long) found in a mound burial at Hopewell Culture National Historical Park, near Chillicothe, Ohio, bear witness to the extensive trade in Yellowstone obsidian during the past 2,000 years. Material from Obsidian Cliff has been found at a number of archeological sites in the Mississippi and Ohio valleys, as well as at numerous sites in the West, products of a remarkable trade network among native people across the continent. *NPS photo by Michael Bitsko, courtesy of Hopewell Culture Historical Park*

long distances in the West and beyond. Obsidian outcroppings are scattered all over western North America; Yellowstone alone has several. A map that attempted to connect all the sources with all the final resting places of obsidian tools, points, and other devices would soon be blackened with crisscrossed lines, some short, some long, and many beginning in Yellowstone. Not only did obsidian travel vast distances from this area, it also was brought here; some flakes and points collected in Yellowstone originated in other places, especially to the west and south. Thus obsidian opens a window on travel patterns and trade patterns in ancient times.[21]

As more obsidian artifacts have been analyzed, they have deepened our appreciation of the importance of Yellowstone in national commerce. The local obsidian has probably been in use at least by regional people for more than 10,000 years. National Park Service archeologist Ann Johnson recently wrote that "no other single lithic material can claim such popularity and utility among so many diverse prehistoric cultures over comparable space and time."[22]

The most interesting questions about Yellowstone obsidian may be how so much of it traveled so far. Excavations in one mound at a Hopewell site in Ohio revealed more than 150 large spearlike blades, and another mound at the same site yielded a collection of obsidian artifacts weighing about 300 pounds.[23] This was probably Yellowstone obsidian from about A.D. 330. Since the early 1960s, when I was a high school student in southeastern Ohio, I've visited many of the Hopewell sites in Ohio and elsewhere in the Mississippi Valley. As I walk the lawns that now cover these sites, and climb anywhere I'm allowed to climb, I often think of Yellowstone, more than 1,500 miles away, and wonder at the combination of spiritual values, aesthetic sensitivities, and market forces that could compel people without domestic livestock or wheels to move such a load of volcanic rock so far. During the peak of the 400-year Hopewell Culture in the first few centuries A.D. obsidian was at least occasionally arriving from various places in the West. Most of it came from Yellowstone.[24]

Obsidian symbolizes the mystery of Yellowstone's early residents and intrigues us with many questions. How many times did obsidian change hands on its way to the Ohio Valley? What kind of "marketing" was involved; was Yellowstone obsidian, for example, known or distinguished from other "brands"? Did the people who buried the obsidian points near present-day Chillicothe, Ohio, know how far it had come? Had any of them actually heard of the Yellowstone area, with its other wonders? On a continent so full of energetic, fearless travelers, did anybody, having heard about Yellowstone, ever decide to visit this strange place out of curiosity or for reasons of spiritual need or intellectual enterprise? Imagine making that trip on foot and by canoe over the course of a couple of years, just to bring home a few precious pounds of treasure.

Yellowstone before the arrival of Euramericans was, like any other landscape, a place of change. Sometimes, when the winters were not too hard, and the climate favored particular life communities, it must have been very hospitable. For centuries it was less hospitable, then it became warmer and drier. Fires, floods, winds, and many organisms (including, we must assume, humans) brought changes to the landscape through the thousands of years prior to its discovery by whites. Even our limited archeological studies suggest that Yellowstone was a busy place at times, what with all the hunters, gatherers, fishermen, miners, and assorted other travelers who came and went over the millennia before white people came along and tacked a couple of centuries of "history" onto the story.

2 | THINGS A LITTLE INCREDIBLE

OUR CULTURE'S PERCEPTION of nature has changed dramatically in the past thirty years. The rise of environmentalism, not only as a major political force but also in academic disciplines ranging from conservation biology to resource economics to environmental history, has stimulated an intensive dialogue on the relationships between humans and the rest of the world. We have learned many things from this. We have learned that past concepts of nature, though useful in their time, are no longer adequate. We now have every reason to believe that what we call nature — a fabulously complex suite of geophysical and ecological processes that our ancestors perceived as behaving in some divinely ordained or mechanistic or even predictable fashion — is a far more unruly, undirected business than we can even imagine.

The idea of nature has been progressively released from our preconceptions, and it seems to require even more conceptual freedom than we have yet given it. For most people, wilderness is nature at its most unruly (where, to resurrect a happy misstatement, the hand of man has never set foot), and as recently as a century ago, that unruliness was not popular; wilderness was a place of wild beasts and demonic presences. But through the eloquence of Henry David Thoreau, John Muir, John Burroughs, and a host of other nineteenth-century travelers, writers, and thinkers, wilderness became not merely good but a kind of quasi-sacred sanctuary; under the pens of these writers, "Satan's home had become God's own temple." [1] Since then we have continued to redefine wilderness, sometimes in philosophical tracts, sometimes in legislation, sometimes in court, but always with an eye to clarifying our relationship with it.

Our perception of wilderness has included the belief that it is outside of our control, free from the kinds of human interference that occur in a settled or "civilized" landscape. Until very recently, for example, most history textbooks portrayed North America (indeed, the whole New World) prior to 1492 as a wilderness. Interestingly, they acknowledged that it was a wilderness with people living in it. These textbooks implied that the humans who lived there were innocent primitives, subsisting on what they grew in small gardens and what they could take from nature's overflow: roots, berries, fish, and the occasional deer or elk. As I suggested in the previous chapter, this view of pre-Columbian North America has collapsed as massive amounts of evidence have shown that humans have been aggressively and creatively shaping this landscape for thousands of years.

But even among those of us who know and accept this evidence, there is a lingering feeling that things were somehow *right* back then, that some fundamental state of harmony existed between humans and the rest of nature and that North America was a kind of environmental Eden until Europeans arrived. To our modern sensibility, only those societies we think of as "primitive" have lived without disturbing the "balance of nature."[2]

Historian Richard White, analyzing the popular perspective of a populated but unspoiled North America ruined by Old World colonists, says that according to this view, "whites are the bearers of environmental original sin."[3] This leaves us with a sort of reverse Eden myth, in which the Garden, rather than being made off-limits to sinners, was in fact invaded by them, chain saws in hand.

The concept of North America as Eden just doesn't hold up under careful scrutiny. Not only do we now doubt nature's tendency to be balanced but we also see many signs that pre-Columbian humans didn't always sustain harmony with nature. Human cultures emerged and faded; human population centers came, exhausted the available resources, and went; climates changed; vegetation communities adjusted; wildlife populations shifted.[4] The pace of the process may have been more stately than it is today, but it was the same process.

Wilderness is now seen as something a great deal more involved than Eden (admitting even that Eden's ecology would make an interesting study). Not only had most of the North American landscapes first viewed by white people been affected by human actions, they had been affected by *European* actions. This is a wonderful and at first puzzling notion, but it is important to many modern dialogues over park and wilderness management. Even a place as remote as Yellowstone may have felt European influences well before the Euramericans arrived in the area. Those influences took many forms, and for all our study and theorizing, we can not claim to know any of them well.

The greatest horrors introduced from Europe were the catastrophic epidemics. The densely populated nations of Europe had fostered the evolution of (and developed resistance to) a variety of "crowd diseases" that when introduced to other parts of the globe became a leading force in what has been aptly called "ecological imperialism."[5] Europeans did not merely conquer the world militarily, forcing their political and religious systems on other areas. Without intending to, they also conquered the world biologically. European organisms — ranging from viruses to plants to birds to livestock to humans — disturbed and even destroyed entire ecological systems that had evolved for millennia without any need for defense against such comprehensive assaults.

In the years following the arrival of Columbus and other explorers and conquerors, Old World diseases, against which American Indians had no defense or immunity, swept large portions of the continent. By 1800, that is, by the eve of the white "discovery" of Yellowstone, at least twenty-eight epidemics of smallpox, twelve of measles, six of influenza, and four each of diphtheria, bubonic plague, and typhus had occurred among native peoples in the American Southeast, Southwest, and Northeast.[6]

The losses of life were incredibly high; one recent estimate places the mortality of all New England Indians at 86 percent by 1639.[7] Though debates continue on the size of North America's human population before 1492, it is clear that millions of people died, most without the faintest idea of where this sudden sickness came from. The marvelous far-ranging travel and trade networks that had once moved Yellowstone obsidian and other goods thousands of miles suddenly became, to borrow a term from archeologist Ann Ramenofsky, "vectors of death."[8] Disease raced far ahead of the Euramericans, with the result that in much of North America, the white explorers and settlers did not see the land as it had been before 1492: "Aboriginal ways of life influenced by entirely American causes changed for many Native American peoples long before they ever saw a European or an African. Aboriginal times ended in North America in 1520–1524, and Native American behavior was thereafter never again totally as it had been prior to the first great smallpox pandemic."[9]

The ecological implications of this wholesale human depopulation were just as profound. Landscapes whose resources had been manipulated — through burning, wildlife harvest, settlement, or agriculture — were abruptly released from that control. At the same time, tribes less susceptible to the epidemics — for example, smaller groups whose isolation and lower population density provided some measure of protection — suddenly had greater power.[10] The biological effects thus generated political ones, as differently affected groups adjusted to the new era, then readjusted as subsequent waves of disease raced across the land.

When François Antoine Larocque, an adventurous French-Canadian trader, visited the Crow living east and northeast of the present park area in 1805, he noted that they were already much reduced by smallpox (from 16,000 to 2,400, according to Larocque), apparently by epidemics in the late 1700s.[11] North of Yellowstone in north-central Montana, smallpox had visited the Blackfeet by 1781, and perhaps earlier.[12]

Livestock diseases also had an impact in the West, especially in the 1800s as white settlement advanced. Bighorn sheep are especially susceptible to domestic livestock diseases, and Yellowstone seems to have supported considerably more bighorn sheep in the early 1800s than it did by the end of the century.[13]

European livestock had other great effects prior to the arrival of whites. The spread of Spanish horses through the West reached southern Wyoming and the Snake River Plain of southern Idaho by about 1700, and, like many other groups, the Yellowstone-area tribes were dramatically affected by the horse.[14] Increased mobility and range changed the way they used the bison, their primary food, and thus the way they used the landscape.

The Bannock provide a telling example of the changes brought by the horse. In 1800 the Bannock were relatively recent arrivals on the Snake River Plain from farther west. Thanks to horses and trade firearms, they wiped out the bison in southern Idaho in the 1840s, then had to make longer annual migrations to other bison ranges farther east. These migrations took them across the Yellowstone Plateau, along what we now call the Bannock Indian Trail. This somewhat variable trail followed traditional routes over the Gallatin Range of what is now the northwestern part of Yellowstone (probably up Duck Creek and down Indian Creek) to Mammoth Hot Springs. From there they rode east across Blacktail Plateau and up the Lamar River Valley, crossing the Absaroka Range through various passes along the east side of the park and dropping into south-central Montana, where they were able to find bison until the 1870s, when the great bison slaughters took place.[15]

Here we have a splendid example of the complex interweaving of American Indian activities and early white history in Yellowstone. The Bannock Indian Trail, one of the park's most famous "native human features," was in good part an artifact of white influence in the form of horses and guns. The trip would not have been necessary without the horses and guns that helped wipe out the bison in southern Idaho, and it would have been impossible without the horses to carry the people and drag their travois such a long distance. We can barely guess at the effects of this increase in traffic by the bison-hunters on Yellowstone's ungulates and other huntable animals; there were no firsthand accounts left by anyone accompanying the Bannock on their trek across the park area.

Like disease epidemics, horses had different effects on different groups, with some groups prospering at the expense of others. Of

A wickiup constructed by American Indians prior to the park's creation in 1872. A few of these have survived into the modern era in remote parts of the park, but they are gradually blending back into the landscape. *NPS photo*

those that frequented the Yellowstone area, the Shoshone of southern Wyoming were the first in the path of the north-trending horse trade and so were mounted long before their most frequent foes, the Blackfeet, who lived farther north. After acquiring horses about 1720, the Shoshone took quick advantage. According to historian Joel Janetski, "Mounted and armed with iron trade weapons, the Shoshone expanded as far north as Saskatchewan, pushing their enemies before them. This success was short lived, however. The Blackfeet, armed with guns obtained from British and French traders at Hudson's Bay, forced the Shoshone back into their historic homelands in Wyoming and Idaho during the last quarter of the eighteenth century."[16]

Thanks to many novels and movie portrayals, we have incorporated the horse-mounted Indian into our stereotypical image of the natural man in tune with his world. We think of the Plains Indians as living in harmony with the vast bison herds. But the horse culture of these tribes was barely two centuries old when it was brought to an end; that was hardly enough time to know if the mounted people would have come to some sort of equilibrium with the bison that they were suddenly able to harvest so aggressively. Also, the Indians' huge numbers of horses were competing with the bison for the native grasses.[17]

Euramericans may have changed commerce in the Yellowstone area in intriguing ways. Studies from other areas have established that when whites set up a trading post in Indian country to gather hides or furs, tribes from ever greater distances responded by harvesting local animals more heavily than they had in the past.[18] Not only could the incentive of trade result in a larger harvest, but such commerce might displace other traditional activities, further affecting the way people used their landscape. In the next chapter we will see how the great fur-trapping era of the early 1800s, in which some local Indians participated, affected Yellowstone decades before the park was established.

Early historians of Yellowstone simplistically pigeonholed entire Indian nations according to certain European values. Hiram Chittenden, whose 1895 history of the park went through many printings and editions and was still recommended as a standard reference when I came to work in Yellowstone in 1972, wrote that the "Shoshones as a family were an inferior race"; the Crow were characterized by "an insatiable love of horse stealing and a wandering and predatory habit," the Blackfeet were "a tribe of perpetual fighters, justly characterized as the Ishmaelites of their race," and the Sheepeaters, a group of Shoshone who were the park area's only permanent occupants at the dawn of the white era, were "feeble in mind, diminutive in stature."[19]

The Blackfeet, except for the brief period mentioned earlier when they were displaced by the Shoshone, ranged freely across much of the Canadian prairie and central Montana north of the park area. Their language, Algonkian, derived from the languages of Canadian groups to the east, but they appear to have been residents of the Alberta-Montana region for perhaps as long as 1,000 years.[20] Noted for their military might, they made occasional visits to Yellowstone.

The Crow settled in the valleys of the Yellowstone and Bighorn rivers to the north and east of the park in the late 1700s, not long before the first known whites visited the park area. They seem to have originated from other Siouan groups farther east along the Missouri River and in southern Manitoba.[21] Through trade systems with the Shoshone, the Crow "may have acquired their first horses as early as 1735."[22] Like the Blackfeet, they traveled throughout the park area, using its various resources and learning it well.

The Shoshone, various groups of which lived south and southwest of the park area, appear to have arrived in the lands around Yellowstone four or five hundred years before the whites. They were "Uto-Aztecan speakers who, within the last 1000 years, gradually expanded north and east across the Great Basin"; that is to say, they were linguistically related to both the Hopi of Arizona and the Aztec of Mexico.[23] Whites often referred to the Shoshone as Snakes; the Snake River did flow through the heart of their domain in Idaho. Oral traditions and historical records indicate that various Shoshone also visited the park area regularly to hunt or gather plants.

The Bannock, close relatives of the Shoshone, have already been mentioned for their conspicuous trail across the Yellowstone Plateau. They were "an enclave of the Northern Paiute" and may have come originally from eastern Oregon as bison disappeared from that area.[24]

The most notable Shoshonean group in the Yellowstone region was the Sheepeaters. Long thought to have preceded the whites into the area by only a few years, the Sheepeaters may in fact have arrived as much as 2,000 years ago. They are the most maligned of the native groups that used Yellowstone. When I came to work in the park in 1972, park educational programs still presented Chittenden's view that the Sheepeaters were culturally deprived weaklings, hiding in a few remote areas of Yellowstone because they simply couldn't survive anyplace else.

Over time I realized the contradiction of this view of the Sheepeaters as failures: they had to be incredibly hardy, adaptable, and resourceful to make a living in an environment as harsh as Yellowstone surely was in the last decades of the Little Ice Age. And as I read the all-too-rare firsthand accounts of them in the journals of early trappers and explorers, it became obvious that they were quite comfortable in their high valley homes. The trapper Osborne Russell, who left us one of the very few early descriptions of these people in his 1835 journal, said that a group of twenty or so Sheepeaters that he had encountered in the Lamar Valley were "neatly clothed in dressed deer and sheepskins of the best quality and seemed to be perfectly happy" and that they were "well armed with bows and arrows pointed with obsidian."[25]

The Sheepeaters acquired their misleading image when they were judged by white values. Their lack of horses and of iron tools and firearms was seen as proof of their backwardness and destitution. The weathered, collapsing remains of their lodgepole tent frames, abandoned in the park and discovered some years later, were judged by whites, who had no knowledge of the efficiency of such housing, as proof of a hard life. Because so few early Yellowstone travelers encountered these people, and even fewer bothered (or were able) to write down what they saw, practically everything that was believed about the lives of Yellowstone's Sheepeaters was based on what was written about the lives of other Sheepeater groups in other places, some quite distant.

The Sheepeaters lived in small groups of a few families, so it has been estimated that the total population of the park area was 150 to 400. They were usually without horses, but they did use dogs to pull their travois. During summer they hunted the high country for sheep and other ungulates, as well as smaller animals, and gathered a great variety of plants. In the winter they made more permanent camps at lower elevation and continued hunting ungulates on their winter ranges.[26]

It has been difficult to determine which of the many archeological sites in Yellowstone were connected with the Sheepeaters, but it is certain that most were not. Many other tribes and groups used the area, and the various signs of activity that Norris noted were the results of many people over time.[27] The famous wickiups, or conical stacks of tent poles, that were identified in several locations (some still survive but are fading fast) were most likely left by the Crow.[28]

The Sheepeaters and the other Shoshone, as well as the Bannock, Crow, and Blackfeet, were all familiar with Yellowstone either through regular use or traditional knowledge. So were other people, including at least the Nez Perce, Kalispel, Coeur d'Alene, Flathead, and Pend Oreille.[29] What is striking about all these groups, at least from the perspective of an environmental historian in the late 1990s, is how little we know of their relationships with and beliefs about Yellowstone. Ethnographic research is now under way, and we can hope that the descendants of these people will share their knowledge and lore of Yellowstone, but it is obvious that we have waited much too long to seek this understanding of the area's earlier human communities.[30]

IN OUR ATTEMPTS to understand the modern Yellowstone landscape, we often wonder how these earlier people used it. It is widely agreed among ecologists, archeologists, and historians that Indian fire was often influential in shaping pre-1492 North American ecosystems.[31] At the same time, there is disagreement over the extent and the purposefulness of that influence. For example, though Indian fires are recognized as an important influence on New England ecology, it appears that, depending upon forest type and the ability of humans to control the fires they started, some parts of that region were burned much more regularly than others.[32]

It is intriguing that a recent review of all the pre-1700 accounts of Indian fires in the eastern United States — that is, an analysis of the original written statements about Indians setting fires regularly and intentionally — revealed a startling lack of actual witnesses to such activities. Of thirty-five early accounts reputed to show that Indians used fire for purposes other than cooking or keeping warm, "no author said that he actually saw the Indians burning the woods. Several, however, indicated indirectly that they had seen this."[33]

The equivocal nature of the historical evidence and the subtle-

An 1871 woodcut by Thomas Moran is the first known image of a fire at Yellowstone. The fire, on Pumice Point on the northwest shore of Yellowstone Lake, is seen from the West Thumb Geyser Basin. Recent tree-ring studies indicate that this area burned around 1867. Moran probably saw evidence of the fire during his 1871 visit to the park with the Hayden Survey, and he brought it to life for publication in *The Aldine*, April 1873. Other early photographs and reports suggest that fires were seen at various locations in the park.

ties of the ecological evidence should make us leery of confident pronouncements about the role of Indian fires in the West, especially in Yellowstone. Elsewhere in North America, Indians were known to use fire for many purposes, including for cooking and warmth, in various ceremonies, to drive game, to gain an advantage in battle, to reinvigorate grazing lands (for game or their own horses), to clear forest undergrowth or land for agriculture, and to signal other people at a distance. It also seems apparent that fires set for some purpose occasionally escaped, burning larger areas than intended. But the use of fire in the West on a scale that would have significant effects on the landscape may have been a comparatively recent addition to native technology. Though humans were in the West by the time the glaciers retreated more than 12,000 years ago, they didn't start to use fire as a "management tool" until 2,000 years ago or so.[34]

Moreover, the great majority of Yellowstone's forests are lodgepole pine, and the consensus among fire ecologists is that high-elevation lodgepole forests in the West were not subjected to intentional burning by Indians. There must have been occasional battle fires, escaped campfires, and other accidents, but Indians had no reason to burn these forests.[35] Thus Yellowstone's lodgepole forests were not significantly influenced by Indian burning. Several fire history studies, based on extensive tree-ring analysis, show that it takes 300 to 400 years following a fire for the lodgepole forests to reach sufficient fuel loads to burn extensively.[36] The shorter fire-return intervals one would expect in an Indian-controlled fire regime simply have not occurred in the park's forests. Following the 1988 fires, some people accused Yellowstone's managers of ignoring "anthropogenic" (that is, human-caused) fire as part of the park's fire history, but the big fires of 1988 burned mostly in these lodgepole pine forests, where there is no evidence of Indian burning.[37]

Yellowstone's landscape is hardly homogeneous, however. Lodgepole pine forests in some portions of the Lamar River drainage in northeastern Yellowstone, especially those on steep south slopes that facilitate fuel drying, have a shorter average fire-return interval, 150 to 200 years.[38] This is still too long a period for human causation to be likely, but it suggests the variability even within a single species, much less across the entire spectrum of species in Yellowstone. Studies of Douglas-fir stands in the Lamar Valley indicated that a "stand-replacing fire occurred somewhere in the 24,000 ha [hectare, which equals 2.47 acres] study area on an average of every 23 years."[39] These fires were relatively small, less than 400 hectares; fires covering more than 400 hectares occurred every seventy-eight years, and really large ones, burning much of the study area, occurred twice, in 1756 and 1988. The intervals and distribution of the fires seem more in keeping with lightning strikes than with intentional or directed burning by people.

The grasslands of the park must be considered separately from the forests. A study of fire scars on trees along the edges of Yellowstone's northern range produced an estimate of fires prior to the park's creation every twenty to twenty-five years on the grasslands (the trees, some of which dated as far back as 1500, were usually scarred rather than killed by grass fires, so one tree might record a number of such events). The researcher thought it "probable that aboriginal man contributed to the frequency of fires."[40]

The northern range was at least intermittently occupied by Indian groups in the nineteenth century, and it is safe to assume it was visited or inhabited in earlier times. One need only drive through the area in the summer to see its hospitable aspects or in winter to see its concentrations of large mammals. If earlier visitors belonged to tribes that burned grasslands elsewhere, they probably did so in Yellowstone as well. In the next few years, as ethnographic, archeological, and paleontological research receives wider attention, and as Yellowstone's various ecopolitical controversies simmer along, more attention will be paid to the influences of American Indians on the Yellowstone landscape.

We do know that various groups of native people used Yellowstone in common with surprisingly little conflict. This area was at the boundary of three distinct cultural groups: Plains, Great Basin, and Intermountain. There is some evidence that Yellowstone was seen by most or all of the region's tribes as neutral ground. One historian has noted that "there are accounts of battles between Blackfeet and mountain men within the park's boundaries; prospectors were also killed by Indians. There are no known accounts of battles between Indian tribes within the park."[41] The evidence for this apparent neutrality is not absolutely conclusive (and there is at least one known account of a battle between Indian groups), but it is persuasive, and all the more intriguing because of another, much more conclusively confirmed, American Indian attitude about Yellowstone.

There is overwhelming evidence that most of the tribes that used the Yellowstone area (especially the hot springs and geyser basins) saw it as a place of spiritual power, of communion with natural forces, a place that inspired reverence.[42] For all the other things that modern society might learn from the American Indian experience, and for all the things that went wrong, even near Yellowstone, in the dealings between Euramericans and Indians, there is this one remarkable reality that binds us together. The magic and power of this place transcend culture; it is a compelling wonder not for just one society but for all humans, whatever their origin.

As the eighteenth century came to a close, although whites probably had not visited Yellowstone yet, their presence was felt by the native people who lived there or visited from nearby. By 1800 word was already out, though incomplete and puzzling, that according to the natives, there was a river and a place of uncommon interest here.

In 1796 Jean Baptiste Trudeau, a Canadian voyageur, wrote what he had heard about it:

> At fifty leagues above the Gros Ventres, to the west of the Missouri there discharges a large river, called the river of the Yellowstone, which is almost as broad and deep as the Missouri. This great river has its source in the mountains of rocks in the western part. Its banks are well supplied with wood. There are found firs, pines, North American firs, birches, cedars, and every other tree. The buffalo and other wild animals rove in herds along its banks. Many little rivers that flow into it abound in beaver beyond all belief.[43]

And in October of 1805 James Wilkinson, governor of the Louisiana Territory, wrote to President Thomas Jefferson, enclosing and describing a "savage delineation on a Buffalo Pelt," which was a map of the Upper Missouri:

> It exposes the location of several important Objects, & may point the way to a useful enquiry — among other things a little incredible, a volcano is distinctly described on the Yellow Stone River.[44]

3 | WILD ROMANTIC SPLENDOR

I T IS CURIOUS that Yellowstone, a place whose name has become so widely recognized, took so long to emerge into clarity in our consciousness. It is less curious, in fact it may have been predictable, that its emergence was troubled with so many doubts and mysteries. From the very beginning, the story — the very idea — of Yellowstone was easy to doubt.

The river for which the park would be named first appeared on an explorer's map in 1796 as the "Rock or Crow River," but on a 1797 map it was named "R. des roches Jaune" (river of yellow stones). The name apparently came from the Minnetaree, a group of Siouan Hidatsas who lived along the lower river when the first whites arrived. Most visitors (and many modern travel writers) assume the river was named for the brilliant yellows of the hydrothermally altered rock in the Grand Canyon of the Yellowstone River, but the name probably came from the many low tan bluffs that line the river far downstream near present Billings, Montana, and that is the part of the river that the Minnetaree would have been most familiar with.[1]

But the river had many names. The Crow, who lived closer to the park area than the Minnetaree did, called it the Elk River, and if they had been the first tribe encountered by whites, the park might bear a different name now. Recently a Crow chief, Dan Old Elk, has suggested an alternative explanation for the naming of the river, one that would exclude the Minnetaree entirely and give the name an especially serendipitous origin. Dan Old Elk maintains that the name "Yellowstone" originated from a misunderstanding by early whites (French-speaking explorers, in this case) of the Crow language. To the untrained ear, the Crow term for Elk River apparently sounded much like the Crow term for Yellowstone River.[2]

To the Blackfeet the park area was known as "Many Smokes," while some Shoshone called it (or at least part of it) "Water-keeps-on-coming-out." Representatives of the Bannock tribe have recently said that their people traditionally knew it as "Buffalo Country." Other less clearly attributed Indian names for the area were "Burning Mountain" and "Summit of the World." Each known name (and it seems safe to assume that there were others) reflects one or more of the park area's distinguishing characteristics: its richness in game, its hydrothermal activity, and its elevation.[3]

Just as Euramericans affected the present park area long before they arrived here, so were they actively trading it among themselves long before they personally staked any claims. Starting in 1603, when the French annexed it (disregarding, as all whites did, the interests and realities of the people who lived there at the time), Yellowstone was regularly traded on the European real estate market. By 1824, thanks to faraway political and military maneuvering by France, Spain, and England, it had gone through fourteen adjustments, sales, and conquests. These exercises were greatly complicated by the park area's position on the Continental Divide, which often resulted in part of it going to one "owner" while the rest went to another. The Louisiana Purchase of 1803 first brought the land draining into the Missouri River into United States possession, but it wasn't until 1824 that the country southwest of the Divide became permanently part of U.S. territory.[4]

The land underwent almost as many long-distance redesignations once it became part of the United States. Between 1803 and 1873 it was at times partly in the territories of Louisiana, Missouri, Oregon, Nebraska, Washington, Dakota, Idaho, Wyoming, and Montana. After eleven variations, it finally ended up in the territories of Montana, Wyoming, and Idaho, at the intersection of which it still rests. Because it had been established as a federal reservation in 1872, prior to the statehood of any of these territories, the park eventually would have many advantages in its self-management;

most later parks, created in existing states, have had to reconcile their needs with state laws and thus have had far less power to decide their own management direction.

I have often wondered about the anonymous and unlettered European wanderers who, sometimes as representatives of their faraway sovereignties and sometimes just on their own, reached the Far West from various directions in the 1700s. I continue to imagine it possible that one of Europe's less well catalogued archives will someday yield an earlier account of Yellowstone adventures than any we now know of. Those of us who enjoy archeological fantasy look out across the 95 percent of the park that has not been surveyed by archeologists and make half-serious jokes about entering a cave and finding a French inscription from the 1770s or a Spanish helmet from a century earlier. Surely one of the most compelling and exciting impulses in the human imagination is to be the first person in a new country. And surely one of the greatest vicarious human experiences is to follow the steps of such a person.

The first white man known to have visited Yellowstone was John Colter, a member of that "foremost of all American explorations," the Lewis and Clark Expedition.[5] After that expedition made its way to the Pacific and returned as far as the Mandan villages on the Missouri River, Colter was granted permission to go in search of fur trading opportunities. One of the first "mountain men" of the West, he spent the next few years prospecting for furs and trade arrangements with the Indians.

In the winter of 1807–08, Colter apparently visited the Yellowstone area; in about 1810 he related his route to Clark, who published it on a map as part of his report on the expedition in 1814. The map shows Yellowstone Lake, the Yellowstone River downstream from the lake, and at least one thermal area in the present park, a hot-spring basin along the Yellowstone near Tower Fall.[6] It would be wonderful to know whether he saw a geyser erupt somewhere along the way and, if he did, how he reacted to the sight.

Many modern writers have mistakenly applied the name "Colter's Hell" to the park, when actually that name belonged to another hot-spring area Colter visited, near the site of present-day

Thomas Moran's woodcut of the Giant-ess gives the water and steam of this geyser an almost architectural quality, rather more like a formal fountain than a natural feature. It was published in *Scribner's Monthly,* June 1871.

Cody, Wyoming. This site is plainly marked as "Colter's Hell" on a number of maps made before the establishment of the park in 1872, and other early Yellowstone travelers, including the legendary Jim Bridger, regarded Colter's Hell as only the site near Cody, but later writers eventually came to apply the term to the entire Yellowstone region. The name, combining a remarkably colorful character with the most pungent of nineteenth-century metaphors for Yellowstone, has proven irresistible to generations of casual journalists.[7]

Eventually many other trappers followed Colter into the Yellowstone country during one of the most romantic eras in the history of North America. Small parties of men, often employed by large, ambitious companies far away (as almost everything familiar was), ventured into spectacular new country every trapping season. Some died, some made a little money, some learned the country well enough to guide settlers and soldiers later, and some found their way to Yellowstone.

What are we today to make of the backwoodsmen and mountain men, whom all preceding generations of Americans have lionized as the vanguard of civilization? Even in the early 1800s, when the mountain men were still alive and active in the Rockies, faraway city-bound people were engaged by the thrill of their fabulous adventures. And near the end of the nineteenth century, in his classic *The Winning of the West,* Theodore Roosevelt echoed a national worshipfulness when he praised Daniel Boone for his "self-command and patience, his daring, restless love of adventure, and, in time of danger, his absolute trust in his own powers and resources."[8] Even in my own childhood — and I am perhaps of the last generation to grow up before satellite mapping made all the world a known country — David Crockett, Kit Carson, Jim Bridger, Jedediah Smith, and their less-storied colleagues represented the ultimate in individual hardiness and self-reliance, the personification of discovery.

The legacy of the mountain men is complex and ironic. We see them as exemplifying a wild, free life, unfettered by social constraints, yet it was commerce and industry that paid their way and drove most of them to the wilderness in the first place. We see them as simple, hardy men, all cast from the same mold, but they were a multinational crowd, with intense and even violent allegiances to their various employers or home countries. And they were interacting with an even more complex set of native cultures, whose own political relationships were as subtle, involved, and convoluted as any in the Old World.

The irony is that the very wildness they represented — both in themselves and in the western landscape — was doomed, in good part by their own activities. As they "explored" the West (a region already explored quite thoroughly by Native Americans), they were preparing the way for hordes of people whose primary goal was to domesticate it beyond recognition. As they adopted the ways of the native people, they were among the first whites to directly, personally affect those native cultures and put them on the long and painful path of subjugation to the ways of white society.

On the other hand, the mountain men did us the great favor of leaving some of the few descriptions of this country prior to the destruction of the great wildlife herds and the massive alteration of the prairie vegetation under agriculture and livestock.

After James Wilkinson's letter to President Jefferson (quoted at the close of the previous chapter), with its tantalizing suggestion of a volcano at the head of the Yellowstone River, no mention was made in writing, as far as we know, of the geothermal activity represented by the geysers and hot springs until a visit in 1819 by a group of trappers led by Donald McKenzie. Alexander Ross wrote that this group reported, "Boiling fountains having different degrees of temperature were very numerous; one or two were so very hot as to boil meat." There are questions surrounding both the location and the year of this account, but like the Wilkinson letter it tantalizes us with the promise of great wonders. Even this brief passage was not published until thirty-six years later.[9] The outside world still awaited a fuller description by someone who could provide a more meaningful characterization of the hot water and a more precise idea of Yellowstone geography.

The first such chronicler we know of was Daniel Potts, a young Pennsylvanian who visited Yellowstone Lake in 1826. In July of 1827 a Philadelphia newspaper published Potts's description of the West Thumb Geyser Basin (though it is uncertain if he was specifically describing the Potts Hot Spring Basin, named much later in his honor):

> At or near this place heads the Luchkadee or Calliforn Stinking fork Yellow-stone South fork of Masuri and Henrys fork all those head at an angular point that of the Yellow-stone has a large fresh water lake near its head on the verry top of the Mountain which is about one hundrid by fourty miles in diameter and as clear as crystal on the south borders of this lake is a number of hot and boiling springs some of water and others of most beautiful fine clay and resembles that of a mush pot and throws its particles to the immense height of from twenty to thirty feet in height The clay is white and of a pink and water appear fathomless as it appears to be entirely hollow under neath. There is also a number of places where the pure suphor is sent forth in abundance one of our men Visited one of those wilst taking his recreation there at an instan the earth

Yellowstone Lake was well known to many wilderness travelers in the early 1800s. This Moran woodcut is from Ferdinand Hayden's *Geological Survey of the Territories* (1871).

began a tremendious trembling and he with dificulty made his escape when an explosion took place resembling that of thunder. During our stay in that quarter I heard it every day.[10]

The "Luchkadee or Calliforn" was what we call the Green River, the "Stinking fork" is our Shoshone River, and the "South fork of the Masuri" would be the Gallatin or the Madison.

After Potts the known or probable visitors amount to a rollcall of legendary trappers, Joe Meek, Thomas Fitzpatrick, Jim Bridger, and Osborne Russell among them. According to a recent compilation of early accounts, whites traveled through Yellowstone's thermal areas during at least twenty-three of the years between 1819 and 1870, and in some years more than one party went through.[11] Thus the park's exploration by whites was a long-drawn-out affair. Even the first "official" exploration parties of the 1870s, as they made their way to Yellowstone full of the sense of discovery, had to admit they occasionally encountered other whites. These less official visitors came frequently, and they took word of what they saw to the settlements, but partly because of what they described and partly because of who they were, they were rarely believed. There was some reason to doubt these trappers, prospectors, and other wanderers. They operated well beyond the social fringe and were part of a growing tradition of tall-tale frontier humor then thriving in, for example, the lower Mississippi Valley (the tradition into which Samuel Clemens was born in 1835). The Yellowstone trapper who became most famous, both as a guide and as a yarn spinner, was Jim Bridger.

A number of Yellowstone tall tales were formerly attributed to Bridger. He was said to have seen the petrified trees of Yellowstone and woven a tale about petrified birds sitting on petrified limbs singing petrified songs. Upon seeing Obsidian Cliff, he was said to have made up a story about a mountain of magnifying glass, which made a very distant animal seem close enough to shoot. Like the erroneous tradition of Colter's Hell, the myth of Bridger as the greatest spinner of Yellowstone yarns was fostered and nourished by generations of western writers, folklorists, and commercial interests. Recent research by Aubrey Haines has revealed that most of the stories attributed to him were either common fare told by various trappers or created later and attached to his legend.[12] The stories remain, however, as enjoyable relics of a day when Yellowstone was not even dimly known to proper white society.

For all their campfire volubility, these early wanderers were not given to written accounts. Most early descriptions of the park are all too brief, leaving us glad for the news but disappointed at the lack of details. Probably the most satisfying document is the journal of Osborne Russell, a literate Maine native who came West in 1834 and passed through Yellowstone several times over the next few years. He gave us our first detailed portrait of the country generally, beyond the narrow limits of the geyser basins. He described abundant wildlife, beautiful vistas, and a country so appealing that one day in the Lamar Valley he was apparently somewhat tempted to settle: "We stopped at this place and for my own part I almost wished I could spend the remainder of my days in a place like this where happiness and contentment seemed to reign in wild romantic splendor surrounded by majestic battlements which seemed to support the heavens and shut out all hostile intruders."[13]

Russell did have reason to worry about hostilities, though he was more the intruder than were the Blackfeet who, in late August of 1839, attacked his party's camp on Yellowstone Lake. After taking arrows in the right hip and right leg, Russell and a wounded friend crawled to safety in the woods. When the friend despaired, Russell proved how easily he could find food in this game-rich country: "He exclaimed Oh dear we shall die here, we shall never get out of these mountains, Well said I if you presist [*sic*] in thinking so you will die but I can crawl from this place upon my hands and one knee and Kill 2 or 3 Elk and make a shelter of the skins dry the meat until we get able to travel."[14] Indeed, Russell died of old age in a civilized bed more than fifty years later. His story is one of the great western movies that have never been made.

By 1840 the trapping era was over. An amazingly small number of men had apparently collapsed many western beaver populations to satisfy eastern and European markets for beaver hats. Changes in fashion and the discovery of alternative materials brought the heaviest trade in beaver skins to an end. But we cannot leave this era without acknowledging a minor milestone of sorts. In 1833, at a trappers' rendezvous, Warren Angus Ferris, a clerk with the American Fur Company, heard some trappers swapping tales about the geysers along the Firehole River. Fascinated, he decided to go see for himself the following summer, thus becoming, in the words of Aubrey Haines, "the first Yellowstone 'tourist' (because his motive was curiosity, rather than business)." At his first sight of the geyser basin, he expressed the wonder of many later visitors: "I immediately proceeded to inspect them, and might have exclaimed with the Queen of Sheba, when their full reality and dimensions and novelty burst upon my view, 'the half was not told me.'"[15]

There is more than one kind of yellow stone, of course, and when gold was discovered in Idaho and Montana in the late 1850s and early 1860s, it was only a matter of time before prospectors began working the streams of the park area. Like the trappers before them, these adventurers were helping to fill in the map. Piece by piece, watershed by watershed, Yellowstone came to be known to a few whites. In the years after the Civil War, visits to the park area increased, and it is often impossible to tell what combination of curiosity and gold fever attracted people. From reading their accounts, one gets the impression that greed was usually predominant, but there is also a lively sense of discovery and adventure, and even a sense of history.

Perhaps the most entertaining of the prospectors' journals was left by A. Bart Henderson. Starting in 1867, he prospected the Yellowstone region for several years, focusing especially on drainages flowing into the Yellowstone River to the north of the present park. He was intrigued by the geysers and hot springs, and in an 1867 journal entry about some hot springs near Yellowstone Lake, he speculated about the fate of Yellowstone — one of the first to do so.

> A short distance below these springs, I found several singular formations, some being in the shape of the lid of a jar, or paint, or shaving box. These singular formations are formed as true as if turned in a turning lathe, in fact very much as if they was. I returned to camp with several very strange specimens, which I packed away very carefully. I consider these the most wonderful specimens that ever was found, & would like very much to spend one summer here. I am anxious to know what this country will develop in the course of time.[16]

Most prospecting attention was focused on the northern end of what became the park. In the late 1860s ephemeral little communities appeared and disappeared on promising tributaries of the Yellowstone, mostly north of the present park. Occasional finds and promising geology kept men like Henderson coming back, though none of them found the big strike they all dreamed of. (Avarice being one of the greatest generators of hope and fantasy, as late as the 1960s there were rumors in the park's boundary communities that park rangers were working a secret gold mine somewhere in northern Yellowstone.) By 1870 seasonal mining efforts were under way here and there; one, at the headwaters of the Clarks Fork, outside the northeast corner of the present park, would soon turn into a rambunctious permanent community, today's Cooke City.[17]

Finally, after half a century of white men wandering in, marveling at, and even mapping Yellowstone, official exploration began. A false start had been made in 1860, when Captain W. F. Raynolds of the U.S. Corps of Topographical Engineers, guided by none other than Jim Bridger, attempted to enter the Yellowstone Plateau from the southeast. They were turned back at least twenty-five miles short of the present southeast boundary of the park by high passes still deep in spring snows.[18] Over the next decade several citizens either proposed or launched explorations, the most notable being the Folsom-Cook-Peterson party of 1869, which traveled up the miners' trail from Bozeman to the Yellowstone River Valley, past Emigrant (already the site of an early ranching and commercial hunting enterprise, as well as a nearby mining settlement), and on up into the park area.[19]

This party visited the Grand Canyon, Yellowstone Lake, and some of the geyser basins, then followed the Madison River Valley back down into the settlements. It being September, they heard elk bugling "in every direction" in the Lamar Valley. Later, while riding through the forest, Cook happened to be turned around in his saddle attending to a packhorse when his own mount suddenly stopped still. When he turned, Cook found himself on the very brink of the Grand Canyon of the Yellowstone River, certainly one of the most dramatic and surprising first sights of that great gorge that any early traveler had.

But when these sober, respectable citizens returned to the towns of Montana, their attempt at exploration was greeted with public skepticism. The established eastern magazines were unwilling to publish what they considered "unreliable material," but enough of the Folsom-Cook-Peterson party's adventures did find their way into print to encourage another party the following year. Indeed, Folsom communicated directly with the leader of that party, Henry Washburn, and made a few encouraging remarks about the need to protect the area, making him an early proponent (one of many) of the national park idea.

These accounts of travel in Yellowstone between 1819 and 1870 have become our primary sources concerning the park's condition on the eve of its establishment. These writings have often been

"The Great Cañon and Lower Falls of the Yellowstone," from Hayden's *Geological Survey of the Territories.*

invoked in the debate about the commonness of wildlife, particularly elk, in the area. People who believe there are now "too many" elk in Yellowstone cite passages from early accounts suggesting that elk were rare or nonexistent here prior to the 1870s, while people who think the elk population is probably not overabundant cite passages suggesting that elk were always here.

Park historian Lee Whittlesey spent many years gathering early accounts of the area, most of which had never been examined by ecologists interested in the elk issue. In 1992 he and I studied 168 accounts of the park area prior to 1882 — more than eight times as many as anyone had evaluated before.[20] We learned that it is impossible to make trustworthy generalizations without having a huge amount of such informal, anecdotal material and that it is apparently very easy to misinterpret whatever evidence you do find.

We concluded that Yellowstone had lots of large mammals in the early nineteenth century, and substantial numbers of elk apparently wintered there. Great numbers of pronghorn (far more than now) were seen, especially in the river valleys that extend out from the park's boundaries. There were herds of bison, and mule deer were common. Bighorn sheep may have been much more abundant then than now. Moose were common only in the southern part of the park, and white-tailed deer were very rare.

Even after examining so many sources (and subsequently many more), we did not share the confidence of many earlier writers that these kinds of "accidental" data were sufficiently detailed to allow for population estimates of any precision. Because the early 1800s was the height of the Little Ice Age, and because some early travelers remarked on snow depths or weather, we suspect that conditions were a good bit harsher then, which may have meant that fewer animals wintered there then than do now.

By the early 1900s it was "common knowledge" among wildlife professionals that the western mountains had held little game prior to the coming of whites and that the large animals like elk and bison had been "pushed back up into the mountains" by settlement of the lower country. This was considered to be true of Yellowstone. Perhaps in some places settlement did have that effect, as it may have had in the Yellowstone area in the closing years of the nineteenth century, when settlement became heavy enough near the park to affect wildlife migrations. But before the 1880s there were no settlements close enough to Yellowstone to push wildlife in any direction. Of the 168 pre-1882 accounts we analyzed, 56 commented on numbers of wildlife, and 51 of those — more than 90 percent — stated that wildlife was abundant. The other 5 accounts didn't explain their belief that animals were scarce (a couple were written by disgruntled unsuccessful sport hunters), so it wasn't clear if they thought the animals had always been scarce, had been reduced by overhunting, or were scarce for some other reason.

This is an overwhelming body of contemporary opinion in favor of wildlife abundance, and the accounts themselves make it easy to believe. Osborne Russell's diaries are full of references to game; in August of 1837 he described the country around Yellowstone Lake as "swarming with Elk."[21] Many other writers reported a similar abundance; phrases like "a hunter's paradise" were common. But there was no societal memory to keep this firsthand knowledge of actual conditions alive. Only forty years later the information was lost, to the eventual confusion of generations of elk researchers, who thought that elk were somehow "unnatural" in this great elk habitat.

Though a number of scientists have proposed, even today, that wildlife was rare or nonexistent in the park in the early 1800s, perhaps the best-known nonscientific statement of that position appeared in Alston Chase's *Playing God in Yellowstone* (1986), a colossal gathering of negative opinions about almost every aspect of Yellowstone management. The author used nine early accounts to make his case. That is of course far too few to rely upon, but it is the way he used them that most clearly reveals how historical analysis of this question has gone awry.

Chase mentions the account of Captain William Raynolds, whose 1860 attempt to enter Yellowstone was thwarted by high snows: "In 1856, scout Jim Bridger warned explorer Captain William F. Raynolds not to try to traverse the Yellowstone plateau, because he would find nothing to eat. 'A bird can't fly over that,' he warned, 'without taking a supply of grub along.'"[22]

But Chase, who has the year wrong (it happened in 1860), has taken Bridger's quote out of context. In fact, Bridger's view of the wildlife of Yellowstone had been published even before the Raynolds expedition, when another army officer had quoted him as saying that "bear, elk, deer, wolf, and fox are among the game." That Bridger was not talking about the entire "Yellowstone plateau" is clear enough in Raynolds's account.[23] By the end of May, Raynolds's party had traveled up the Wind River and reached a point north of Union Pass, about twenty-five miles south of the southeast corner of what is now the park. To get closer, they would have to climb over a high ridge and drop down into the headwaters of the Yellowstone River drainage, then proceed down the river to Yellowstone Lake and beyond. But Raynolds discovered that the snow was too deep on the high ridge ("Directly across our route lies a basaltic ridge, rising not less than 5,000 feet above us"). Raynolds gives us no reason to think that when Bridger said "a bird can't fly over that without taking a supply of grub" he was referring to the several thousand square miles of the Yellowstone Plateau; the mountain man was obviously talking about that high, snowbound pass.

Raynolds's account, in fact, makes clear that game was abundant in the country they traveled. For days before deep snow stopped them, the party had been encountering game, including "abundance of buffalo 'signs.'" They had no reason to fear that they wouldn't encounter more game on the other side of the ridge; they just couldn't get over it.

Chase also cites Ferdinand Hayden out of context, in perhaps the most famous misused quote in this debate, and further errs by misconstruing the report left by Captains Barlow and Heap, who led Hayden's military escort through the park at the same time: "The Hayden expedition of 1871, though it employed professional hunters, reported finding only one animal, a mule deer, on the entire trip. The party of Captains Barlow and Heap, army engineers who explored the park in 1871, exhausted their food eight days before the end of their trip and had to send out for more."[24]

Here is what Hayden actually wrote:

> Our hunters returned, after diligent search for two and a half days, with only a black-tailed deer, which, though poor, was a most important addition to our larder. It seems that during the summer months of August and September the elk and deer resort to the summits of the mountains, to escape from the swarms of flies in the lowlands about the lake. Tracks of game could be seen everywhere, but none of the animals themselves were to be found.[25]

Hayden made it clear that he believed animals were as common as their tracks suggested, and he later became an active campaigner on behalf of protection for the park's abundant wildlife. Moreover, other members of his party did see animals and reinforced his report of tracks. Hayden's group frequently split up to cover different areas in their survey, and various members of his military escort, under Captains Barlow and Heap, frequently mentioned seeing animals, including several elk they shot, as well as tracks and other sign.

Near the Lower Geyser Basin they reported that "tracks of deer, elk, and buffalo in great abundance were seen," and on the upper Yellowstone River, near the park's south boundary, "signs of game abound, among which were found the tracks of the grizzly and black bear, mountain-sheep, elk, and deer." North of Sour Creek, "the wood abounded with game-tracks, several elk and deer being seen just in advance of our train."[26]

Dr. A. C. Peale was one of several members of the Hayden party that year who kept a diary, and it is full of interesting references to wildlife. On August 9, for example, he reported a missed shot at an elk, and on August 11 their hunters killed three elk. As to the matter of exhausting their food, there were provision shortages, but what they ran out of were items one cannot obtain in the wilderness. Peale reported on August 15 that "all our flour has been used and we have to live on meat coffee & tea."[27] These early parties were often on short rations of one sort or another, depending as they did on getting meat through hunting and on rationing the supplies (sugar, flour, coffee, and so on) they had to bring with them. Vague references to a shortage of store-bought provisions is no proof that the wildlife population was small.

The Hayden party of 1871, perhaps partly because it was large and noisy, partly because the animals were in higher country, and partly because they were unlucky, wasn't as successful at hunting as were many other parties. (That, presumably, is why it is called "hunting" instead of "finding.") The following year the Hayden party did a lot better. William Blackmore, a member of the 1872 party, wrote in his diary that in a three-week period in late July and August, the five hunters in his party of about thirty men killed thirteen antelope, sixteen elk, two deer, eight bear, and assorted smaller game. On this trip Dr. Peale arrived at their camp at Mud Volcano following an especially successful day of hunting and "found them all enjoying roast elk meat . . . the place looked like a meat market, there was so much meat about."[28]

The notion that large western mammals were displaced from the plains up into the mountains by settlement is a complex one, and it will probably endure in regional folklore for a long time. It seems highly improbable that free- and far-ranging herds of herbi-vores that had spent several millennia adapting to prairie life could abruptly move to the mountains and adjust to an entirely different behavioral and ecological regime. Rather than some animals "find-ing refuge" in the mountains, it seems more likely that some animals that had always lived in the more remote, high-elevation habitats were the only ones left after settlement of the lower country and that these remaining animals were presumed to have fled there.

Humans do have profound effects on the ways wildlife use the environment. For example, in some places in the West, as settle-ment advanced, some animals accustomed to moving from summer ranges in the high country to winter ranges in lower valleys may have been denied access to those ranges; thus they may have spent more time more densely concentrated in areas where they had for-merly not stayed during winter. This type of "displacement" of wildlife from the lower country is also assumed as fact in the wildlife management business, though the notion appears not to be as care-fully thought out as it should be.

The notion of displacement is routinely applied to Yellowstone. After the area farther down the Yellowstone River Valley was settled heavily in the 1890s and later, elk attempting to migrate from sum-mer ranges in the park to winter ranges in the valley ran into both hunters and property barriers. How the elk responded to the block-age of their migration routes is unclear. Some people think they simply toughed out the winters in ever greater numbers in the park; others suggest that perhaps the migratory segment of the herd was wiped out, and the animals that had always wintered in the park continued to do so. Neither position has been proven, but the his-torical evidence does, I think, indicate that elk were wintering in the park prior to 1872. Additional study of the archeological and paleon-tological record should help clarify this question, but it seems im-probable that we will ever have a precise idea of how many elk wintered in the park area over the long centuries before 1872.

Twentieth-century changes in vegetation in Yellowstone, espe-cially those caused by the elk's very heavy use of woody vegetation such as willow, aspen, and cottonwood, have been interpreted as evidence that the animals are "unnaturally" concentrated. It is quite clear that in some places, especially along the park boundaries and in the feeding grounds set up for these animals in the early 1900s, the elk have at times concentrated heavily, and elk certainly do hammer the woody vegetation hard all winter. However, the grasslands on the park's winter ranges have proven able to support large numbers of elk year after year, so the question remains why these elk would not have used these same hospitable winter ranges in the winters before settlement. Indeed, it may be that the park can now support more wintering elk than it did 150 years ago. Climate change, especially the gradual warming since the end of the Little Ice Age in the mid-1800s, may have made the park an easier wintering area.[29]

Another difference between wildlife in the park today and in the early 1800s is in the uses humans have made of it. Historians and ecologists have for many years theorized about the effects that Indians had on local large mammal populations. The many accounts of Yellowstone prior to 1872 indicate that the various neighboring tribes freely traveled through the area, but these accounts don't give us much detail about their hunting activities (there isn't a single useful account of the Bannocks on their trail in the park, though they used it for decades during this period). All these accounts really do is provide the historian with the occasional tasty vignette, just enough information to inspire conjecture.

As explained in the previous chapter, Indians created a variety of "works" to help them kill game. There is evidence of some buffalo jumps (where bison were intentionally stampeded off cliffs to kill them) in the lower country near the park, and one possible buffalo jump site has been identified in the park. But in the writings of the first white visitors to the area in the nineteenth century, we find no firsthand accounts of such jumps or of other mass-killing sites in action. But we do find numerous accounts of Indian hunting and other manipulation of wildlife populations in or near the park area. In 1860 William Raynolds noted extensive evidence of Indian activity in the Wind River drainage south and southeast of Yellowstone:

I have frequently heard that the Snake Indians keep the buffaloes penned up in the mountain valleys, and kill them as their necessities require. Our camping ground for the night is evidently one much used, as the remains of numerous lodges and hundreds of lodge poles cover the ground, and it is evident that a camp at this point would effectually "pen" anything not winged that should chance to be in the valley above it.[30]

And after Osborne Russell and his companion were shot by Blackfeet Indians in 1839 they hid near the shore of Yellowstone Lake, where they watched an Indian hunting party of about sixty people "shooting at a large bank [band?] of elk that was swimming in the lake killed 4 of them dragged them to shore and butchered them which occupied about 3 hours. They then packed the meat in small bundles on their backs and travelled up along the rocky shore about a mile and encamped."[31]

Russell left several other accounts of Indians either hunting or with game in hand. During his meeting with the Sheepeaters in the Lamar Valley, described in the previous chapter, his party "obtained a large number of Elk Deer and Sheep skins from them of the finest quality and three large neatly dressed Panther Skins in return for awls axes, kettles tobacco ammunition etc."[32] The many skins on hand might suggest that the Indians were killing more game than they needed in order to trade the skins with whites, but Russell's party was the first they had seen in some years, and they actually fled at his approach, only returning when he convinced them he was peaceable. Russell also noted that the Indians had "killed nearly all" of the beaver in the area (beaver being preferred even to elk and bison for food by some tribes) and had singed the fur off the beaver hides, "being ignorant of the value."[33] Singed beaver hides were not of interest to white trappers, and Russell sounds a little disappointed that the Indians were ruining the hides this way, but this further suggests that this group of Indians, at least, were not yet familiar with the white trade in beaver skins. Any effects these Sheepeaters were having on the local wildlife (reduction of numbers, change of distribution, or change in behavior) were probably the result of their own needs rather than of white commerce.

On the other hand, in September of 1866, when A. Bart Henderson met a group of Sheepeaters on the Graybull River east of what is now the park, he was there "for the purpose of trading skins &c with them, as we knew they had hundreds of fine sheep skins and furs of all kinds."[34] Perhaps by Henderson's time there were enough whites in the area to induce the Indians to kill animals for trade. Incidentally, Henderson made several other references to hides in his possession during his years in the area, including a cache of twenty-seven bear skins gathered in 1870.[35]

The accounts of Russell, Henderson, and others suggest that white and Indian hunting and trapping may have had considerable effects on pre-1872 wildlife populations. Russell's comments indicate that the Indians, even with no trade incentive from whites, had depressed or eliminated the beaver population of a sizable drainage. Judging from their effectiveness elsewhere, it seems that the numerous trappers who visited Yellowstone almost certainly could have done the same.[36]

Yellowstone on the eve of its formal discovery and establishment as a national park was already a culturally complex and ecologically subtle place. It was as wild as any land in the lower forty-eight, a storehouse of the native species and ecological processes of the pre-Columbian American West, but it was also, in the modern jargon of historical preservation, a cultural landscape. It was already a powerful stimulant to the human imagination and had been a source of power for human souls for a long time. But even its most seasoned travelers and most creative storytellers could hardly imagine what it was about to become.

4 | A PUBLIC PARK

THE INITIAL RELUCTANCE of the world to believe the wild tales of Yellowstone's many wonders served only to heighten interest in the place when their truth was finally confirmed. So late in the exploration of the West, when the frontier was closing fast, such fresh and spectacular wonders must have seemed all the more remarkable. Part of Yellowstone's early appeal, both as a tourist attraction and as an idea, must have had to do with its being a last frontier itself.

No other early visit to Yellowstone, not even Osborne Russell's journal of the 1830s, has so engaged our interest and appealed to our longing for vicarious adventure as the Washburn-Langford-Doane expedition (hereinafter the Washburn expedition) of 1870. Though it was not the first exploration of the park, it captured the American imagination almost immediately and has held it ever since. Excited by stories (especially from the Folsom-Cook-Peterson party) of strange sights on the upper Yellowstone, the Washburn expedition was organized in mid-August and set off from Bozeman well supplied for an extended trip. The group had a very good idea of what they were going to "discover." Washburn carried copies of Cook's and Folsom's diaries, as well as a map of Montana and northern Wyoming, including Yellowstone, just published by his office, which included much of Folsom's information from the year before.[1] Most explorers and discoverers aren't as well supplied as these men, but that doesn't lessen the impact of their findings. Here was the full story at last: the major geyser basins defined, the great falls of the

Yellowstone River measured, the mountains climbed, and the mysteries revealed.

There would be no denying their reports, because the party consisted largely of prominent citizens of Montana and official federal representatives — a military escort under Lieutenant Gustavus Doane. Henry Washburn was surveyor general of Montana Territory, Nathaniel Langford had spent several years as internal revenue collector for Montana, Walter Trumbull was the son of an Illinois senator, and the others were merchants, attorneys, and politicians.[2]

Traveling up the Yellowstone River, they followed what would become a popular tourist route, missing Mammoth Hot Springs, then heading across the Blacktail Plateau to Tower Fall. They climbed and named Mount Washburn, followed the Yellowstone River to Yellowstone Lake, then skirted the east shore and circled the lake as far as West Thumb. One party member, Truman Everts, got lost and wandered for more than a month before being rescued in northern Yellowstone.[3] After spending as much of their time and supplies as they could afford searching for Everts, the rest of the party visited the Upper Geyser Basin, then followed the Madison River down and out of the present park area and back to the Montana settlements. Like so many others, they wrote of abundant wildlife, but their great contribution was in the full, accurate descriptions of a remarkable array of hot springs and geysers. In various reports and articles, they effused at great length about this hot pool or that geyser. Theirs might be thought of as the first grand tour, a trip of endless wonder, and for most of them it was the great event of their lives.

Soon after entering what is now the park, they came upon a hot-spring area on the slopes of Mount Washburn, which they christened "Hell-Broth Springs" (now Washburn Hot Springs). Cornelius Hedges, noting that "doubtless the sources of this heat, if not of the water, are the great internal fires in the innermost bowels of the earth," ruminated on the demonic feeling of the place: "In earlier ages fancy would have peopled the vicinity with grimy ghosts and demons dire, trooping in the triple darkness of storm, shade, and night to hold unhallowed carnival about such an infernal looking smelling and sounding place, bowl, and contents. But science has so demoralized fancy that it will probably succeed poorly in peopling Hell-Broth Springs."[4]

He sounds a little disappointed in the sensibility of his time, as if Yellowstone deserved a more fanciful belief system than science could provide. It is entertaining to wonder how Hedges would have reacted to the eventual discovery in the hot springs of an incredibly complex set of hot-water ecosystems "peopled" by uncounted species of microscopic life forms that have been of far-reaching benefit to human society.

Human fancy was indeed hard pressed to keep pace with all that the explorers saw. At the Lower Falls in the Grand Canyon, Hedges admitted that it was difficult to know which to admire more, the sheer immensity of the show or its actual features: "At first the grandeur overtops and absorbs all other considerations, while the beauties only come out to appreciation by time."[5] They saw a dozen geysers in action in the Upper Geyser Basin. The most poetic moment of the trip may have occurred when, just as they emerged from the dense forest onto the edge of the basin, they were greeted by a geyser: "Judge, then, of our great astonishment on entering this basin, to see at no great distance before us an immense body of sparkling water, projected suddenly and with terrific force into the air to the height of over one hundred feet. We had found a real geyser."[6] This moment alone should have earned the Washburn party a sort of literary immortality; the geyser that would become a world symbol not only of Yellowstone but of fidelity itself seemed to have waited through the centuries for its chroniclers, and at the instant of their appearance greeted them with an eruption. The coincidence helps explain the magical quality that these men, and many who have followed them, attached to the Washburn visit. They stayed long enough to see that this geyser was a regular, almost predictable performer and named it Old Faithful.

Other geysers also overpowered their senses. Washburn described one that they also named:

William Henry Jackson took the earliest known photograph of Old Faithful in eruption during the Hayden expedition's 1872 survey of the park. *National Park Service*

Standing and looking down into the steam and vapor of the crater of the Giantess, with the sun upon your back, the shadow is surrounded by a beautiful rainbow, and by getting the proper angle, the rainbow, surrounding only the head, gives that halo so many painters have vainly tried to give in paintings of the Savior. Standing near the fountain when in motion, and the sun shining, the scene is grandly magnificent; each of the broken atoms of water shining like so many brilliants, while myriads of rainbows are dancing attendance. No wonder, then, that our usually staid and sober companions threw up their hats and shouted with ecstasy at the sight.[7]

We see in these descriptions the basic elements that still characterize the experience of Yellowstone's hydrothermal scenery. The weirdness fascinates and attracts us, and then the beauty rises to awe and stun. All is brilliant light and ominous shadow, alternating dazzling prismatic displays with the "dark, dismal, diabolical aspect" of each place.[8] The ebb and flow of the waters gives the show length and change, so that we become aware of subtlety as well, whether in the play of refracted light in a pool's depth or the delicate scalloping of mineral deposits along its edges.

As historians begin to seriously study the evolving aesthetics of Yellowstone's geothermal features, the papers of the Washburn expedition must be an important primary source.[9] Not only did members of this party give us unusually careful accounts of what they saw and how they reacted to it, their writings were widely read and formed the basis of some of the park's first guidebooks. With the Washburn expedition, wonder assumed a primary place in written accounts of Yellowstone. The fantasy and hyperbole of the mountain men were superseded (though never entirely replaced) by the glowing, emotional enthusiasm of more self-consciously civilized observers.

By 1870 many personalities involved in the establishment of the park, still two years in the future, were already embroiled in controversy. The more I read of Yellowstone Park's early administrative and legislative history, the more I realize how convoluted its paternity was and how many people were anxious to take some credit for the idea. But many of them have been forgotten, and the story much simplified.

Since the turn of the century, the creation of Yellowstone has been told as a near-fable in which the idea for the park came into being on the evening of September 19, 1870, as Washburn and his friends sat around a campfire at the junction of the Firehole and Gibbon rivers. The next day they would follow the Madison River (formed by that junction) back home, and their sense of opportunity and responsibility weighed heavily. After various party members had suggested ways to profit from the area's wonders (such as by staking claims to profitable tourist sites), Cornelius Hedges asserted that the area was too important for commercial exploitation and should be made into a national park. The men agreed and vowed to fight for the protection of Yellowstone's wonders. This is the institutional legend that has inspired generations of conservationists, rangers, and park visitors.[10]

One hundred and two years later a plaque was dedicated at Madison Junction in honor of that campfire conversation, which led to the birth of Yellowstone and of the national parks. The campfire story, this spontaneous outflowing of good will and energy, this immaculate conception of a great idea, still has wide currency in the literature and speechmaking of the national parks. The story portrayed the park idea as having such intuitive force of rightness that it was immediately embraced by all who heard it. For park managers seeking to justify or enlarge their meager budgets, the campfire story provided a rhetorical position of moral unassailability. It also provided the park movement with perfect heroes: altruists who were so committed to protecting wonder and beauty that they would forgo all thought of personal gain. And it put the creation of the park movement in the hands of the people whose possession of it would have the most symbolic power: regular citizens.

But the legend is not true. Some historians had long been skeptical of the campfire story; in 1948 historian Hans Huth referred to it as a "sentimental legend," and in 1960 National Park Service historian Carl P. Russell called it a "mistaken story" and said that "it is not necessary to make such an unsupported claim in order that Yellowstone National Park may be lighted by an extra blaze of glory."[11] In the 1960s, under intense scrutiny by Yellowstone historian Aubrey Haines and by Richard Bartlett, a prominent historian of the West, the story fell apart. The campfire conversation may not even have taken place, and if it did, it hardly mattered in the history of the park.

None of the original diaries, letters, or published articles by Washburn party members even mentioned such a conversation that evening, though they wrote of many far less momentous discussions. Hedges's own diary said nothing of the evening's activities, and the next morning's entry commented only that he didn't sleep well for "thinking of home & business."[12] In 1904 he published an edited version of his 1870 diary and became the first member of the Washburn party to refer to the campfire conversation, modestly saying that he suggested they work to preserve the place as a national park, "little dreaming that such a thing were possible."[13] In 1905 Langford published an edited version of his own diary, in which he included a much more full account of the conversation, and the legend was born.

Though Hedges seems to have been an honest man, Haines's research revealed that Langford was a tireless and unethical self-promoter who left a legacy of shifty dealings and indignant business associates.[14] For example, there is the matter (one of great importance to the various contenders for Yellowstone's fatherhood) of which person first used the term "national park" in their discussions. Langford claimed to be the one. In the 1890s, when Hiram Chittenden was preparing the first edition of *The Yellowstone National Park, Historical and Descriptive* (1895), Langford sent him a letter supposedly transcribing a quotation taken from the *New York Tribune* of January 23, 1871, in which Langford was reported as having given a speech in favor of the creation of Yellowstone as a "national park." Repeated searches by historians have failed to find any such quotation in any New York paper of the time, but Chittenden, trusting Langford, published the spurious quotation, which became a staple of Yellowstone history.[15]

In Langford's sizable collection of papers at the Minnesota Historical Society, two important items are missing (Langford was, in Haines's words, "a literary string saver," so the documentation is extensive): the scrapbook of clippings that would have held the *Tribune* clipping if it existed and Langford's original pocket diary (one of many in the collection) carried on the Yellowstone trip. Haines, having learned so much of Langford's slipperiness, could only ask, "Were they disposed of for a reason?"[16]

We cannot prove that the legendary conversation happened, but on the other hand we cannot prove it didn't. We can only wonder why the most important intellectual achievement of the trip, one that changed the lives of several of the participants forever, went unmentioned for so long, among a group of men often singled out for their achievement (and thus given abundant opportunity to retell their story). Like Haines, I am inclined to think that some sort of discussion may have occurred around the campfire that night but that it meant little to any of them or to Yellowstone.[17] Langford's low reputation and seamy ambitions intrude on my thinking at every turn. Perhaps more important, the story of that September campfire leaves out most of the background of the making of Yellowstone National Park.

Yellowstone as the product of human culture is much more realistic than Yellowstone as the sole creative property of one man. As Hans Huth, Aubrey Haines, Roderick Nash, and other historians have shown, the park grew out of a long, if halting, movement among European cultures to create parks and preserves of many kinds. The earliest example in the American West was Yosemite Valley, given by the United States to the state of California in 1864 so that its extraordinary scenery might be preserved. The language of the act creating Yellowstone National Park in 1872 is strikingly similar to the language used in the Yosemite cession.[18] Yellowstone did not spontaneously appear; it grew from earlier experiments in shared public land that had already given us sites as diverse as the village greens of New England, New York's Central Park, and the Yosemite Valley. It was a great leap, in fact, from the protection of relatively small sites to a very large one, in excess of 2 million acres, but it was only one leap in a journey begun long before. In the history of this journey, Langford's fabled gathering of sainted altruists at Madison Junction might appropriately merit a midtext footnote about apocryphal tales rather than prominence on the first page.

The true story is far more complex. The creation of the park involved many moments of inspiration and many more of successful campaigning. In 1865 the territorial governor of Montana, Thomas Meagher, and a group of companions were snowbound at the St. Peter's Mission in west-central Montana. Their host was Father Francis Xavier Kuppens, one of many people who had visited the Yellowstone area, and he told them what he had seen there earlier that year. According to Kuppens's own account, "Meagher said if things were as described the government ought to reserve the territory for a national park. All the visitors agreed that efforts should be made to explore the region and that a report of it should be sent to the government." Among those present during the conversation was Cornelius Hedges.[19]

Folsom later claimed that in 1869 he and others in his party had had a conversation near Madison Junction in which they agreed that the area "ought to be kept for the public in some way." (However, the conversation is not mentioned in any of their journals and thus has the same dubious flavor as Langford's story of the following year.) None of the men in the Folsom-Cook-Peterson party used the term "national park," but Folsom said he shared this sentiment with Washburn when the latter was preparing for his 1870 trip.[20]

By 1870, when the Washburn party was still forming, Jay Cooke's Northern Pacific Railroad needed backing for its planned route through Montana Territory. Nathaniel Langford met with Cooke early that summer and convinced him that the wonders of Yellowstone could be a useful device for promoting the line.[21] Thus even before visiting the park area, Langford knew its commercial possibilities and was communicating with the one commercial enterprise — the railroad — most able to take legitimate advantage of those possibilities. Within two months of his return from Yellowstone, Langford was hired by Cooke to deliver twenty lectures on Yellowstone; the first was given on January 19, 1871, in Washington, D.C.[22]

In the audience was U.S. Geological Survey administrator Dr. Ferdinand V. Hayden, who became interested enough in Yellowstone to obtain congressional funding to survey the area that summer. He and his team had an adventure nearly the equal of the Washburn party's and brought back a host of specimens, measurements, photographs (by William Henry Jackson), and illustrations (by Thomas Moran) to flesh out the public portrait of the place.

Then, on October 27, 1871, just after his return to Washington, Hayden received a letter on Jay Cooke's letterhead. It was from A. B. Nettleton, an agent of the Northern Pacific Railroad, and it forwarded to Hayden an idea suggested by Judge William Kelley of Philadelphia, a friend and business associate of Cooke's and a longtime railroad booster. Kelley, according to Nettleton, proposed that "Congress pass a bill reserving the Great Geyser Basin as a public park forever — just as it has reserved that far inferior wonder the Yosemite valley and big trees. If you approve this would such a recommendation be appropriate in your official report?"[23] Hayden, of course, decided that it would. Nettleton seems to have been the first to put the word "park" on paper in reference to Yellowstone.

The winter of 1871–72 was a busy one for the park promoters. The bill to create the park was introduced into both the House and the Senate on December 18, 1871, and Langford and the rest of what historians have identified as the "Montana group" (especially Hedges, Samuel Hauser, and Montana's newly elected representative, William Clagett) agitated for its advancement as best they could, perhaps most effectively through Langford's continued speeches and two articles in *Scribner's Monthly* (June 1871 and February 1872).[24] Langford was not yet advocating a park in print, and his promotion of the railroad was understated, but he was raising the public's awareness of the wonders of Yellowstone. Hayden, meanwhile, through his writings (an article of his also appeared in *Scribner's* in February 1872) and his powerful political connections, saw to it that congressional interest was activated; he displayed some of Jackson's superb photographs and Moran's vivid watercolor field sketches, along with geological specimens, in the Capitol rotunda. And at all times representatives of the Northern Pacific Railroad were moving quietly in the wings, apparently engineering the most important parts of the campaign while letting (whether intentionally or not) the key public figures seem to function independent of such influence. The Senate bill, S. 392, made its way through committee first and was signed by Ulysses S. Grant on March 1, 1872.

The motivation of the creators of Yellowstone has been a troubling issue for many people. When Haines exposed the many flaws in the campfire story, he sent a shock wave through the National Park Service. Some administrators immediately recognized the sense in his account, while others were deeply offended. Horace Albright, an often heroic figure in the park service's first years, was still a vital presence in the conservation community in the 1960s, and he fought bitterly and effectively against the demythologizing of the campfire creation story. He, more than anyone else, had employed the moral purity of the story to promote the goodness of the parks and had turned the story into a secular genesis for the conservation movement. It was unthinkable to him that Yellowstone did not start at Madison Junction.

The only hope for a reasonable understanding of the origin of Yellowstone National Park is in admitting that none of this was simple. Human nature was not on holiday. The people who created Yellowstone were not exempt from greed, any more than they were immune to wonder. Some cared more for the money, some for the beauty. Some were scoundrels, some may have been saints. It is true that Langford and others were eager to take railroad money to promote the park, but that is not in itself proof of evil intention. I have yet to find any reason to suspect that Cornelius Hedges, for example, had anything but the best interests of the public at heart. Hayden, a powerful and ambitious science administrator, is prob-

Thomas Moran's woodcut "Crater of the Castle Geyser" (Upper Geyser Basin) illustrated Nathaniel Langford's article in *Scribner's Monthly,* June 1871. Images like this, inaccurate in scale (the men and animals are much too small in proportion to the formation) and in detail (Moran had not seen the geyser basins and did not understand the deposition process), gave the world its first look at the wonders of Yellowstone.

ably even more interesting than Langford; his impulse was to further the work of his survey, and thus his own career, but as a result he made an enormous contribution to our knowledge of Yellowstone and to the protection of the park. Perhaps most significant, while the unbridled corporate impulses of the Northern Pacific Railroad would over the next fifteen years place Yellowstone at considerable risk, the railroad would also be the foremost means of public access to the park for the first half century of its existence. The railroad shaped the Yellowstone experience more than any other factor before the automobile.

The campfire myth is not the only oversimplification of the story of Yellowstone's creation. In his provocative book *National Parks: The American Experience,* historian Alfred Runte argued that Americans suffered from a "cultural insecurity" that drove them to create parks as a way of proving that their landscapes (and therefore they themselves) were a match for Europe's long, rich human history and culture.[25] Parks were set aside "first as symbols of national pride, and, in time, as areas for public recreation."[26] To demonstrate this for Yellowstone, he quoted explorers — Charles Cook, Langford, Gustavus Doane — who described various geological features in architectural terms: towers, spires, pillars, terraces, fountains. To Runte this proved that these men were seeking to compensate for their culture's lack of European monuments by showing that America could be proud of its *landscape's* architecture. Pride in landscape is a very interesting idea, one that deserves consideration in the later history of the national parks, but in the case of Yellowstone Runte's argument is entirely conjectural.

First, in their praises of Yellowstone, none of these men mentioned that its features proved America's equality with Europe. Runte had to infer that; for example, he quoted Doane that the geyser basin along the Firehole River "surpasses all other great wonders of the continent."[27] Doane was talking about the *North American* continent, but Runte jumped to conclude that "it followed that the scenery of the Old World, especially the Alps, had found its equal in the Rocky Mountains as well as the Sierra Nevada."[28] This is all conjecture. Langford and Doane both compared Yellowstone's geysers to other geysers of the world, including those of Iceland and Tibet, but said nothing about the Old World or the Alps. Langford's entire emphasis was on the superiority of Yellowstone to the rest of *American* scenery, and Doane's special emphasis was on the great scientific (rather than scenic) interest of Yellowstone.

As for the architectural comparisons, many aspects of young, raw landscapes are blockish or towerlike. Many geological formations remind people of buildings. Others remind them of the moon or an Indian chief. The flowing water of a hot spring deposits its minerals as gravity dictates, often resulting in terracing. Mudpots remind people of pudding. Do Yellowstone's dozens of thermal features that were named early on the Devil's this or Hell's that prove we envy Hell? Of course not. All these comparisons prove is that we seek to associate the new with the familiar.

When Haines stirred up the agency with his revelations about the campfire story, he obviously assumed that he was simply straightening out some facts and restoring historical reality to the park's origin. But in fact he was arguing religion with some very determined zealots. Historians have mostly learned better, but the plaque is still there at Madison Junction. The Madison campfire story, like many "creation myths," is valuable not for its accuracy but for its rhetorical force. The campfire story is still told, but some who tell it realize that, like the famous speech of Chief Seattle now often invoked by environmentalists, it is poor history.

The decade following the Civil War was not a time of notable government foresight. The public domain was being chopped up and parceled out as fast as possible, and with all manner of corruption. The idea of saving a piece of land for future generations — other than future generations of investors and speculators — was quite odd, not only to legislators but to much of the public. But thanks to the hard work of Hayden, Langford, and others, Yellowstone National Park came into being.

The act of 1872 set aside a large rectangle of land (a vaguely drawn box that, it was hoped, would take in all of the known wonders and any others hidden nearby) that was "hereby reserved and withdrawn from settlement, occupancy, or sale under the laws of the United States, and dedicated and set apart as a public park or pleasuring ground for the benefit and enjoyment of the people; and all persons who shall locate or settle upon or occupy the same, or any part thereof, except as hereinafter provided, shall be considered trespassers, and removed therefrom."[29]

An especially interesting element of the debate over setting aside Yellowstone had to do with its possible worth for other purposes. When the park was being discussed in Congress, its supporters found it helpful to argue that it wasn't really good for anything else. As one congressman put it, "It is a region of country seven thousand feet above the level of the sea, where there is frost every month of the year, and where nobody can dwell upon it for the purpose of agriculture."[30] Alfred Runte takes a fairly extreme position on this statement, claiming that "clearly its approval hinged on whether or not the park would interfere with the future of the West as a store-house of natural resources,"[31] but this conclusion doesn't seem clear at all. Yellowstone's advocates in Congress did repeatedly assert that the land was not good for anything else, but few lawmakers questioned whether the land was really useless. I suspect that once the Northern Pacific threw its weight behind the park, it was going to happen.

But as Runte correctly points out, "The enabling act bore no 'inalienable' clause."[32] Yellowstone could be *un*created by Congress if, as one representative put it, "it shall be found that it can be made useful for settlers."[33] Yellowstone's legislative foundation, now seemingly so secure, was initially quite insecure.

When the legislation was signed by the president, one Helena newspaper lamented that "the effect of this measure will be to keep the country a wilderness, and shut out, for many years, the travel that would seek that curious region. . . . We regard the passage of the act as a great blow struck at the prosperity of the towns of Bozeman and Virginia City."[34] In this respect the politics of the creation of nature reserves has not changed much. It doesn't matter how often, and in how many places, the protection of large natural settings has proven to be a financial bonanza to the surrounding communities; each time the locals have to learn the lesson for themselves, kicking and screaming for a generation or so until they notice how much more money they're making than they used to.

On the other hand, another Helena paper, in favor of the park, claimed that it would "redound to the untold good of this Territory, inasmuch as a measure of this character is well calculated to direct the world's attention to a very important section of the country that to the present time has passed largely unnoticed. It will be the means of centering on Montana the attention of thousands heretofore comparatively uninformed of a Territory abounding in such resources as mines and agriculture and of wonderland as we can boast, spread everywhere about us."[35] Not a word here about the aesthetic (much less spiritual) value of saving the land or of making it available to the diverse recreational needs of the national public; it all came down to cash.

"Yellowstone Geysers," a gatefold engraving from Hayden's *Geological Survey of the Territories* (1872), dramatically depicts the character of a number of Yellowstone's hydrothermal features. It captures the delicate scalloping around the pools, the remarkable variety of form, and the shape of the formations with great precision.

Little has changed in the way national parks come into being. They are still created and then maintained in a rich and sulfurous atmosphere of love and fear, wonder and boosterism, awe and greed, with a desperate measure of high hopes. As unsettling as this combination of forces may be for the participants in the process, it is improbable that any other process would work at all. For all its great beauty and fabulous wonder, for all the near-religious devotion of its adherents, and for all its world fame as a milestone achievement of human society, the park must still make its way in the less lofty realm of political economy.

5 | ECOLOGICAL HOLOCAUST

THIRTY MILES NORTH of the park boundary, well downstream from the confining reaches of Yankee Jim Canyon, the Yellowstone River Valley widens out to flat, broad benches, and the cottonwood-lined river meanders in long, slow turns. Archeology, early accounts, and common sense all indicate that this was excellent game country, rich in resources that had made it hospitable to hundreds of generations of American Indians. The first white settlers were the three Bottler brothers, Frederick, Henry, and Phillip, who established a ranch near the present site of Emigrant, Montana, in 1868, four years before the park was established. Entrepreneurial agriculturalists, they raised some livestock (mixing in an occasional captured bison or elk calf) and started a garden, quickly creating an important supply center and way station for the miners, travelers, and adventurers lured to the valley by reports of its various treasures and wonders. Fred, the family's foremost hunter, soon discovered that game was abundant in all directions.

On July 18, 1871, Ferdinand Hayden's U.S. Geological Survey of the Territories, consisting of some twenty men, arrived at the Bottler ranch after a difficult wagon trip from Fort Ellis, near present-day Bozeman. They were on their way to Yellowstone, where they would confirm the reports brought back by earlier parties and would also pioneer the scientific work that soon earned the area the title of the world's foremost outdoor laboratory. Among Hayden's party was a young photographer named William Henry Jackson, whose views of Yellowstone and other western landscapes would earn him immortality both for their artfulness and for their contri-

William Henry Jackson's photograph no. 203 shows the Bottler Ranch, near present-day Emigrant, Montana, about thirty miles north of the park, in July 1871. By this time hide hunting was well under way in the Yellowstone River Valley. *National Park Service*

bution to conservation. Jackson took many photographs on this trip, but one of the most powerful, even haunting, was made at the Bottlers' place.

Jackson's photograph no. 203 shows five men standing, leaning, or sitting along a crude rail fence. Behind the men in the near distance, just in front of a grove of small trees, stands a sturdy-looking log cabin; it appears to have two doors side by side. But the photograph is dominated by a large shed on the right, perhaps forty or fifty feet long; its roof is made of wide sawn boards, but its sides are open. At first glance, it appears to have rough, vertical log walls, but a closer look reveals that the "wall" is really a solid row of large animal hides. The shed is full of skins, hung tight one against the other, reaching the full length of the two visible sides of the building. Some of the hides may actually be entire carcasses, perhaps hung to drain before butchering or sale. From the back of the building a long

"The Successful Hunter," a William Henry Jackson photograph from 1872, shows Fred Bottler (left) and other hunters on the Hayden Survey with several bull elk they had killed near the Grand Canyon of the Yellowstone. *National Park Service*

pole or framework extends for another fifteen or twenty feet, and this is piled high with what appear to be skins of smaller animals, perhaps deer or pronghorn. One of the five men, the only one squarely facing the camera, has a half-grown pronghorn kid standing next to him. It appears to be leaning on him, but judging from the position of the man's hand, he may be holding it close with a leash. Every time I notice the kid, standing so near the evidence of such wholesale carnage, I wonder again about the complexity of our relationships with wild animals. Every time I look at the shed, I realize again that Fred Bottler had been busy that spring.

The fifteen years following the Civil War were a time of accelerating profligate slaughter of western wildlife resources. Advances in tanning technology generated huge markets for wildlife hides in the United States and abroad. This was the era not only of the well-known destruction of the last great bison herds but also of the virtual elimination of many other wildlife populations. The hide hunters were remarkably efficient, able to kill and skin thousands of animals in a very short time.[1] No region with large populations of ungulates was exempt from the slaughter, and Yellowstone fell victim in its turn.

We don't know exactly when that turn began. The Bottlers were aware of some of the park area's wonders before Hayden visited, but there is no way of telling if any of the hides in their shed that day came from Yellowstone; I suspect that most were from closer by. The historical evidence indicates that hide hunting was rampant in the park area for much of the 1870s. The park's first superintendent, Nathaniel Langford, had essentially no budget and no support staff. He visited the park only briefly now and then, so we are dependent upon the accounts of visitors for our knowledge of the slaughter.[2] Most visitors — at least the ones who wrote about their trips — came in the summer, missing the worst of the killing, which took place in winter or spring.

But in one year, 1875, a fortuitous combination of visits provides us with a glimpse of the park's worst decade. Philetus Norris, who would two years later become the park's second superintendent, made his second visit to the area that July (in 1870 he had gotten as far as the slopes of Electric Peak, along what would become the park's north boundary, but unseasonably high water in the streams had almost drowned his guide, Fred Bottler, and they had had to turn back). This time he made it through the park and was appalled to discover the destruction under way. In an unpublished memoir he described it:

> The Bottler Bros. assure me that they alone packed over 2,000 elk skins from the forks of the Yellowstone, besides vast numbers of other pelts, and other hunters at least as many more, in the spring of 1875. As the only part of most of them saved was the tongue and hide, an opinion can be formed of the wanton,

unwise, and unlawful slaughter of the beautiful and valuable animals in the Great National Yellowstone Park.[3]

By "the forks of the Yellowstone," Norris meant the Lamar River Valley in northeastern Yellowstone Park, that being winter range for large herds of elk and bison. Norris predicted imminent extinction for the ungulates unless the slaughter was stopped.

Norris gives us a total of roughly 4,000 elk taken that spring: 2,000 by the Bottlers, and "at least as many more" by other unnamed hunters. Meanwhile General William E. Strong, visiting Mammoth Hot Springs with a large party of military dignitaries, reported similar destruction:

> An elk skin is worth from six to eight dollars, and it is said that when the snow is deep, and a herd gets confused, one hunter will frequently kill from twenty-five to fifty of these noble animals in a single day. Over four thousand were killed last winter by professional hunters in the Mammoth Springs Basin alone. Their carcasses and branching antlers can be seen on every hillside and in every valley. Mountain sheep and deer have been hunted and killed in the same manner for their hides. The terrible slaughter which has been going on since the fall of 1871 has thinned out the great bands of big game, until it is a rare thing now to see an elk, deer, or mountain sheep along the regular trail from Ellis to Yellowstone Lake.[4]

Norris and Strong reported on areas that were some distance apart, so between them we hear of 8,000 Yellowstone elk killed in the course of one winter and spring.

George Bird Grinnell, at the start of an extraordinary career in natural history, anthropology, and conservation, also visited the park that summer, with an army survey party under Captain William Ludlow. Grinnell reported that "it is estimated that during the winter of 1874–'75 not less than 3,000 elk were killed for their hides alone in the valley of the Yellowstone, between the mouth of Trail Creek and the Hot Springs."[5] Trail Creek joins the Yellowstone River more than forty miles downstream from the park boundary, so it is impossible to know how many of Grinnell's 3,000 elk were part of Strong's 4,000, but it is clear that the slaughter of elk was enormous all along the drainage of the Yellowstone, from well inside the park to far down the valley.

In fact we know little about these numbers except that they were very large. Ludlow also complained about the slaughter, but he heard of only 1,500 to 2,000 elk killed near Mammoth, as opposed to the 4,000 Strong reported.[6] On the other hand, these men were reporting on selected portions of the elk range; other killing probably was going on in other areas in or near the park, as the hide market's appetites demanded. The miners working around the northeast corner of the park were for many years among the park's most notorious poachers, and it is safe to assume they were active in this period too.

Even a region as unpopulated and rich in large mammals as Yellowstone could not sustain such a harvest for long. The Bottlers, and probably others, were almost certainly working the Yellowstone Valley north of the park as early as 1869, and by the early 1870s the killing could have taken on the industrial scale it did in so many other regions. Whether 1875, the only year for which we have any reported numbers, was the highest year is unknown. The following year was one of little public travel because of "Indian trouble" elsewhere in the West (the Battle of Little Bighorn occurred in June), so either fewer people were around to witness the slaughter or fewer hunters were willing to hunt, or both.

Though a number of observers in the later 1870s supported Strong's contention that the game had been thinned out, quite a few others did see large numbers of animals, which suggests that the destruction was not complete. In late October 1876, Lieutenant Gustavus Doane surprised a herd of "at least two thousand elk" in Hayden Valley in central Yellowstone and encountered elk on several occasions in the southern part of the park as well.[7] Other travelers made similar, if more modest, reports.[8] Even Strong, who in 1875 was as dismayed as anybody by the destruction, noted that large mammals were still common in the wilder country in the park, and Norris said that "these animals are still plentiful around the falls and the great geysers."[9]

The slaughter of Yellowstone wildlife has usually been told as a kind of redemption tale: this terrible thing happened, but we overcame it and made things right.[10] The good guys acted in time and saved the day. But this was not an isolated, free-standing story that ended when the slaughter ceased. The effects of the killing were many, and we are still living with its consequences, some of which are only now being considered.

Hunting, for sport or subsistence, was legal in Yellowstone National Park through the 1870s. In the first years, when services were minimal or nonexistent, visitors either brought their food in or hooked or shot it along the way. The act of Congress creating the park required only that the secretary of the interior "provide against the wanton destruction of the fish and game found within said park, and against their capture or destruction for the purposes of merchandise or profit." "Wanton destruction" was not defined carefully enough, however. A review of the accounts of travelers in this period shows that even the ones who were technically allowed to kill animals did so excessively, at least by the standards of good sportsmanship or by the standard of killing only what was needed to feed the hunter. The free-for-all mood of early hunting in the park was exemplified by a member of Archibald Geikie's party in 1879: "Andy's rifle was always ready, and he blazed away at everything. As he rode at the head of the party the first intimation those behind had of any game afoot was the crack of his rifle, followed by the immediate stampede of the mules and a round of execration from Jack. I do not remember that he ever shot anything save one wild duck, which immediately sank, or at least could not be found."[11]

Unfortunately for the animals, many sport hunters were better shots than Andy. But it was the illegal hide hunters who did the most obvious and massive damage, despite regulations against their work. Shortly after assuming the superintendency in 1877, Norris published a new prohibition against market hunting and hired assistants to patrol the park (quickly dubbed "rabbit catchers" by the locals);

these men varied widely in their skills, but the best of them were among the park's truest friends. By 1879 Norris believed the slaughter was over, though he feared that the increasing numbers of visitors would kill more and more animals for food.[12] The exact end of the large-scale killing of Yellowstone wildlife has proven difficult to pinpoint, but it does appear that by 1880 or 1881 the worst was past and that market hunting was significantly reduced. As the park showed promise of being good for the regional economy, as the surrounding territories developed not only their own game laws but their own sportsman's organizations, as public indignation over market hunting increased, and as the market changed, the destruction of park wildlife on an industrial scale declined.

But by 1880 the very idea of Yellowstone as an institution had also changed. The slaughter of animals had outraged some forceful characters, George Bird Grinnell among them. From his pulpit as editor of *Forest and Stream*, Grinnell barraged American sportsmen and nature lovers with dozens of short notices on threats to the national park.[13] Yellowstone, initially established almost solely to protect its geological oddities and vistas, became the focus of a different conservation struggle, to protect wildlife. As sportsmen and other conservationists watched the destruction of wild animals across the country, they looked with almost desperate hope to a few isolated places as potential sanctuaries for the last herds. No place seemed to give them as much reason for hope as Yellowstone.

The wildlife conservation movement, the product of a variety of impulses, operated on many levels in society. The industrial revolution, which progressively distanced a larger proportion of people from the suffering of domestic animals, was a factor in the growth of the humane movement, though concern over the welfare (even the rights) of animals had existed for centuries. The development of a sporting subculture, with many local fish and game clubs as well as influential national publications, led to the active promulgation of restrictive game laws to ensure the survival of favored species (thereby inadvertently protecting other species that used the same habitats and spelling doom to the predators that hunted the favored species). Advances in science led to a fuller understanding of and

Philetus Norris, Yellowstone's second superintendent (1877–1882), was one of the most colorful in the park's long history. A self-described mountaineer, he was taken with the romance of the western wilderness and dressed in full buckskins to look the part of the adventurer he surely was. *NPS photo*

familiarity with some elements of the natural world. Such broad developments affected a growing number of citizens, many of whom may have had no particular focus for their concern over wildlife but who collectively were developing a stronger and stronger conscience concerning wild animals.[14] By the 1870s, that conscience was taking hold, and when appealed to by wildlife advocates, could be made to feel guilty.

So it was that dissatisfaction with the destruction of wildlife generally, and growing opposition to the slaughter of Yellowstone's animals in particular, led to a momentous development in park policy. On January 15, 1883, Secretary of the Interior H. M. Teller, pressured by Missouri's Senator George Graham Vest, instructed the superintendent (by now Norris was gone, replaced by the grumpy and ineffective Patrick Conger) that neither sport hunting nor subsistence hunting was to be allowed:

> The regulations heretofore issued by the Secretary of the Interior in regard to killing game in Yellowstone National Park are amended to prohibit absolutely the killing, wounding, or capturing at any time of any buffalo, bison, moose, elk, black tailed or white tailed deer, mountain sheep, Rocky Mountain goat, antelope, beaver, otter, martin [sic], fisher, grouse, prairie chicken, pheasant, fool hen, partridge, quail, wild goose, duck, robin, meadow lark, thrush, goldfinch, flicker or yellow-hammer, blackbird, oriole, jay, snowbird, or any of the small birds commonly known as the singing birds.[15]

This list tells us much more than at first appears. Whoever compiled it (probably a clerk in Washington, D.C.) didn't know much about the park, because it includes animals not native there (mountain goats, pheasant, quail, prairie chicken) and mistakenly assumes that bison and buffalo are different species. More important, it tells us that predators had no significant standing in the eyes of managers; the list includes only a few carnivorous furbearers (otter, marten, fisher) that had obvious commercial value. In its neglect of the predators, the new regulation only maintained what was already a tradition in the young park: the destruction of the carnivorous species, especially the large ones. For, though the wild-life slaughter of the 1870s forever redirected the park from its simple mission of protecting nature's oddities into an increasingly complex one by making it an enormously important game reserve, predators would wait many years for the respect accorded their prey.

But before considering the predators, it is worth following an-other thread, the one connected to sportsmen, the most visible and the most directly influential group in this critical period in Yellow-stone's history. At its simplest, their campaign to outlaw hunting in Yellowstone might seem an extraordinary act of altruism: they locked themselves out of one of the nation's last great hunting grounds. But their vision was broader than the park, and it revealed early glimmerings of an ecosystem-scale perspective that often seems lost on their modern descendants. Sportsmen wanted Yellow-stone safe from hunting exactly because that safety was *good* for hunting. The leading figures in the hunting community understood that the park was summer range for huge numbers of animals, many of which migrated to winter ranges outside the boundaries. They realized, therefore, that the park could serve as more than a game reserve; it could serve as a game *reservoir,* from which surrounding public lands would be restocked in perpetuity by the annual move-ments of protected animals. Grinnell repeatedly asserted the value of the park as "a breeding ground for big game which will furnish sport for hundreds of hunters."[16]

The 1883 change in the management of Yellowstone wildlife thus accomplished two things, both of which have echoed down the dec-ades, challenging us more all the time. For one thing, it both raised the importance and changed the role of wildlife in Yellowstone. Elk, bison, and other animals were no longer just walking lunchboxes or handy targets; they almost immediately assumed a primary role in visitors' enjoyment of the park. Yellowstone pioneered the noncon-sumptive use of large mammals among western recreationists.

For another thing, the fate of the park became forever con-nected to the fate of the surrounding lands. The migrating elk and other species carried symbolic lines hooking the park's wildlife habi-tat to the surrounding wildlands. They also carried with them the economic incentives to protect those wildlands, as the hunters themselves became a major regional cash resource. Though the concept of an expanded park had surfaced earlier, Teller's 1883 wildlife policy probably should be seen as the first official salvo in the battle to define and then save Greater Yellowstone.

But park expansion was far from the most pressing concern at the time. The need to protect park animals was agreed upon, but the definition of protection was not. Norris, for example, foresaw a day when Yellowstone's wildlife would be commercially farmed and managed in a way that modern wilderness advocates would find quite objectionable. Intensive husbandry of landscapes was simply assumed in his time to be a human prerogative, and took surprising forms. As the park's administrator, Norris could institute any policy he chose, as long as he could obtain funding. He recommended that "two or three spirited, intelligent herdsmen" should divide their time between raising domestic animals and domesticating the park's bison herds: "These, by practical rearing, and by sale of the young to zoologists throughout the world, and by judicious slaughter and sale of their flesh, pelts, and furs, and also of those still wild, might render them permanently attractive and profitable to the park and to the nation in its management."[17]

Norris was passionate about this goal, which he saw as the best chance to save the animals because they would pay their own way. With carefully regulated hunting and carefully managed harvests of various species, the park's large mammals could be an attraction not only to the eye but also "to the palate of the countless health and pleasure seekers, when elsewhere unknown, save in the natural history of extinct species." Like many of his time, Norris was convinced that these animals were doomed by the market hunting then being practiced: "If our people are ever to preserve living specimens of our most beautiful, interesting, and valuable animals, *here,* in their native forests and glens of this lofty cliff and snow encircled 'wonderland,' is the *place* and *now* is the time to do it."[18]

This vision of Yellowstone as a huge outdoor zoological garden and meat distribution center was not to be realized (though at times a lot of meat was shipped from the park for other reasons), but in other, less costly ways Norris did establish far-reaching policies, if only through passive approval of practices already occurring. In his annual report for 1880, Norris expressed his own peculiar view of the way nature worked in Yellowstone while discussing the park's beaver:

> Unmolested by man, who is ever their most dangerous enemy, the conditions here mentioned are so favorable to their safety that soon they would construct dams upon so many of the cold-water streams as literally to flood the narrow valleys, terraced slopes, and passes, and thus render the Park uninhabitable for men as well as for many of the animals now within its confines. In consideration of this I have not seriously interfered with the trappers, who have annually taken from the Park hundreds, if not thousands, of the valuable skins of these animals.[19]

Norris's only problem with this custom of unregulated trapping was that it made no money for the government, so he suggested that in the future trappers should have to pay a fee for the privilege.

But setting aside his apocalyptic view of beaver dams (the park's watersheds simply do not allow for the kind of flooding he feared, and they could not support beaver in the numbers needed to do the damming), we are left with Norris's statements about the destruction of beaver as an underappreciated report of a very big splash in the ecological system, one that has rippled through the system ever since. In the early 1900s, the beaver, whose numbers were probably continually suppressed until the 1890s, cashed in on a burgeoning aspen food source that had flourished during the period of suppression. The beaver increased so dramatically and alarmingly that park managers invited a researcher to study them.[20] And fifty years after that, both journalists and conservationists assumed that the beaver population reported by that first scientific study in the 1920s was in fact typical and that the park could support high numbers of beaver, rather than the population irruption being at least partly an artifact of human tinkering in the 1870s.[21]

The legacy of the park's first decade may have been most potent in predator control. In his recent textbook on wildlife management, James Peek begins a very helpful discussion of predators by quoting biologist Werner Negel, who defined a predator as "any creature that has beaten you to another creature you wanted for yourself."[22] Predators may have been more despised in nineteenth-century America than in earlier times. As Thomas Dunlap observed, "Perhaps it was the specter of the Darwinian struggle for existence or uneasiness about the dark underside of industrial America, but turn-of-the-century naturalists loathed predators even more than their predecessors had."[23] There were probably many other reasons for this loathing, including an intense national pride in the conquest of a continent: predators, like native people, were at worst a threat to everything white society stood for and at best merely a nuisance.

Throughout the West it was common practice, of an almost religious intensity, to kill predators large and small by any means. The hide hunting of the 1870s gave those who were also interested in killing predators a powerful tool: an abundance of carrion, irresistible to many predators and easily poisoned. Norris, a man of his time, enthusiastically favored poisoning the carcasses left to rot by the hunters, and by 1880 he believed that wolves were "nearly" exterminated and that mountain lions had been greatly reduced.[24] A review of the historical records of this period, combined with a review of the effectiveness of similar poisoning and trapping campaigns elsewhere in the West, provides persuasive evidence that the wolves of Yellowstone were largely exterminated by 1880 rather than by 1930, as is widely believed. The official predator control program launched by the federal government on public lands in the early 1900s may have been little more than a mopping-up operation on leftover wolves in Yellowstone.[25]

The role of predators in maintaining and controlling prey populations has undergone intensive study, often accompanied by controversy, in the past few decades. Though most people probably still see predators and prey as existing in a simplistic "balance of nature" that only humans disturb, ecological thinking has moved far beyond that, into a much more complex arena. Although predators do sometimes keep prey numbers down and thereby limit their own food source, other factors are also now recognized as important. The availability of winter food, which is a function of climate, can strongly affect herbivore populations and therefore the numbers of predators that depend upon the herbivores. Competition between predator species can affect the prosperity of each predator type and of the favored prey species. Competition between prey species for food or space can do the same. Diseases, whether native or exotic, may sweep through a predator or prey population and shift the balance in favor of a formerly less successful species. Human hunting can reduce predators, prey, or both and can alter the way animals use the land. Human uses of the land, such as development for homes, agriculture, logging, mining, or recreation, always favor some species over others and often simply eliminate species. Fires can alter habitats to favor different species.[26] In the real world of a large wild setting, many of these factors are at work at once, and their interplay is both elegant and difficult to sort out.

The wolf provides a good example of this complexity. Modern population modeling exercises that were done in conjunction with planning for the recovery of wolves in Yellowstone suggest a great variety of possible scenarios for wolves in the park.[27] But wolves are only one player in this performance. Incorporate grizzly bears, coyotes, black bears, mountain lions, and dozens of smaller predators and scavengers, and the picture becomes so complex that we would be arrogant to assume we fully comprehend its direction or potential for variability.

The abrupt ecological disruptions that had occurred in Yellowstone by 1880 included the removal of American Indian influences, the massive slaughter of ungulates (which not only removed huge numbers of animals but also may have altered the behavior of those remaining), the wholesale removal of the beaver (the foremost riparian landscape engineer), and the determined killing of predators. Later generations would continue, complicate, and complement these actions in many ways, for example by building hundreds of miles of roads through the center of many of the park's richest wildlife habitats. Road building directly displaced some species and had untold local effects on plant communities and, where roads followed rivers, on stream processes. On top of these disruptions, ongoing changes in climate, which affect everything from ungulate forage to fire patterns, further complicated the picture.

We now know that ecological settings, once disturbed, do not automatically tend to return to their predisturbance state. The whole notion that nature tends toward equilibrium conditions is now questioned, if it has not already been disproved. When humans suddenly knocked the props out from under the established wildlife "order" in Yellowstone, a great many relationships in the ecosystem changed. We cannot assume that once the elk slaughter ceased, as it seems to have by the early 1880s, the elk simply went back to using the land as they had prior to 1870. Indeed, how could they if, as seems to be the case, their predators were also reduced? We know that when wolves are removed from an ecosystem, coyotes thrive, and when coyotes thrive, foxes suffer. When wolves return, foxes may prosper and coyotes suffer. Effects of changes in the numbers or species of predators ripple out to many other species, from the smallest to the largest. In 1872 moose were rare except in the southern part of the park; did the destruction of wolves and possible reduction of bears have anything to do with the moose's quick colonization of the rest of Yellowstone over the next half-century or so? When humans induce changes in a predator-prey system, they rarely just cause it to collapse; more often they set in motion processes that may not naturally tend toward a stable state or may not reach such a state before humans induce more changes.

At the time of the slaughter, the area had just emerged from the Little Ice Age and was still undergoing powerful climatic changes. The first twenty years of the park's existence coincided with an increase in effective precipitation (a combined measure of temperature and precipitation) that may have been the deciding factor in a surge in aspen growth across the park. Tree-ring studies reveal that practically all of the aspen trees now growing old and dying in northern Yellowstone sprouted between about 1870 and 1895, just when the two foremost aspen predators — beaver and elk — were being reduced in numbers on a large scale.[28] The aspen remind us that when considering a historical change in one element of an ecological system, one must keep in mind what other elements would do in response to that change. The layers are many and are linked in various ways.

For example, what impact did the poisoning of elk carcasses have on the less glamorous but still ecologically significant smaller predators, such as wolverine, fisher, marten, weasel, fox, bobcat, mink, and lynx? How were they affected by the commercial trapping that Norris endorsed? What shifts or trends in their populations had been set in motion by 1880? To what extent are their modern populations reflections of those trends? And what have those trends meant for *their* prey species?

IF THIS portrayal of relations among Yellowstone wildlife as a free-wheeling ecological crapshoot is a bit too unsettling, let us turn to a more familiar part of the Yellowstone story, one many Americans know through experience or legend: the bears. The park was only a year old when it recorded its first known case of breaking and entering by a bear. James McCartney, proprietor of a primitive hotel at Mammoth Hot Springs, was in the habit of storing game meat in one of his cabins. One March night in 1873 a bear of unnamed species forced entry and made off with some venison. McCartney overloaded a "set gun" (more often known as a "spring gun" today, this was a firearm, usually a rifle or shotgun, rigged to fire when a wire or string was tripped) with "three inches of powder and five large balls." The bear's next entry resulted in "one musket with stock badly shattered, the barrel bursted, one window broken, and a dead bear lying in the center of the cabin."[29] It was the opening act of a long and often violent relationship between bears and humans in Yellowstone's developments.

After writing two books devoted to the bears of Yellowstone, I am still amazed by the complexity of our relationship with them. Grizzly and black bears were the park's most powerful predators — the only animals ever to hurt hundreds of humans in the park — and we have treated them with far more affection and forbearance than we treated the less dangerous predators, which hardly ever hurt anyone. We could do no less, for in dealing with what anthropologist

Paul Shepard has described as "the most significant animal in the history of metaphysics in the northern hemisphere," we were at the mercy of our own culture and every culture it grew from.[30] The bears were too much like us, too entangled in our sense of ourselves, to be summarily written off along with the other predators. For most of Yellowstone's history we have studiously and sometimes explicitly denied that bears even were predators, though they have by now killed at least five people in the park and injured many hundreds of others; in the same period there is no record of a wolf or mountain lion attacking or injuring a person in Yellowstone, except for minor injuries from captured animals.

At first the bears fared no better than the other animals. Norris himself killed some; he related one particularly exciting episode in which a charging grizzly bear absorbed at least seven shots before dying. The uncontrolled market hunting and sport hunting of the 1870s could have been hard on bears, partly because of their commercial and sporting appeal and partly because they are masterful scavengers and might have succumbed in good numbers to the poisoned ungulate carcasses (from which they no doubt chased many wolves). However, I find that accounts of Yellowstone in the 1880s speak enthusiastically of the abundance of bears. Judging from what we know about the extended period of time it takes to "recruit" a widespread bear population to a localized food source (such as a garbage dump), I suspect that the era of hide-hunting and poisoned carcasses may not have lasted long enough to draw in bears from all the remote corners of the park, so a fair number were still around, both in and near the park, when the poisoning and shooting were over.[31]

But something else also came to the bear's rescue. The metaphysics that Paul Shepard referred to took hold of our imagination, and the bear assumed the role of entertainer, tourist attraction, garbage disposal, and, eventually, national icon. With improved protection, the bears found their way onto our garbage piles and into our hearts. By the late 1880s they began to show up, at first in small numbers, in the dumps near the various park hotels, and within a remarkably short time they had become one of the must-see sights on a park visit. Thus began one of the most colorful, instructive, and controversial chapters in the management of Yellowstone and perhaps in the history of wildlife management in North America. Eighty years after those first bears cautiously poked their noses out of the forest in the direction of the hotel dumps, grizzly-bear management would become the single greatest driving force in the movement to protect not only Yellowstone National Park but also the much larger Greater Yellowstone Ecosystem, of which the park was both the symbolic heart and the ecological center.

But even the complex attitude we have displayed toward the bears does not complete the portrait of wildlife management in the park's early years. We were accustomed by centuries of experience to dealing with different types of animals in different ways, and the park tended to follow custom. Secretary Teller's 1883 prohibition of public hunting in Yellowstone signaled the permanent separation of two types of park wildlife in the eyes of the public and of park managers. Hunting of mammals and birds (except the predators, of course) was prohibited, but fishing was not. Early surveyors were quick to notice that 40 percent of the park's area was devoid of fish. Free of ice for only 12,000 years or so, this volcanic landscape featured a host of natural barriers in the form of insurmountable waterfalls, so fish had not yet found their way into some park waters that are now world-famous for great fishing. Many small headwater streams had no fish, and a surprising number of larger waters, including Lewis and Shoshone lakes and most of the Firehole River drainage, were, in the parlance of fishermen, "barren."[32]

Actually they were anything but barren; they were home to a rich invertebrate fauna and to a flora whose diversity was probably heightened by the numerous geothermal sources, which introduced both heat and an assortment of chemicals into the streams. The Firehole River, which drains the park's most spectacular and famous geyser basins, looks "almost as if short sections of many different streams from many different places were spliced together and the aquatic life within each was made to live near totally alien environments."[33] For more than 10,000 years these unique aquatic habitats had been developing and tailoring life communities that responded to their strange and various characteristics. But these life communities, though of great interest to naturalists, were judged insufficient to the needs of sport fishermen. Modern fly fishermen will enjoy Rudyard Kipling's condescending description of the Firehole in 1889 as "a warm and deadly river wherein no fish breed."[34]

As the late nineteenth century saw the near-destruction of American big game, it likewise saw the rise of managed fisheries. The development of fish hatchery technology, the rise of fish and game clubs as an active part of the conservation movement, and the creation of both state and federal fisheries management agencies all resulted in more intensely managed aquatic resources. The "improvement" of fishing became a national obsession, as fish from distant drainages and even distant continents were dumped willy-nilly into North American waters to satisfy the growing appetite for recreation. As usual, Yellowstone mirrored the national experience; its managers began to wish for ways to improve the barren waters. The ways existed, and soon the technology would turn Yellowstone into an angler's paradise.

Yellowstone's wildlife came through the reckless slaughter of the 1870s in much better shape than did most wildlife populations in the West. By 1885 elk populations were already rebounding; indeed, as early as 1883 local newspapers carried reports of thousands of elk wintering in the park. Some of the predators were virtually gone, but others, including the bears, coyotes, and perhaps even the mountain lions (which Norris had also pronounced as greatly reduced), were either becoming more abundant or at least holding on. Some species had been through the worst that our best intentions could dish out, and the worst they would see in the park's long history. Others, like the bears and the trout, were just beginning to interest us.

In only fourteen years — that is, from the creation of the park until the U.S. Cavalry assumed control in 1886 — the park's animals had unwittingly participated in perhaps the most intensive on-the-job training ever imposed upon ignorant, well-intentioned resource managers. Out of that period emerged a park with a far broader and more ambitious mission than it had been given in the act that created it. Yes, Yellowstone existed, as the Roosevelt Arch at the park's North Entrance reminds us daily, "for the benefit and enjoyment of the people," but both the benefits and the enjoyments were being redefined as the realities of ecology and the appetites of the public were revealed to the park's managers. So much was left unsaid in the act that created the park that, in the words of historian John Reiger, "the battle over the future of Yellowstone National Park was, in a sense, a battle over the language of the act that created it."[35]

6 | Privations and Inconveniences

R IGHT FROM THE START we called it Wonderland. Countless early guidebooks, tour brochures, and promotional
articles used the term, which became common among the tourists as well. To the Northern Pacific Railroad, the park's most tireless and effective promoter, the name Wonderland applied rather
vaguely to the whole northwestern United States, but it stuck most
determinedly to Yellowstone, probably because there really was
more wonder here.[1]

In the 1870s only a few hundred people reached the park each
year, but they were vocal in their amazement, and because many of
them were influential or prominent citizens, word spread quickly of
the glories of what at the time was formally known as "the Yellowstone National Park" (after other national parks were created, "the"
was dropped). Until the 1880s most visitors were from nearby states,
but after 1883, as the railroad's publicity campaign geared up, the
park began to attract the attention of more and more long-distance
visitors (President Chester A. Arthur's visit in 1883 was exhaustively
reported in the world press).

Nathaniel P. Langford, self-advertised hero of the park's creation
(he was fond of joking that his initials, N.P., stood for "national
park"), became its first superintendent in 1872. With no budget,
no facilities, and little public support, he accomplished very little,
which may have been his intent. Aubrey Haines has suggested that
Langford's inaction, besides being the result of no funding, was also
caused by his continuing association with the railroad, aimed at
"preventing the development of strong concession interests in the

Park until such time as the Northern Pacific pushed its tracks close enough to dominate the development of visitor facilities."[2]

Langford visited the park only twice during his five-year administration. His one annual report, produced in 1873, outlined the problems facing not only the manager but also the visitors, explaining that the park could be reached only by pack train, "a mode of travel attended with many privations and inconveniences."[3] What visitors found when they arrived was as wild as it was wonderful.

By 1879 the park still had only eighty-nine miles of what might generously be called roads. Travelers had also established more than 200 miles of passable or recognizable trails that took them to the major attractions. Travel writer Carrie Strahorn described the roads in 1880 as having been "cut through the timber over rolling ground, with stumps left from 2 to 20 inches above the ground, and instead of grading a hill it went straight up on one side and straight down on the other."[4] Some of these original grades can still be seen, faintly making their way through the forests of northern Yellowstone, and though they often do grind straight uphill (wagons and coaches must have unloaded the passengers on those grades, or the horses couldn't have made it), others wind hopefully back and forth across the slopes, as if looking for a gentler path but never really finding it.

If Wonderland was to become a resort matching its name, as its promoters hoped, it would need much more than tolerable roads. It would have to provide pleasant accommodations, trustworthy places to eat, and good transportation. Someone had to decide where people should stay, what they should eat, and how they should travel. Thus began the often uneasy but entirely necessary three-way relationship among the federal government, the public, and the park concessioners.

Today, with an increased awareness of the ecological effects of any development in a national park and an ever-intensifying public scrutiny of all government management of natural resources, all commercial enterprises in national parks are distrusted or seen as merely a necessary evil. Former Yellowstone superintendent Robert Barbee has referred to this suspicion as the "money-changers in the temple" mentality, suggesting that it takes a comfortably simplistic view of what concessioners do. Yellowstone provides us with the full spectrum of case studies, from the very worst to the very best, in commercial hospitality in a park.

One of the many differences between the way we perceive the park today and the way its first visitors did is in this very issue of the role of concessioners. Every historian who has written about the early days of Yellowstone has taken the side of those who wanted less development rather than more, and some have argued the case with an almost embarrassing intensity. We are accustomed to a certain level of development in Yellowstone, and anything more jars our sensitivities.[5]

At first there were practically no comforts for tourists. James McCartney, Harry Horr, and Matthew McGuirk had established modest (according to some early accounts even that adjective was too flattering) facilities centered on thermal pools in the Mammoth Hot Springs area, McCartney and Horr at the springs themselves and McGuirk down along the Gardner River to the east. They provided a rude sort of shelter in a cabinlike hotel, a bathhouse or two for those seeking the "healing" waters, and rough but ample fare in the form of locally shot game. Slowly others arrived who were willing to risk their energy and resources on the chance that the park would eventually attract enough money to justify the effort.[6]

Some of these early concessioners, even setting aside modern environmental biases against development, were scoundrels or worse, but many were genuinely fond of the park and conscientious about providing good service. As the years passed, the reliable ones usually outlasted the fly-by-night schemers, so for most of the time, at least after the very rocky first decade or two, tourists apparently felt passably well served.

Essentially there were two types of concessions. The first was the outfitter or manager of a single little operation. In the park's administrative archives, these are represented on some odd pieces of hotel stationery, requesting permission, in pinched script, to bring in a party of tourists on such-and-such a date, begging the honor of a prompt reply and all of that wonderful formal language now vanished from our customs. The other type was the larger corporation, generally favored by early park service managers after 1916, if only because it was easier to watch over a few big businesses than many small ones or because the big ones could provide more consistent service.

My favorite scoundrel among the small operators was E. C. Waters, who from 1889 until 1907 ran a steamboat tour business on Yellowstone Lake. Even on paper Waters is instantly dislikable. He wrote stacks of long, simpering, obsequious letters to the various superintendents, responding to the many complaints and accusations that flew his way. He used his political influence to help get rid of a superintendent he especially disliked, he was implicated in at least one attempt at poaching; and he generally behaved in the manner of the worst stereotypes of the sleazy park concessioner. The nadir may have come when he established a small zoo on Dot Island in Yellowstone Lake, where one visitor reported seeing an elk so hungry (apparently Waters was feeding them garbage from somewhere) that it actually ate meat.[7]

But the real risks to the park's overall welfare were not from individual small concessioners. To the extent that the park's resources and the tourists' visits could be really ruined, only a big concessioner could do it right. The first to emerge was the Yellowstone Park Improvement Company, or YPIC.

Today even the name would make most park defenders nervous; we would object that the last thing wild nature needs is "improvement." But at the time the term did not necessarily bode ill. Like many of the political-economic stories of Yellowstone, the tale of the YPIC is convoluted enough to be a short book in itself — a greed-and-graft potboiler of the Gilded Age, with silk-vested entrepreneurs directing their nefarious plot from elegant eastern drawing rooms. The YPIC was (to employ appropriately sinister language) the corporate front for a group of businessmen, most noteworthy of whom was C. T. Hobart, superintendent of a planned branch of the Northern Pacific Railroad (NPRR) that would run from the main line up the Yellowstone River to the park.[8]

The NPRR was always a presence in the more important deliberations of this sort. Clark City, some fifty-two miles north of the park on the Yellowstone River, renamed itself Livingston in the early 1880s in honor of an NPRR official. That same year the miners just outside the northeast corner of the park named their community Cooke City in honor of the NPRR's Jay Cooke, so hopeful were they of his attention and eventual investment in a branch line to their area — a branch line running, if at all possible, through the park.

Of course the money for concession development had to come from somewhere, and most western citizens couldn't wait for more railroads to be built; the boosterism of a recently settled region had little sympathy with anything that slowed progress toward more settlement. I suspect that if a poll had been taken of Americans in 1880, asking if railroads should be run to the major attractions in Yellowstone, an overwhelming majority would have said yes. To them the railroad was the very soul of the future; what could be wrong with swift, efficient travel around Wonderland?

However, if polled about the YPIC, those same Americans might not have reacted so affirmatively, not because they feared the damage the concessioner might do to Yellowstone (most did not care), but because the company was such a blatant scam. Even in those days, the terms that the YPIC wanted were outrageous. Through its agreement with the secretary of the interior, the company sought to acquire exclusive rights to cheap rental of a *square mile* of land surrounding each of the seven biggest visitor attraction areas. It was allowed to cut timber elsewhere at will, rent other lands as needed, and exercise a variety of other extremely generous freedoms in the new park.

The public, politicians, and scientists protested, but the outcry did not stop the YPIC from constructing the first of the several huge hotels that would eventually appear in the park. This was the National Hotel at Mammoth, four stories high and more than 400 feet long. Laborers worked through the winter of 1882–83, using local lumber (the stumps are still visible on the lower slopes of Terrace Mountain to the southwest) and living on game from the park. They completed enough of the giant building for the hotel to open for the summer. But when the YPIC could not pay them, the builders staged a sit-in (still living on park game) in an unsuccessful attempt to

The immense National Hotel was constructed at Mammoth Hot Springs by the scandal-ridden Yellowstone Park Improvement Company in 1883. Frequently modified, it served visitors well into the twentieth century. Note the stagecoaches loading passengers. *NPS photo*

force their employer to pay their back wages. Instead the YPIC went bankrupt, and the National Hotel ended up in the hands of the NPRR.

Such was the start of the serious hotel business in Yellowstone. Less pretentious hotels were established at Mammoth Hot Springs and near the Lower Geyser Basin in the mid-1880s, and tent camps also began to flourish. The NPRR became ever more visible and active in setting up concession operations to serve its railroad passengers, and it was merciless in forcing out competition. For many years writers would tell hilarious and appalling stories of the strange service provided by park concessions, but by the 1890s it was entirely possible for visitors to get around the park in fair comfort, with every hope of encountering hospitality of a rude sort, and often much more.

If the 1870s was the decade of Yellowstone's worst ecological disruption, the 1880s can be seen as the decade of greatest risk from wholesale development. In its development of the park's tourist trade the NPRR, an aggressive and extraordinarily powerful American corporation, followed the business impulses of the day and the example of almost every other resort area in America. The railroad long attempted to lay track clear to the geyser basins, and well into the 1890s Cooke City residents hoped that the railroad might reach them as well, through the Lamar Valley and Soda Butte Creek. It's hard to imagine these railroads in the park today without wincing, and even then there were quite a few people who did not think the park needed so much improvement. The resistance the NPRR met in its attempts to reach these goals, which no doubt its leaders saw as entirely honorable, must have surprised them. The NPRR track reached its terminus near the north entrance in 1883, and the Union Pacific reached the west entrance in 1901, but no tracks entered the park.

Opposition to wholesale development of the park came from many quarters. Key legislators, most notably Missouri senator George Graham Vest; well-placed journalists, especially George Bird Grinnell; and others fought to contain development and to protect the park from being reduced in size in the 1880s and early 1890s. In fact, without the "park grab" (actually a series of moves over more than a decade, all designed to consolidate or enlarge NPRR's control) by the Yellowstone Park Improvement Company and its descendent corporation, much that was accomplished in the rapid evolution of park management probably would not have been possible. Without Grinnell's dozens of editorials and articles in *Forest and Stream* and continual public pressure from other sources, the campaign to protect Yellowstone's wildlife would certainly have had less public exposure.[9] The specter of wholesale development horrified enough of our forefathers to prevent the park from taking that direction.

It is entertaining, in a perverse sort of way, to imagine what the park would be like if it had been developed like the busier portions of the Poconos or the Adirondacks: a patchwork of private holdings, ski slopes, lodges, condominiums, mini-malls, and pretty lakes lined with "camps" and cabins. Driving through the park and looking at it with a real estate agent's eye gives one a different feel for the land-scape. The Antelope Creek drainage of Mount Washburn is a fabu-lous ski hill, Hayden Valley is an obvious golf course. It is less entertaining, but very instructive, to realize how close the park came to that fate. The battle was fought early enough in the park's history that the stakes were still largely hypothetical; had the number of visitors already been large and clamoring for more amenities, devel-opment would have been much harder to fight off.

But Yellowstone was as undefined for the visitors as it was for the developers and the legislators. The matter of what people should do once they got to the park was no little problem. From the first, some visitors displayed the behavior that has made the word "tourist" a worldwide term of derision. They left campfires burning, carelessly starting fires. They took axes to the delicate sinter formations in the geyser basins, hauling off tons of fragments. They abused the geysers and hot springs in many other ways, laundering their clothes in them, jamming an incredible assortment of junk down the vents, and provoking geysers to erupt by "soaping" them. As already described, they slaughtered the animals, blazing away at everything they saw.

But as Aubrey Haines has observed, what should we have ex-pected of them?

> Captain Ludlow typified them as prowling about "with shovel and axe, chopping and hacking and prying great pieces of the most ornamental work they could find. Men and women alike joining in the barbarous pastime." Perhaps this is unfair, for how were those plain country people . . . to know how they should act? No one had told them. Indeed, it was only in the rudeness of their action that they differed from the scientific visitor who used his hammer to break off a piece of exquisite hot-spring filigree for his specimen sack. These people were vandals all, whether their trophies served a parlor knick-knack cabinet or a museum exhibit case.[10]

Ludlow wasn't the only traveler to express exasperation with the insensitivity of the average tourist. One especially galling practice was the scratching of names in the delicate geyserite of the thermal basins. Owen Wister, who first visited the park in 1887, asked, "Why will people scrawl their silly names on the scenery? Why thus disclose to thousands who will read this evidence that you are a thoughtless ass?"[11]

Wister also captured the conflict that confronts all parks, of just how much development to allow for the "benefit and enjoyment of the people." In a conversation he had in 1891 with a woman who favored a then-active proposal to build an elevator to the foot of the Lower Falls of the Grand Canyon, the woman criticized him for elitism:

"But why should your refined taste," objected a lover of the multitude to whom I told this, "interfere with the enjoyment of the plain people?"

"Have the plain people told you or anybody that the one thing they lie sleepless craving for is an elevator to go up and down by those falls the way they do in hotels?"

"They would like it if it was there."

"Of course they would. Is that a reason to vulgarize a supreme piece of wild natural beauty for all time? How are the plain people to learn better things than they know if you lower to their level everything above it?"[12]

And there you have one of the greatest challenges of national parks: striking a balance between catering to public taste and elevating it, always in the hope that those in charge of the parks actually know what good taste is.

Yellowstone required us to stretch our awareness in many ways, for the legislation creating the park did not tell people how to act. At every step along the way, the public, the park managers, and the resource itself would have to resolve what was and was not appropriate. The creation of the park in 1872 launched the American public, indeed the world public, on a search for Yellowstone in the

Stagecoaches ready to begin the tour from the National Hotel around 1890. *NPS photo*

grandest sense: not just to learn what was there and enjoy it, but to make sense of it in the context of their times.

Historians of travel have emphasized the tourist industry's requirement that major destinations provide a highly standardized experience, but these historians have given an unrelievedly sinister tone to what happened in Yellowstone as the visitor experience became defined and institutionalized. As one recent historical study commented, "The same socioeconomic and cultural currents which have dictated events on the balance of the American landscape — that is, the command and control of nature to serve an industrial market economy based on acquisition and possession — also transformed the feral Yellowstone wilderness into a packaged, consumable product."[13] Another historian, speaking more broadly, summed up the irony of tourism in a world where travel is hardly the adventure it once was: "Travel as tourism has become like the activity of a prisoner pacing a cell much crossed and grooved by other equally mobile and 'free' captives. What was once the agent of our liberty has become a means for the revelation of our containment."[14]

There is no question that Yellowstone tourism was the product of effective, highly organized marketing — that the park was "packaged as an object of cultural desire."[15] And it took only a few years for the park tour to firm up along a single route with predictable stops at the best-known features. There is, however, a great deal of question about what that packaging meant to the average visitor and what the alternatives were. Statements about the packaging of the park clearly imply that this is a regrettable, if not tragic, sacrifice of Yellowstone's true potential as a source of enjoyment, but it never becomes clear what the alternative experience would be. Historian John Sears has complained that "despite the vast natural areas of the park that remained unvisited by the average tourist, Yellowstone was curiously artificial. . . . Its natural wonders were theatrical and the impact of these curiosities as elements in a show was reinforced by the trappings of the tourist culture which sprang up around them."[16] These are important points, but traditional academic historians are perhaps a little too comfortable in their hindsight and are ignorant of the fragility of "the vast natural areas of the park that remained unvisited."

I have often thought how much fun it would be to go back in time, knowing what I know now, and take one of the standard tours of the park in the early days. Would I react as did Rudyard Kipling, who began his account of an 1889 visit with the lament "Today I am in the Yellowstone Park, and I wish I were dead"? Kipling was appalled by the attitudes of the tour group he encountered at Cinnabar, the rail terminus near the north entrance: "It is not the ghastly vulgarity, the oozing, rampant Bessemer-steel self-sufficiency and ignorance of the men that revolts me, so much as the display of these same qualities in the women-folk."[17] Or would I, like Frederic Remington on an 1893 visit, marvel at the park's most adventurous stretch of road, over the newly constructed Golden Gate trestle, then reflect on how its wonder was reduced because "as the stages of the Park Company run over this road, every tourist sees its grandeur, and bangs away with his kodak."[18]

It is true that the park's promoters were fairly successful in selling Yellowstone, not only to those who would buy train tickets, hotel rooms, and all the other services but to a distant populace who found even knowing of such a strange place to be worthy recreation. We have not adequately considered the extent to which public knowledge of the young park was the result of photography and artwork; the combination of pictures and words reached far in acquainting the world with Yellowstone's wonders. In 1897 *Harper's* editor Charles Dudley Warner was not exaggerating when he wrote that "all the world knows, from the pens of a thousand descriptive writers and from the photographs, the details of these marvels."[19]

Today there is widespread concern among conservationists that Yellowstone is "overcrowded," a condition that affects not only the well-being of the park's resources but also the quality of the visit. I am convinced those concerns are valid; at some time, perhaps forty years ago, perhaps longer, we became so numerous in Yellowstone that we crossed some threshold of use that resulted in an unacceptable diminishing of the experience.[20] From that perspective it is easy to view the aggressive promotion of the park in earlier times as a harmful thing. But from the perspective of the people who wanted to visit the park, who yearned for whatever combination of its features that they found rewarding, the promotion of Yellowstone must have seemed entirely good and appropriate.

The trivialization of a spectacular natural area's real beauty and power through the standardization or "packaging" of the visit is always regrettable, but it is hard to imagine how else public use of Yellowstone might have proceeded. Visitors in the park's first decade, often relying on their own hunting skills to feed themselves and following their own judgment about where to go, how to acquire firewood, and how to treat the fragile thermal features, amply demonstrated that Yellowstone could not long afford this highly individual approach to its enjoyment. It is both naive and absurd to imagine that people at that time would display the environmental awareness needed to accommodate large numbers of unrestrained visitors without serious impact on the landscape. The only way to move large numbers of people through Yellowstone and allow them the opportunity to view the recognized "wonders" (primarily the geological and geothermal features) was through industrial tourism.

Indeed, we may be grateful that it worked out that way. For all the now-regretted things that early managers and concessioners did, their development of a recognized Yellowstone experience did serve to protect "vast natural areas of the park" from random and uninhibited use until attitudes relating to those areas matured to the point that managers understood how to handle the problems.

What may be most remarkable about the Yellowstone tour is how quickly it achieved a stable form that in some ways has not changed. It may have taken a trapper or prospector months to reach the Yellowstone Plateau from St. Louis or farther east; a great learning occurred in that long journey that later visitors would not share. But by 1883, when the NPRR Park Branch Line reached Cinnabar, it was possible for a family in New York City to board a train and reach the park in about the same time as it would take to drive that distance today in a car. Yellowstone was abruptly and universally available and would need all the organization and standardization it could get.

The visit, whether it took five days, seven days, or several weeks, contained the same elements. Depending upon where a visitor entered the park, the starting and ending points varied, but the classic "grand tour" began with the geyser basins and concluded with the canyon, the scenic finale. The loop road, essentially complete in its present form by 1905, has dictated the terms of the average visit ever since. Independent travelers in their own conveyances (labeled "sagebrushers" for their habit of camping at will along the roads) had the opportunity to vary the pace and route, but few departed from the main roads.[21]

The shortcomings of the view that the commercialization of Yellowstone simply victimized the tourist can be seen in visitors' reactions to the experience. Certainly the average tourist, knowing essentially nothing of what Yellowstone had to offer, depended heavily on park managers and commercial services to lead the way to the "attractions." John Sears has said that directions to all the tourist attractions were quickly spelled out: "The raw material of nature was rapidly transformed into a cultural commodity by reproducing and marketing verbal descriptions and pictorial representations of these places, by building roads and bridges so that tourists could reach them, by constructing facilities to accommodate the tourists, even by the act of naming their features (a process which in important ways defined their cultural meaning)."[22]

There is a good bit of hyperbole here. The raw material of nature, unless it was smashed into oblivion by souvenir-hungry tourists or shot to death by poachers, remained as raw as ever. We now know that roads and bridges can have all kinds of effects on ecological processes, effects that weren't understood by early park managers, but even at its height, development didn't cover one percent of the park. Decisions *were* made about which of the "raw materials" were required stops on a park visit; in that process, the raw materials may indeed have become conceptually different than they had been prior to the park's establishment, but the difference is not as simple or as easy to measure as Sears seems to believe.

It is true, though, that once there were professional guides and guidebooks, tourists were directed not only to where they should go but also to what they should *feel* about what they saw. This process, too, has been portrayed as fairly sinister and manipulative, but again it seems to have been precisely what the visitors wanted and needed. The quality of the guidebooks and other sources of information was often quite high, considering the limitations of the available information in the late 1800s and early 1900s; the sentiments promoted in the standard park guides were often as lofty as they were lamely expressed. The "homogenization" of the visitor experience could just as easily be viewed as an essential educational process. By today's standards, the guidebooks leaned heavily on a romantic view of the Wild West and failed to explain the ecological and geological wonders we now appreciate. Yellowstone was being given an image; its character was being defined and institutionalized.

At that time the search for Yellowstone led us to the development of what has been called "personality of place." With the benefit of hindsight we can see that by 1900 the park already had a complex personality, however shallow the commercial portrayals of it may seem to us. Besides its obligation to protect geological wonders, the park was quickly given a bundle of additional informal responsibilities, as a repository of a stylized western experience (stagecoach rides, campfire cookouts and talks), as a protective forest covering for the headwaters of some of the west's most important watersheds, as a refuge for wildlife no longer welcome in settled areas, and as a resort where universal vacation activities, from swimming to riding to dancing, could be enjoyed. Some of these uses were widely known, some were familiar only to a few. Yellowstone was being defined, not just by the promoters and managers, but by the visitors themselves. Visitors, as much as the tourism industry, passed the word of Yellowstone to many people who might never visit the place but who now had some idea of its personality. And as this personality became known, so did the visitor's awareness of the recreational possibilities here and how best to enjoy them. What was happening was not merely the standardization of the experience; people were learning how to act.[23]

To assume that most, or even many, visitors responded precisely as the guidebooks implied they should is to sell human nature short. The early accounts of Yellowstone — whether diaries, articles, promotional brochures, guidebooks, or scientific reports — may not be reliable indicators of what most visitors really got from the experience. Many were written by professional journalists and travel writers, a self-conscious and untypical crowd if ever there was one. These accounts are a rich and important source of information about the early visitor experience, but even today public attitude surveys reveal surprising and unexpected reactions to Yellowstone.

I repeat an opening statement of this book: We did not create Yellowstone National Park one day early in 1872. Instead, on that day we embarked upon an ongoing process that is based upon our always growing knowledge of the park and upon our changing attitudes about our relationship with nature. We will always be establishing Yellowstone. Every visitor participates in the search for Yellowstone; each first-timer sets out on a new journey of discovery. The vehicles of that discovery — whether television travelogues, the received wisdom of other visitors, publications, a road system, a hotel and campground network, a stagecoach, a mule, a pair of hiking boots — are modified over time, but they are at last only vehicles for each person's search. The intellectual and aesthetic resources of the individual come into play, and provide the Yellowstone experience with endless permutations, no matter how regimented the trip may seem or be on the surface. We may lament the limitations that commerce and culture place on the Yellowstone experience, but we must never underestimate the resourcefulness of each visitor in finding his or her way to the wonder of the place.

Once the tourist industry took hold and the park visit was standardized, the personal journey of discovery succeeded or failed only as a matter of degree. The experience rapidly became very well defined and achievable; except in the most unlikely circumstances, such as the fires of 1988, hardly anyone could fail to view Old Faithful in eruption, or the Grand Canyon from Artist Point. Almost any visit met the minimum standard of a "good" visit as defined by our culture. But even in the first years of the park, from that minimum standard rose a galaxy of opportunities, from the brief glimpse of a mule deer fawn from a stagecoach at dusk, to the unique combination of events occurring each evening at the old bear-feeding grounds, to a brief romantic interlude along the rim of the Grand Canyon.

The experience of our ancestors, decked out in full-length dusters and thumbing their guidebooks, may have fallen short of our own hopes and expectations for a Yellowstone visit, but we must judge our forebears gently, for they found much in Yellowstone. If the place had not lived up to the unofficial name of Wonderland, and if these people had not carried home such lively stories of its marvels, no amount of commercial promotion could have succeeded in making it the goal of one of America's foremost public pilgrimages. If Yellowstone had not been an authentic global wonder, it would have settled into the role of a regional attraction, more on the scale of New York's Catskills or the Wisconsin Dells.

WE CANNOT leave our early visitors without checking in once more on the people who had been coming to Yellowstone for 10,000 years: the Indians. In 1879 Superintendent Norris, who frequently expressed concern over hostile Indians, built an imposing blockhouse on a small hill adjacent to Mammoth Hot Springs. Throughout the 1880s complaints were published in the national press of Indians hunting or traveling in the park, and they were blamed for any number of fires, some of which they may have set.[24] But even before Norris's arrival in 1877, the resident Sheepeaters had been moved to reservations in Wyoming and Idaho. In 1878 the Bannocks were stopped, by military force, from moving around so much.

The most famous episode in the park's Indian history was the flight of the Nez Perce tribe in 1877.[25] About 750 of the Nez Perce, a very patient group of people who lived in eastern Oregon, refused to settle on a reservation as required by the U.S. government. They set out in the spring of 1877 from their homeland to reach the lands north and east of the park. Along the way they engaged the U.S. Army several times quite successfully, but eventually they were caught and defeated near the Canadian border in Montana Territory as they attempted to reach the Canadian Sioux lands. Some did escape into Canada, but more were placed on reservations. The whole "war" is now seen as one of the most tragic episodes in the sordid history of the subjugation of Native Americans; it made one of their leaders, Chief Joseph, a folk hero for his wisdom and eloquence in the face of the losses his people endured.

The Nez Perce passed through the park in late August and early September, pursued by General Oliver O. Howard and 600 soldiers. They entered from the west, traveled up the Madison River, kidnapped some tourists in the geyser basins, crossed the Central Plateau to the Yellowstone River just north of the outlet of Yellowstone Lake, then followed Pelican Creek up to the upper Lamar River and eventually left the park across the Absarokas. They did not know the way, and the time they lost in the park was time they couldn't afford. Though the leaders preferred not to harm anybody, some younger warriors were not so discreet; in various skirmishes and attacks two tourists were killed, and a few others were taken prisoner and forced to act as guides.

Oddly enough it was during this period, even after the forced settlement of various native groups that used the park regularly and after the Nez Perce incidents, that perhaps the most intriguing perceptual legacy of Native Americans in Yellowstone was firmed up; this was the belief, held by many people, including historians and park managers, that Indians were afraid of the park area.[26] By 1877, when Norris became superintendent, it was widely believed that Native Americans held the geysers in "superstitious awe" and were afraid to venture there. It isn't clear what those who held this theory made of all the Indians, including the Nez Perce, who came into the park to hunt or otherwise move around.

It would be easy to see this theory as a conscience-soothing justification generated by the whites for taking the land from the Indians — "they never wanted it in the first place" — but I doubt that such motivations had much to do with it; at the time whites seemed to feel no need to justify the massive relocation and destruction of Indians throughout the West. More likely, people fell for this story because it fit nicely with the prevailing stereotypes of the Native Americans as simple savages. As I mentioned earlier, the tribes that used Yellowstone in fact revered the area and its geothermal features. The idea that they were afraid of it may have come from accounts of Christianized Indians who, having been introduced to the concept of Hell, saw in Yellowstone a spooky resemblance to the whites' descriptions of the place.

INDIAN OR WHITE, visitors to Yellowstone were captured by its magic. Writers left breathless accounts of wonder upon wonder, and if they saw it as nature's sideshow rather than as some more profound window into the wilderness, they were no less appreciative.

Even John Muir, that most prominent of geological evangelists, abandoned his passion for mountain scenery when he hit the basins:

> Geysers, however, are the main objects, and as soon as they come in sight all other wonders are forgotten. All gather around the crater of the one that is expected to play first. . . . While tourists wait around a large geyser, such as the Castle or the Giant, there is chatter and small talk in anything but solemn mood; and during the intervals between the preliminary splashes and upheavals some adventurer occasionally looks down the throat of the crater, admiring the silex formations and wondering whether Hades is as beautiful. But when, with awful uproar as if avalanches were falling and storms thundering in the depths, the tremendous outburst begins, all run away to a safe distance, and look on, awe-stricken and silent, in devout, worshipping wonder.[27]

At the time of Muir's visit (1885), visitors were allowed to get close to the thermal features, but soon afterward they were kept at a "safe distance" most of the time. The experience of the geysers was evolving too. In many ways Yellowstone was being redefined, a process that would be hastened a year after Muir's visit, when the cavalry arrived to save the day.

7 | A SINGLE ROCK

Most visitors to Yellowstone in the mid-1880s may have had a great time, but prospects were bleak for the survival of the park. Nathaniel Langford and Philetus Norris each served five years as superintendent, but between 1882 and 1886 three men held the job in quick succession. Patrick Conger was ineffective from 1882 until September of 1884; Robert Carpenter was a crook whose "crass and venal attitude toward management of the Park led to his early removal" the following June; and David Wear was a capable, strong-willed superintendent who, during his year in office, was unable to dig himself out of the hole created by his predecessors.[1] The park was an administrative failure, threatened on all sides. In March of 1883, accepting the need for more supervision and protection of Yellowstone, Congress authorized the hiring of a park police force. Known as assistant superintendents, many of those hired were ignorant, ineffective political appointees. A few, most notably George L. Henderson, came to love the park deeply and made lasting contributions, but most were simply unable to accomplish anything meaningful.[2]

A clear window into this period is provided us by a neglected hero of the early conservation movement, William Hallett Phillips. In the summer of 1885 a House special committee had provided the young park with a powerful statement of direction, urging that "the park should so far as possible be spared the vandalism of improvement. Its great and only charms are in the display of wonderful forces of nature, the ever varying beauty of the rugged landscape, and the sublimity of the scenery. Art cannot embellish them."[3] Here was a new vision, enlarging on and clarifying that of the park's organic act thirteen years earlier. The "forces of nature" were presumably the geysers and hot springs, but the landscape itself (rather than just a few specific spots) was now more explicitly recognized as part of the park's value. But the committee, predicting the doom of the wildlife if the poor protection of the superintendent and his assistants continued, concluded that the park should be turned over to Wyoming when the territory achieved statehood. That same summer Secretary of the Interior Lucius Quintus Cincinnatus Lamar sent Special Agent Phillips to investigate conditions in the park.

In his report Phillips summarized the misbehavior and contract violations of the various concessioners (or leaseholders, as he called them). Announcing that "many of such leases were granted to unfit persons," he assembled a dismaying list of offenses: facilities constructed entirely outside the bounds of the agreed-upon sites, universal violation of the park's policy of no alcohol sales, "unsightly" ramshackle structures cluttering up the major features, seventy-one people jammed into a tent camp with only twenty-one beds, and hotel "privy bowls . . . more or less filled with human excrement; some even overflowing upon the surrounding floor."[4] Of all park concessioners, only the photographer F. J. Haynes was not violating his lease in some way.

Of equal concern to Phillips was the park's sad legal situation. Without the force of law behind park regulations, even a competent administrator had no way to control the lawbreakers. In March of 1884 the Territory of Wyoming passed a law providing for justices of the peace and constables of that state to patrol the park and arrest and try vandals and poachers, but complaints poured out about these Wyoming officials, some of whom abused their power to the great disadvantage of park visitors. Phillips couldn't imagine where Wyoming got the authority to set up such a system, and he was angered by its abuses. Interestingly, one of his complaints was that visitors were arrested even if they picked up a small piece of obsidian or geyser formation; even the park's defenders did not yet fully understand the ultimate damage that could be caused by such casual souvenir collecting.

Phillips criticized the 1883 Teller memo that prohibited hunting, pointing out that it omitted many species that were still hunted (especially bears, a popular target in the park): "The consequence has been that under the excuse of hunting bear and other animals not on the enumerated list, the large game in the Park which the Government is so much interested in protecting have been slaughtered."[5]

It is a time-honored tradition in Yellowstone to invoke the park's founders to prove that one's own opinion is right, to argue that "we should do . . . [fill in your favorite opinion] . . . so that Yellowstone will live up to the dreams of its creators." On the matter of game protection, Phillips distinguished himself as one of the first park defenders to indulge in creative interpretation of Congress's intentions. He maintained that "preservation of the great game" was one of Congress's "three objects" in creating the park, though game protection is only peripherally mentioned in the act.[6]

Phillips made an eloquent plea for increased authority for the park's managers, a strong federal judicial presence, and a wholesale cleanup of the shadier concessioners. He reinforced the statement of the House special committee that "if there is one object which should be kept in view more than any other, it is that of preserving the Park as much as possible in a state of nature"; from that principle he went directly to a concern on many conservationists' minds, that "a railroad through the Park would go far to destroy its beauty, and besides is not demanded by the public."[7]

As mentioned in the last chapter, a chorus of voices was already demanding better protection and management for Yellowstone. Phillips's report was an outstanding statement of the park's most urgent needs, adding weight to public fears for the future. Eventually, most of the guidelines he proposed would be enacted, though not in the way he had imagined.

There were many active sportsmen in the American military in the late 1800s, and some were effective and prominent conservationists. For Yellowstone the most often cited officer-conservationist is General Philip Sheridan, a Civil War veteran who in 1882 urged that the park's eastern and southern boundaries be greatly extended (forty miles to the east!) to encompass more wildlife range.[8] This was the most amibitious of many expansion proposals over the next half-century. On December 11, 1882, George Bird Grinnell gave Sheridan's report extensive coverage in *Forest and Stream.* Grinnell, like Sheridan, had seen the future of the West, and in Yellowstone he also saw its salvation:

> For many years we have hunted and traveled and fished and trapped and mined and fought Indians over the length and breadth of the great West. We have seen it when it was, except in isolated spots, an uninhabited wilderness: have seen the Indians and the game retreat before the white man and the cattle, and beheld the tide of immigration, once small like a tiny mountain stream, move forward, at first slowly, and then, gathering volume and strength, advance with a constantly accelerated power which threatens before long to leave no portion of our vast territory unbroken by the farmer's plow or untrodden by his flocks. There is one spot left, a single rock about which this tide will break, and past which it will sweep, leaving it undefiled by the unsightly traces of civilization. Here in this Yellowstone Park the large game of the West may be preserved from extermination; here, like the almost extinct aurochs of Lithuania, it may be seen by generations yet unborn.[9]

Like Captain Ludlow in 1875, Sheridan in 1882 proposed that troops be used to patrol and protect the park. A year later, influenced by Sheridan's report, Missouri senator George Graham Vest saw to it that the Sundry Civil Appropriations Bill for 1883 provided that the secretary of war supply troops to protect the park, should the secretary of the interior feel they were needed. Then in 1886, with congressional debate deadlocked over what to do about the park and no funding forthcoming, Vest's foresightful action paid off: the military was asked to help. Thus began one of the American military's most unusual peacetime assignments, protecting Yellowstone and then several other parks. They did so with uncommon energy, thanks in good part to the strong conservation sentiment

The soldier station near Tower Fall shortly after the turn of the century. This was one of the outposts along the park's main road from which soldiers patrolled the major developments, camping areas, and backcountry trails. *NPS photo*

among some prominent officers. And they arrived, with a cinematic flourish, just in the nick of time.

On August 17, 1886, Captain Moses Harris, with Troop M of the First Cavalry, arrived at Mammoth Hot Springs, where he immediately established Camp Sheridan.[10] That camp was gradually replaced by Fort Yellowstone, a larger and more attractive post. Most of the National Park Service buildings on the level plain east of Mammoth Hot Springs today were built as Fort Yellowstone by the army between 1891 and 1916; the War Department was said to have lavished more than usual attention on making the post attractive because it received more foreign visitors than any other American army post except perhaps West Point.

The commanding officer of Fort Yellowstone, at first a captain in the U.S. Cavalry and, as the post grew, a major, was known as the "acting superintendent," so temporary was this assignment imagined to be. He dealt with two superiors (and kept two sets of administrative records); as commanding officer of Fort Yellowstone he took his orders from the secretary of war (often directly), and as acting superintendent of Yellowstone National Park he was supervised by the secretary of the interior. Over the thirty-two years during which the army protected Yellowstone, a number of outstanding officers held the position of acting superintendent. Some were made honorary members of the Boone and Crockett Club and became eloquent spokesmen for the conservation movement.

The U.S. Cavalry proved quite capable of protecting the place. The operations of concessioners received much closer scrutiny, soldier stations were established along the major tourist routes, and patrols were set up to guard against poachers. The tales of these patrols and their exploits, especially in the winter wilderness, rival the adventures of the trappers: after spending a long day on skis weighing several pounds each in abominable weather, they would hole up for the night in a tiny box of a cabin (or sit up at a small fire outside all night if necessary), then continue the next day across country where one mistake meant freezing to death.

The poachers were often lifelong backwoodsmen who knew the country better than anyone else alive, and even if a patrol caught one, their options were limited by the inadequacy of the park's legal protection. Here the military showed a flair not only for persistence but for improvisation. With no legal recourse other than expulsion, the soldiers "found ways" to make the punishment suit the crime. If they caught a particularly objectionable character committing some serious violation of park regulations, they could hold him in custody (locked in the guardhouse) and write to the secretary of the interior for instructions — which could take a very long time. If they caught him near the north boundary, say, they could march him on foot, in front of a mounted trooper, all the way to the south boundary, expelling him there with the information that all his gear was at the north boundary, and he had to go around — not through — the park to pick it up.

The army imposed upon the park just the sort of order and regimentation that was needed. Visitors began to understand why they shouldn't do all the harmful things that had seemed like such fun, and even if they didn't understand, they found they couldn't get away with it. The operators of the many commercial enterprises began to get a better idea of their responsibilities toward the public. Best of all, it became clear that the park was going to last.

Fort Yellowstone was not the most popular assignment for soldiers, and the army rotated new troops to the park each year, so the soldiers had little chance to get to know the place well. If it weren't for the small corps of civilian scouts, the soldiers would have been much less effective, especially in their backcountry patrols. The scouts, gathered from among the region's rougher element, proved able to deal with the worst lawbreakers, and they taught batch after batch of new soldiers what Yellowstone needed. But they couldn't teach them to like the place, and isolation and cabin fever were frequent problems for the soldiers. At one point shortly after the turn of the century, Fort Yellowstone had one of the highest desertion rates in the country.

But for the most part the army honored the assignment heroically; the title of historian H. D. Hampton's book *How the U.S. Cavalry Saved the National Parks* is not much of an exaggeration. The artist Frederic Remington, himself an enthusiast of wild western landscapes, captured the nation's growing mood of pride in Yellowstone in language that is at once poetic and practical after a visit in 1893:

> Americans have a national treasure in the Yellowstone Park, and they should guard it jealously. Nature has made her wildest patterns here, has brought the boiling waters from her greatest depths to the peaks which bear eternal snow, and set her masterpiece with pools like jewels. Let us respect her moods, and

let the beasts she nurtures in her bosom live, and when the man from Oshkosh writes his name with a blue pencil on her sacred face, let him spend six months where the scenery is circumscribed and entirely artificial.[11]

The army also played a fundamental role in institutionalizing the park experience when they refined and completed the road system. In 1883 the U.S. Army Corps of Engineers was assigned to lay out and construct the park roads. They did so with a sensitivity to landscape that would amaze many modern conservationists, who have come to regard the Corps, because of its levee and dam building in later years, as the enemy of natural settings. Over the next three decades, under the inspired guidance of such engineers as Dan Kingman and Hiram Chittenden, the Corps developed a usable system of roads that fit as well as was possible into the landscape.[12]

It was not an easy place for road building. Chittenden complained about what the park's complex geological legacy meant to the builders: "The first difficulty arises from the wretched nature of the material through which the roads pass. Unquestionably there is no other spot of equal area on the face of the earth where there is such a remarkable variety of substances, and such curious combinations, in the composition of the soil."[13]

He compared the variety of conditions encountered in building a mile of park road to what one would normally encounter "in building a turnpike from Portland in Maine to Portland in Oregon."[14] That may have been an overstatement, but without question the work was an awful chore. Today, despite improvements in equipment and engineering, and the realignment of many grades, maintaining the park's road system is still enormously costly. Paving didn't start until after the National Park Service was created in 1916; prior to that, stagecoach passengers were issued full-length dusters to keep their clothes relatively free of the fine choking dust kicked up by the traffic (the major coach lines tended to run convoys of coaches from point to point, so passengers in any but the lead coach saw a lot of dust). Starting in 1902, Chittenden developed a system of water wagons that sprinkled to keep the dust down, but it wasn't until 1915 that his proposal to oil the roads was finally enacted, probably, in part, in response to the automobiles that would arrive that year.

Road construction and improvement proceeded by fits and starts. A substantial appropriation in one year might be followed by very little the next; during much of the army period, Congress had an exasperating tendency to delay passage of the annual appropriation until the season was so far advanced that little could be accomplished.

The Corps of Engineers didn't so much create the road system as complete it with exceptionally good taste and heroic engineering. The landscape and the locations of the attractions people most wanted to see dictated the routes as much as anything else did. Early tourists found their way to the park's famous features by following obvious drainage courses and passes, creating a number of minor alternative paths and a fairly obvious set of major ones. In the late 1870s Superintendent Norris laid out and pioneered the rough course of more than two thirds of the 140-mile grand loop that led visitors to the main attractions at Mammoth, the geyser basins, the lake, and the canyon, but even Norris was responding in part to the already recognized routes early visitors had followed. Still, the Corps of Engineers vastly improved on Norris's primitive tracks in every respect, from alignment to surface to aesthetics, and Yellowstone historians have unanimously praised the Corps's accomplishment.

By 1903 the lower half of the grand loop, connecting Old Faithful, West Thumb, the lake outlet, the Grand Canyon, Norris, and Madison Junction, was in place, and there were reasonable if unimproved roads connecting this loop with the north, west, south, and east entrances. By 1905 the upper part of the loop was in place, connecting the canyon with Tower Fall, then following the general course of the old miner's road west toward Mammoth and east to Cooke City.

In most national parks roads have an important role as interpretive devices. There continues today a tension between the urge (sometimes regarded as a legal obligation) to "modernize" park roads and bring them up to some national standard and the equally compelling desire to preserve their quality not as roads but as "auto

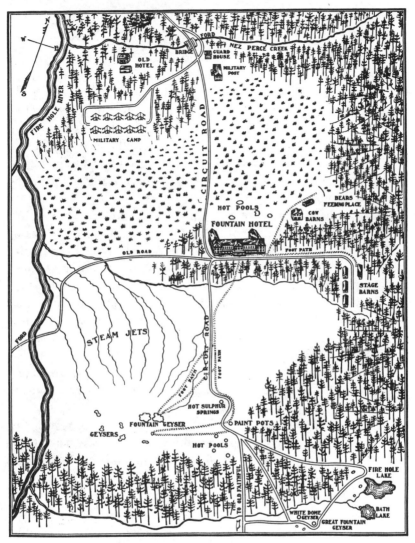

The Lower Geyser Basin in 1909, from Campbell's *New Revised Complete Guide and Descriptive Book of the Yellowstone National Park*. Notice that there are two hotels, the Marshall ("Old Hotel," top left) and the large Fountain Hotel, as well as many barns and other outbuildings, a "Bears Feeding Place," a military post and guardhouse, and a large summer encampment for troops. None of these structures survives today. The area has largely been restored, and vegetation has been allowed to regrow over the building sites. The amount of developed acreage in the park probably peaked before 1920 and has declined substantially since then.

trails." The latter approach affords the now-rare charm of driving a winding forest road at a slow speed, but it also enhances the road's role as an educational tool. Unlike most other public roads, park roads do not exist merely to move people from one place to another as quickly and safely as possible, nor are they built merely to do as little damage to the setting as possible. They are the principal means of public enjoyment of the park, compelling visitors by their very nonmodernness to take their time and take part in the landscape as they pass through it.[15]

Roads, however, are the bane of today's wilderness advocates, and though Yellowstone is not legally defined as wilderness, it is in fact one of the last great wild areas in the lower forty-eight states. Its road system still generates considerable resentment among people who would prefer to see the park's wilderness not subdivided by busy highways, with their many ecological effects on the surrounding country.[16] The army engineers may have shown unusual sensitivity in the design and construction of roads, but they still tended to build them either through the middle (very bad), or along the edge (perhaps even worse) of many of the park's richest riparian zones, because those are the prettiest places, which people want to drive through.

A tour of the archival records of park road building reveals the same kinds of now-nightmarish possibilities as does a review of Superintendent Norris's ambitions for managing and exploiting park wildlife. At various times roads were proposed, and even surveyed, over such fabulous wilderness areas as Bighorn Pass and the Thorofare region in southeastern Yellowstone. Like the elevator once seriously considered for the Lower Falls in the Grand Canyon (a builder actually applied for a permit in 1889), these roads that never happened are now seen as narrow escapes, but they again demonstrate the serendipitous process by which Yellowstone evolved.

PERHAPS THE most important aspect of managing Yellowstone was caring for the animals. The wildlife policies of the earlier civilian superintendents and those of the army differed primarily in the latter's far greater ability to act on its beliefs. Like Norris and his fellow civilian superintendents, the acting superintendents of the army period believed in aggressive management to make the most of the park's potential as a wildlife reserve. By the time the army arrived, that potential included the following definitions: a reservoir to perpetually restock game ranges outside the park; a "last stand" wildlife museum to preserve animals that only decades earlier had inhabited the entire West; an unfenced zoological garden for the enjoyment and enrichment of visitors who rarely saw such animals elsewhere; an angler's paradise, where fish were as abundant as in presettlement times; and a vast outdoor laboratory where all facets of the park, from geology to entomology, could be studied by researchers. Even by 1900 wildlife conservation was a complex matter that combined a number of impulses of numerous elements of society, from bird watchers to bear hunters to bison breeders. Sportsmen were the most effective single group in promoting conservation at this time, especially of the game animals, but they were hardly the only people who appreciated wildlife or saw its value in Yellowstone.

Like Norris, some of the army acting superintendents toyed with what now seem especially odd notions about uses for Yellowstone. For example, various animals were considered or proposed for introduction, including reindeer and a number of game birds. At the time the idea apparently seemed a logical extension of the park's use as a game reserve; why not stockpile species of special interest, even if they were not native? As experience with wildlife management accumulated in the United States and elsewhere, it became abundantly obvious that introducing nonnative species is virtually never without cost to the native species, and such introductions were soon perceived as aesthetic intrusions upon the integrity of the setting as well.

But most attention was paid to the protection of a key group of species, already established as "noble" animals by centuries of sportsmen and naturalists: the ungulates. These hooved herbivores — elk, bison, deer, moose, pronghorn, and bighorn sheep — were admired by sportsmen and nonsportsmen alike. The bison seemed most urgently in need of attention. Though the numbers of most other grazers rebounded from the slaughter of the 1870s, the bison

Bison poacher Ed Howell (right) escorted by army scouts, February 1894, probably at Norris Geyser Basin. The photograph was taken by F. J. Haynes, whose party, just then starting a winter tour of the park, met Howell and his captors on their way in from Pelican Valley, where Howell had been caught killing park bison. The dark shape in the snow to Howell's right is probably his dog, which he wanted to kill because it failed to alert him to the scouts' approach. *Haynes Foundation Collection, Montana Historical Society, Helena, Montana*

population continued to decline. Amazing as it seems, within a few years of the time when the bison market was dealing in hundreds of thousands of hides, by the early 1890s a single trophy head could bring more than one hundred dollars, so quickly did we go from abusing abundance to prizing rarity. Yellowstone, as home of the last few free-roaming bison in the United States, was a prime target for poaching, and the few hundred estimated bison of the early 1880s had become a few dozen by the early 1890s.[17]

The saving of the Yellowstone bison is a story that provides the park with one of its truest connections to the mythic Old West, where good guys and bad guys fought it out in the wilderness and where right triumphed in the end. On February 13, 1894, a civilian scout and a trooper, on a winter patrol funded in part by Acting Superintendent George Anderson's personal funds, captured a poacher named Ed Howell in Pelican Valley, where Howell had just killed several of the park's very few remaining bison. The capture involved a risky rush by the veteran scout, Felix Burgess, on skis across a broad expanse of open snow to get within pistol range before Howell (armed with a rifle) or his dog saw him coming. Burgess and the trooper then escorted Howell on an arduous return trip to Mammoth. As luck would have it, Emerson Hough, a young correspondent from *Forest and Stream*, was in the park at the time, and, encouraged by park personnel, he wrote the story and rushed it back to George Bird Grinnell in New York, who published it in the magazine. The public outcry was great enough that an act "to protect the birds and animals in Yellowstone National Park," locally known as the Lacey Act after the Iowa congressman who introduced it (not to be confused with the more famous Lacey Act that forbade interstate transportation of wildlife for commercial purposes), was passed on May 7, 1894.[18] The Lacey Act finally put legislative weight behind park regulations, making the army's job a great deal simpler.

But still the bison seemed likely to disappear, so in 1902 Congress appropriated $15,000 to purchase some bison from domestic herds (even at that time bison were not in danger of extinction; there were many private herds, as well as wild herds in Canada). These animals were brought to Yellowstone and mixed with calves captured from the wild herd, and for the next half-century Yellowstone was in the buffalo-ranching business. After the population had been built up, the animals were eventually weaned from ranch care and released. The entire saga, from the arrest of Howell to the closing of the ranching operation in the 1950s, has long been regarded as one of the shining successes of the wildlife conservation movement, though the glow of achievement faded during subsequent controversies over bison management, which are discussed in a later chapter.

Other park wildlife was flourishing. Of all the ungulates, the elk were most abundant and held the public interest most consistently. By the early 1880s, when large-scale market hunting ceased in Yellowstone, elk populations inside and outside the park had been substantially reduced. North of the park, especially, it seemed that these animals had been essentially destroyed or reduced to very low numbers. Over the next two decades, as the numbers of elk increased under the protection of the army, relatively few people in the region seemed to consider that the populations might simply be returning to their preslaughter levels or distribution. The almost unanimous view among visitors to the region before 1880 (which I reviewed in Chapter 3), that elk and other wildlife were abundant, was soon replaced with the opposite view, that few animals had inhabited these mountains prehistorically.

It is difficult to explain how this belief changed so quickly, but it probably resulted from the short memories of most area residents. By the late 1870s, well before any significant settlement of the Yellowstone Valley north of the park, the elk had been much reduced. Most area residents arrived after the slaughter, and people have a tendency to presume that the form of the landscape they first remember it having is its "right" form.

But for army managers in the 1890s, and for many later writers who have tried to understand the history of Yellowstone elk, what happened was quite simple: suddenly there were more of them, and more all the time. In the 1890s and for a few years after that, the high rate of reproduction was a matter of pride, because it proved that the park's protection was making a difference. But then satisfaction was replaced by concern and eventually alarm. "Plenty" of elk became "too many," though few people in that day had the ecological acumen to consider the question "Too many for what?"

In *The Northern Yellowstone Elk* (1982), Douglas Houston has done more than anyone else to sort out what happened to the elk during this period.[19] He notes that though the army superintendents routinely reported that the elk were increasing, their actual tallies suggest otherwise. Their numbers seem to have reached a certain level and then hovered there, rising or falling depending upon environmental conditions. Meanwhile the acting superintendents published confusing reports, varying which of the park's eight elk herds they included in their totals, sometimes counting summering elk only or both summering and wintering elk, and in other ways providing a tangled and inconsistent record. As early as 1891 Acting Superintendent Anderson reported that "conservative estimates place their numbers at 25,000," and though occasional later estimates were higher, for the next twenty years the reports that claimed the elk were increasing also confidently stated there were between 25,000 and perhaps 40,000 in the park.[20]

No doubt it looked good on reports that these animals were doing so well, but I don't think that the officers were intentionally exaggerating the numbers. Instead, they were trusting their local advisers: scouts, friends, and others who had lived in the area longer than they had and who were quite earnest in their convictions that elk were a whole lot more common than they used to be. But the first attempts to actually count the animals are a gigantic muddle. Houston's examination of original records, such as diaries and the reports of the field personnel responsible for the counts, turned up many irregularities. In the years 1912 to 1914, for example, the counts of the largest herd, the northern one, were made in the spring over a period of three weeks or more, by scouts who started at the lower elevations and worked their way up the drainages, counting elk as they went. But at that time the elk were migrating up those same drainages on their way to summer ranges; the same individuals were obviously going to be counted more than once. In those years the scouts reported between 30,000 and 35,000 elk in the northern herd.

These numbers became controversial early on, when U.S. Forest Service personnel pointed out the inadequacies of the counting system. In 1916 and again in 1917, more reliable interagency counts of the northern herd (conducted by scouts moving in the opposite direction from the elk) yielded an estimate of less than 12,000 (9,564 were actually counted) for 1916 and less than 18,000 (10,769 were actually counted) for 1917. But confusion and disagreement continued, no doubt fueled by political rivalries between the various agencies, culminating in the worst single misconception about Yellowstone elk in this period, that the winter of 1919–20 caused a massive die-off, on the order of 14,000.

Rather like the famous and now challenged (if not completely discredited) claim that as many as 100,000 deer died in the winter of 1924–25 on the Kaibab Plateau of Arizona, the great Yellowstone elk winterkill has made its way into the literature of wildlife management. It seems to have been largely an artifact of wild miscalculations: first, of how many elk were alive at the beginning of the winter (somehow the old estimate of 25,000 was revived), and second, of how many were alive at the end of the winter (nobody counted them, but an estimate of 10,000 to 12,000 emerged). The die-off was largely the product of arithmetic conducted far away, most notably by the park superintendent, who was then in Washington. As Houston pointed out, "No one present at the time ever suggested natural mortality of that magnitude."[21]

By this time elk were a national issue among conservationists, and Yellowstone was center stage, not only for the reported die-off but also for a controversy over the management of the Jackson Hole herd, some of which summered in Yellowstone. Not only managers but also sportsmen and other concerned citizens recognized that the winter ranges of Yellowstone-area elk were being settled and that action had to be taken to keep the elk from starving in the short run and disappearing entirely in the long run.

The management of elk presented great challenges to the army, the most important of which they did not really understand. An underlying presumption of most wildlife management decisions was that the primary goal was stability — to have a large herd of elk whose number did not change dramatically. The officers must have understood that it would be "good" to report increasing herds of ungulates for only so long; at some point there had to be "enough." But they had no clear way of determining how many were enough. In the face of an ever-varying environment, in which even modest climate changes could cause dramatic alterations in the productivity of winter ranges, the unspoken intent of the managers was to achieve stasis. They were demanding of themselves the great power required to dampen the perpetual oscillations of the system, when they didn't understand that the system lived by oscillation.

In some matters, though, the army's job seemed simple enough. One especially straightforward question was what to do about predators. One of the first official acts of the park's first military administrator, Captain Moses Harris, was to follow William Phillips's advice and outlaw all public hunting of all species. He did not do this because he thought the predators deserved protection but because he figured that allowing the hunting of any species would lead to abuses of the regulations and result in the illegal killing of more elk and other protected animals than the carnivores could possibly kill anyway.[22] If anybody was going to kill predators, it would be the officials who ran the park.

Predators were being exterminated throughout the West, of course. Grizzly bears, wolves, mountain lions, and smaller predators had no political constituency, and only a few people mourned their passing. As the western ranching economy geared up, predators became, like the Indians before them, an impediment to progress, and like the Indians, they were persecuted relentlessly and in many cases were eradicated.

Popular portrayals of predator control in this country have been too simplistic, based on the idea that the removal of predators will always cause the prey numbers to increase, sometimes disastrously. We now know that this result can occur, but we also know that the removal or even the addition of a predator may not have such clear-cut results in a given system.

We also know that the early advocates of predator control were not entirely naive. In 1897, when Acting Superintendent S. B. M. Young reported that some coyotes had to be killed because, he believed, they were killing too many elk calves, antelope fawns, and grouse, he acknowledged that destruction of coyotes might favor an increase in "gophers," who might then overharvest grasses.[23] Eleven years later, during Young's second term as superintendent, he received the following letter from President Theodore Roosevelt:

I do not think any more cougars (mountain lions) should be killed in the park. Game is abundant. We want to profit by what has happened in the English preserves, where it proved to be bad for the grouse itself to kill off all the peregrine falcons and all the other birds of prey. It may be advisable, in case the ranks of the deer and antelope right around the Springs should be too heavily killed out, to kill some of the cougars there, but in the rest of the park I certainly would not kill any of them. On the contrary, they ought to be let alone.[24]

By then, however, the army had been killing predators for a decade. In 1907, for example, building on earlier orders, the scouts and noncommissioned officers at the soldier stations were "authorized and directed to kill mountain lions, coyotes, and timber wolves. They will do this themselves, and will not delegate the authority to anyone else."[25] In the first thirty-five years of the twentieth century, army and National Park Service personnel killed more than 100 wolves, 100 mountain lions, and 4,000 coyotes.[26] We have spent the rest of the century trying to understand what that campaign of destruction cost us.

BY MOST of their own measures, Yellowstone managers, defenders, and promoters at the beginning of the twentieth century regarded the park as a grand success. It was now well protected both on the ground and legislatively. More and more visitors were finding their way there, and the concession services were steadily improving. The perhaps premature sentiment expressed by William Phillips in 1886, that the park had become genuinely "national," was now true.

What made it possible for the park to last through this most perilous quarter century? Was it merely good luck, or was Yellowstone National Park such a good idea that it simply had to work? Over the years, historians have nominated a number of forces as reasons for Yellowstone's survival, but I think it is impossible to name a single preeminent cause. The aesthetic enthusiasms of many people, from Cornelius Hedges to Rudyard Kipling, were certainly a factor; the park's extraordinary features appealed to what historian Katherine Early has described as a "genteel romanticism" for wild beauty.[27] The activation of industrial tourism increased public awareness of the park just as the resulting pressures for development compelled park defenders to test and refine their ideas about what kinds of tourism should be practiced here. The raw greed of many people, from the well-scrubbed urban financiers (who knew from the beginning that these were not "worthless lands") to the vilest poachers of pregnant bison cows, provided an enemy for the defenders to rally against. The high-minded idealism of gentleman sportsmen like George Bird Grinnell produced articles that ceaselessly hammered on the public conscience, but it was not just a small elite group of sportsmen who cared about Yellowstone; Grinnell had no trouble enlisting the support of thousands of rank-and-file hunters and fishermen who cared. The random individual heroism of Felix Burgess, G. L. Henderson, Harry Yount, and countless others brought victory in this or that skirmish along the way. And the army, whose physical presence and unceasing sense of duty stabilized park administration and policies, became the means by which all Yellowstone's friends saw their park protected and enshrined in world culture.

One last legacy of the army days must be mentioned here, for its consequences were far-reaching. When Captain Moses Harris arrived in Yellowstone that August day in 1886, one of the first duties he assigned his men to was fighting a fire south of Mammoth Hot Springs, by all accounts the very first involvement of the federal government in firefighting on public lands. The soldiers were frequently called upon to fight fires over the next thirty-two years. From that modest beginning grew a vast, multi-agency, high-technology bureaucracy employing many thousands of people — the world's largest and most expert firefighting team, a century deep in experience, training, and wisdom. And in 1988 they all came home.

8 | Big Men with Fine Personalities

I N THE EARLY 1900s, while the management of Yellowstone was evolving rapidly, the entire national park movement was trying to define itself. By 1915 there were thirteen national parks and eighteen national monuments, and the system showed every sign of continuing to grow, but for most practical purposes, nobody was in charge. The parks were administered in a variety of ways by a variety of agencies. As one conservationist put it, "Nowhere in official Washington can an inquirer find an office of the National Parks, or a desk devoted solely to their management. By passing around through their departments, and consulting clerks who have taken on the extra work of doing what they can for the Nation's playgrounds, it is possible to come at a little information."[1] The parks needed more bureaucratic support, of course, not only so that their direction might be more unified but also so that someone in the government would champion their cause and their many practical needs.

The idea of a centralized national park administration rattled around in the federal bureaucracy for years before the National Park Service was created on August 25, 1916. The National Park Service Act charged the new agency to "conserve the scenery and the natural and historic objects and the wildlife therein and to provide for the enjoyment of the same in such manner and by such means as will leave them unimpaired for the enjoyment of future generations."[2] Countless writers have since pointed out the apparent contradiction — conserve these things yet provide for their enjoyment by a growing number of people — but the statement offers us more than this one dilemma. Notice especially that it started with scenery. That was not an accident or a rhetorical flourish. The experiment that led eventually to our current understanding of the value of parks had barely begun; they were still thought of primarily as places where magnificent vistas were preserved for public viewing. Yellowstone had unique geothermal features along with the more traditional scenery at the canyon, the lake, and a few other places along the grand loop road. Today, with our greatly heightened awareness of the significance of "unsightly" ecological processes in changing and shaping park landscapes, the traditional definition of scenery has begun to fall out of favor. The old view, now sarcastically characterized as "scenery is greenery," has been supplanted by one in which fire, avalanches, windstorms, floods, mudslides, and other disturbances are respected as essential, process-forcing events. Scenery itself is a confusing, evolving resource.

But though the National Park Service Act reinforced the purpose of parks in terms of scenery, it also represented a significant shift in balance. The 1872 act creating Yellowstone Park had vaguely specified that the park's features should be protected somehow, but the park service act more clearly put protection of the resources — whether scenic, historic, geological, or biological — on an equal footing with public use. "Enjoyment" may not have been any better defined than it was in the 1872 act, but "unimpaired" implied more than had been suggested earlier about just how far protection could be taken.

On the other hand, Yellowstone visitors and managers still had a pretty generous definition of enjoyment. Many activities that would later be questioned were considered just fine (assuming they were considered at all). The park's biological character was appreciated by the early visitors and protected by the early managers — according to the attitudes of the times. Those attitudes were, in general, far more openly anthropocentric than those of most park defenders today; benefit and enjoyment were simple enough concepts, and not all that many people were coming to Yellowstone anyway; what harm could they do?

Ranger-naturalist Philip Martindale (right) leading a group of visitors at Old Faithful, July 1930; the Old Faithful Inn is in the background. Notice that they are walking across the hot-springs formation, a common practice at the time. The formations are now protected by confining foot traffic to boardwalks. *NPS photo*

In 1926 Yellowstone superintendent Horace Albright wrote, in a letter to an applicant for a summer ranger's job:

> We want big men with fine personalities, and experience in the out-of-doors in riding, camping, woodcraft, fighting fires and similar activities. . . . Remember there is no vacation in the work and mighty little money. If you want to come for pleasure you will be disappointed. If you want a summer in the Park as an experience in outdoor activity amid forests and a

fine invigorating atmosphere, apply if you are qualified. Otherwise, please plan to visit the Yellowstone National Park as a tourist.[3]

The rangers (thanks in good part to Albright's effective image promotion) quickly became known not only as protectors of the park's resources but also as the soul of the place. National park and forest rangers became a symbol of self-sufficiency, goodness, and a wholesome, nature-filled world. This image has never entirely faded, despite great changes in the realities of the work and the attributes of the rangers themselves. Even today, when the ranger profession is infinitely more complicated administratively, now that women (and small men with lousy personalities, for that matter), minorities, and others that Albright would have rejected have been successfully integrated into the profession, and the media periodically run stories about this or that crisis in rangering (low pay, bad housing, and poor training are trotted out most often as threats to the trade), the image still holds for most people.[4]

To the average American, rangers probably still stand for some abstract "good" more than they stand for any of the agencies that employ them. They are our equivalent of Canada's "Mounties" — Dudley Doright with brains, skill, and a field guide to animal tracks in his hip pocket. The ranger is the person every visitor looks to for answers to questions or solutions to a problem. Many visitors just want to see a ranger, the representation of some vague romantic vision of the Old West (a vision at least partially corrected and vastly enriched by an environmental conscience virtually nonexistent in that West). For all the changes that rangering has undergone since the park's early days, I continue to believe that, as I once wrote, "Surely the ranger is one of the most important cultural achievements the national parks can aim to protect within their boundaries."[5]

The ranger's role in Yellowstone was evident in many romantic portrayals in stories, films, and books, one of my favorites being the popular children's book *Cubby in Wonderland,* first published in 1932. The author, Frances Joyce Farnsworth, used the travels of a black bear sow and cub in the park as a vehicle for describing Yellowstone's most important features. Prominent among those features was the ranger, whom the animals described as "our friend":

> "I think he is splendid," said Cubby. "If I were a little people instead of a little bear, I'd want to be a Ranger when I grew up. I wonder if he knows how much all the little bears and otter babies and everything else, out here, like him?"
>
> "He has lots of friends," said Mrs. Otter, "and he gets well acquainted with all the wild things in the Park. I suppose a Ranger sees things that we do, and knows more about our ways than any other people in the world. He's kind to us."[6]

Yellowstone recruited some of its first rangers from the ranks of the soldiers and scouts who had worked in the park before 1918. This transition would have worked more smoothly than it did but for the political maneuvering that seems never to end around national parks. In 1916, when the National Park Service was created, local business interests around Yellowstone, concerned that they would lose revenue if the army was replaced by the smaller ranger force, exerted enough political influence to withhold funding from park service managers for two years. During that time the soldiers continued to patrol the park, but some of the potential rangers, already released from military duty and in need of work, drifted away.[7] Those who stayed and became rangers were witness to extraordinary developments in Yellowstone.

It had all started innocently enough with what almost everybody saw as simple improvements in visitor services. By 1891 tourists with fifty dollars or so could board a stagecoach belonging to one of several transportation companies and bounce around the park for five or seven days, disembarking here and there to splash around in the hot springs, hike through the major geyser basins, take a short boat ride on Yellowstone Lake, and risk the crumbly ledges of the Grand Canyon of the Yellowstone River. The brightly painted (most were yellow) coaches became a big part of the adventure, if only because visitors spent so much time aboard them. The drivers cultivated colorful personalities (and even more colorful vocabularies), charming the dudes with wild stories of the old days.

Long before the rangers, and almost before the bears, the stage-coaches were part of the magic of the place, a central prop in Yellowstone's development as a "theatre of the Wild West."[8] By 1900, thanks to Owen Wister, Frederic Remington, and a host of other writers and artists, the Wild West was an important part of the American idea of itself, and Yellowstone played to that romance through its stagecoaches, which were a mainstay of transportation long after they had become rare elsewhere. Even today the stage-coach cookout offered by the hotel company T. W. Recreational Services at Roosevelt Lodge (itself a satisfying and successful play to the Wild West legend) continues that tradition. Visitors love it, and I rather enjoy it myself. Some observers might see it as a kind of Hollywood trick played on naive tourists, but it's hard to imagine any harm in charging visitors for a safe, modernized version of a stagecoach ride. Along with viewing the park's geological and eco-logical wonders, a visit to Yellowstone has come to mean encounter-ing earlier versions of the park experience as well. Here is a 1922 description of a retired coach that had been parked in front of the Mammoth Hot Spring Hotel:

> Here, too, is the old stage coach that in its lifetime had wit-nessed many a thrilling adventure; its sides still show the scars from the bullets of the "hold-up man" and the hostile Indian. This is the same old Deadwood coach in which proudly rode many a potentate of the old frontier days. Its doors still swing on leather hinges; its red paint is blistered with the sun, the snows, the rains, and the frosts of many long years. And yet, the old veteran seems to bob a welcome to us, even now amid the fumes of gasoline, mingled with the sulphurous vapors of the hot springs of Yellowstone.[9]

Much of this was not true of Yellowstone's stagecoaches (although there were several stagecoach holdups in Yellowstone, there was no gunplay). Visitors are still attracted to the historic stagecoach parked by a hotel, which probably reminds them of some personal version of western history, mythic or accurate, romantic or cynical.

The first automobile to enter Yellowstone Park arrived in 1902. It was an 1897 Winton, driven by Montanan H. G. Merry. Hurrying past the confused troopers at the North Entrance, Merry made it partway up the hill to Mammoth (an 800-foot climb) before the Winton gave out. The troopers caught up with him and had their horses tow him the rest of the way to Fort Yellowstone, where the acting superintendent politely explained that he would have to leave because cars scared the horses; his punishment before leaving the park, according to Merry family tradition, was to take the officer for a ride.[10]

In 1915, after several years of growing pressure from local automobile clubs, and after long public debate and resistance from park managers and interest groups, Yellowstone officially admitted automobiles (the first car issued a permit was a Model T Ford from Minnesota). Most roads were one-way, with strict schedules and speed limits as a kindness to all the horse-drawn conveyances still in the park.[11]

But it was obvious to most people that the stagecoaches and wagons had to go. By 1916 the need to accommodate automobile traffic gave the newly created National Park Service a convenient excuse to streamline Yellowstone's concession operation. The various stagecoach companies and smaller teamster operations were replaced by one large transportation company. At the same time related enterprises, including the permanent camp system, were required to consolidate. The old concessions disposed of 700 used coaches, 2,000 horses, and related gear, and the new Yellowstone Park Transportation Company placed a $400,000 order with the White Motor Company for 116 buses.[12]

It is hard to imagine another year in the park's history that would bring such prodigious changes to the park as 1916 did, not even 1988, with its globally famous and politically explosive fires. In a period of only twelve months in 1915 and 1916, the National Park Service was created and the internal combustion engine was admitted to reign in Yellowstone. In the short haul what the creation of the

The first cars arrive at Wylie Hill, site of the Old Faithful Wylie Camp, August 15, 1915. The system of permanent camps along the park roads provided an alternative to camping on one's own or staying at the more expensive lodges and hotels. *NPS photo*

park service did most successfully was pave the way for the fabulous success of motorized transportation. The 52,000 visitors of 1915 (an exceptionally high number) rose to 80,000 in 1920, to 154,000 in 1925, and to 227,000 in 1930. More than 80 percent of the 1915 visitors came by train; about 10 percent of the 1930 visitors did. In 1940 the number of visitors rose to half a million, and except for the years of World War II it has climbed ever since: a million in 1949, 2 million in 1965, and 3 million in 1992.[13] The park has not grown larger, the mileage of roads available to the public has declined, the number of

Car camping with a Model T Ford, 1923. *NPS photo*

campsites and hotel rooms and cabins declined and then leveled out long ago, but still people come, more and more every year, virtually all of them in cars. Where once dozens might watch Old Faithful at once, now hundreds, even thousands, gather on the boardwalk around the cone; in the Upper Geyser Basin, perhaps more than anywhere else, the sense of the park as a national shrine on the scale of the Washington Monument or the Statue of Liberty is clear in the volume of foot traffic to and from the huge parking lots.

The quick trip around the park in the stagecoach became a far quicker trip in a car. The 1920s and 1930s saw the upgrading of roads throughout the park, as well as of the approach roads from surrounding towns. The park roads were mostly blacktopped by World War II, and the faster surfaces allowed for the closing of many small facilities (such as lunch stations) that had been necessary in the slower days of horse travel. National Park Service campgrounds were constructed at several locations to break visitors of the habit of casually pulling off into the sagebrush for the night. A variety of other facilities — stores, gas stations, quick restaurants — also appeared, all to the advantage of the car travelers who very soon were the majority of visitors. (In 1962, when my family made its pilgrimage from Michigan to the western parks, we saw Old Faithful, Mammoth Hot Springs, Tower Fall, the canyon, and the lake all in the same day and still found time to stop and gawk at — but not feed, because my father believed in obeying the law — dozens of bears.)

All of these changes were part of a national trend, of course, as the tourist industry got rolling and the delights and economy of car camping became known. In 1905 there were 78,000 licensed motor vehicles in the United States; by 1921 there were 10 million.[14] The Good Roads Movement, started by cyclists in the 1890s, became a national campaign among automobilists, leading to a number of national and regional initiatives, including the National Park-to-Park Highway. By the 1920s this expansive loop, composed of sections of many different state and federal roads, was promoted as the way to visit Glacier, Mount Rainier, Crater Lake, Lassen Volcanic, Yosemite, General Grant, Sequoia, Grand Canyon, Mesa Verde, Rocky Mountain, Grand Teton, and Yellowstone, as well as many smaller parks and monuments not far out of the way.[15]

However, the park service was not about to surrender traditional park values to the automobile, any more than an earlier generation of park defenders could tolerate surrender to the railroads. It was clear that the car would bring more people to the parks to experience something that cars were quickly making impossible elsewhere. Eric Sandeen recently wrote an excellent summary of how the National Park Service leaders, especially its first director, Stephen P. Mather, viewed the coming of the car:

> Through Mather we can see the overwhelming impact that the automobile has had on Yellowstone. The development of good road systems outside the parks had by 1922 made the Park roads seem substandard. The Park-to-Park Highway movement, which encouraged tourists to pioneer the road between,

say, Yellowstone and Crater Lake, promised more road-weary families who would be accustomed to viewing scenery at speed and would not tolerate traffic jams or the unseemly jostling of worn-out roadbeds. Mather looked down the road and saw what was coming. Against the phalanx of approaching headlights, his argument focused on the preservation of a Yellowstone experience that was anachronistic, that encouraged people to step out of the twentieth century and, if not into the forest primeval, then at least into a more relaxed tourism that predated the internal combustion engine.[16]

The excitement America felt in its great automotive and road-building binges of the first half of the twentieth century may be hard to understand now, accustomed as we are to cars and highways. But several parks bear witness to the earlier mystique of car travel. Glacier, Rocky Mountain, Zion, Yosemite, and other parks were given new attractions in the form of "engineering marvels" — automobile roads and tunnels carved from raw cliff walls and improbable grades. These routes opened vast sections of wildland to easy access and attracted people to drive a road as much for its qualities as a human achievement as for its usefulness as a pathway into the park's heart.[17] Yellowstone's road system already existed, but the Yellowstone experience was much affected by this philosophy; the roads over the park's high passes (especially Dunraven and Sylvan) and the Beartooth Highway northeast of the park were appreciated and promoted for their own merits. But driving in the park was to be different from driving in other places; the roads, thanks in good part to the foresight of the army engineers, were self-consciously and firmly called and maintained as "auto trails." Responding to the unavoidable technological pressure of the automobile, the park service found a path between fruitless resistance and outright capitulation, giving us a few places where driving (and now snowmobiling) was not supposed to be an end in itself but a way to keep the landscape in view and in mind.

As the welcoming of the auto suggests, the National Park Service assumed a hospitable stance to visitors in its first decades, far more than the army commanders of Fort Yellowstone had. Though it did not run the hotels or stores, it was the genial host behind all the bustle, and park service leaders made sure the invitation was sent out widely. Mather was from the first a great believer in the democratization of the parks. He truly believed everybody should be able to enjoy them, but he also believed that the more people who did, the easier it would be to justify reasonable appropriations. In the late 1920s Mather's successor, Horace Albright, was known even among park service people as "the nation's innkeeper," a not entirely complimentary label among people already worried about the parks' resources.[18] Mather and Albright were above all else outstanding champions of park needs through a larger pro-park constituency.

Yellowstone and the other national parks launched educational programs that at last began to fulfill the parks' long-standing promise as great public classrooms. Thanks in good part to donated funds, handsome, rustic museums were built at key locations in Yellowstone. A separate division of rangers, known as naturalists or interpreters, established the evening campfire programs, nature walks, and other activities that have become such an important part of the park experience. In the 1927 *Ranger-Naturalists Manual* for Yellowstone, Horace Albright wrote that Yellowstone hired fifty-two seasonal rangers to assist the thirty-one permanent rangers and four buffalo keepers. He exhorted his ranger-naturalists with a zeal that characterized the park service's sense of mission for many years:

> We have a two-fold mission. We represent the Secretary of the Interior and the National Park Service as hosts to the People of the World. Each tourist is our personal guest. We are the faculty of the biggest summer school of nature study on earth, — a school of 200,000 pupils! Our glorious task is, in John Muir's words, "To entice people to look at Nature's loveliness." Our statements must be exact and cautious beyond possibility of question. And we mustn't hesitate to show our boundless delight in the marvelous and beautiful world we have to interpret.[19]

The ranger-naturalists, a small subdivision of the rangers, probably did more to shape the public impression of rangers than all the rest, because each of these men (almost all were men until well after World War II) talked to thousands of tourists, contributing much to the image of the ranger as both self-reliant woodsman and expert naturalist. However, they have been given too much credit as the originators of public education, or "interpretation," in the parks. As early as 1931 an editorial in *Nature* magazine praised the National Park Service, which two years earlier had created the Branch of Research and Education, and the ranger-naturalists, who had been giving talks in some parks for a decade or so, for filling a real void:

> A visitor to the parks fifteen years ago possessed no such opportunity. He had to be content with sightseeing tours enlivened by the jokes of Munchausen-minded guides who did not know a marmot from a cony. While this satisfied the "gape-and-run" variety of tourist, it pleased neither the curious-minded who went back home with thousands of questions unanswered, nor the Park Service officials, who realized the wealth of natural history latent in the parks.[20]

But like the campfire myth, this version of history left out a great deal. Interpretation in many forms, including publications, formal guided tours by qualified naturalists or geologists, and interpretive signs, was going on in Yellowstone long before the rangers arrived. The most impressive of these early educators was George Henderson, one of the first assistant superintendents of the park in the 1880s, who established a natural history museum at Mammoth, wrote a popular park guidebook, and conducted countless widely praised tours of the park's features.[21]

RICHARD BARTLETT's observation that "a changing America has always had an impact upon Yellowstone"[22] is especially true of the tourist trade. In a recent study of the evolving use and commercial development of the Upper Geyser Basin, Karl Byrand has identified four periods in the visitor experience of the area since the park was established. From 1879 to 1904 the heaviest emphasis was placed upon the geysers: the basin's "uniqueness as a thermal landscape and the reliability of Old Faithful Geyser appear to be the chief selling points."[23]

In the second period, 1905 to 1940, the geysers were still promoted as an extraordinary feature, but more attention was paid to the tourists' comfort. The stupendous Old Faithful Inn became an important part of the visit, with dances and surprisingly fancy dinners. Swimming, fishing, horseback riding, and other forms of recreation received more attention, and the old-fashioned campfire was formalized into a nightly social program, complete with singalongs and other entertainment. In 1919 the park's most famous, best-loved guidebook, the *Haynes Guide,* which was regularly revised and published for more than sixty years, "was the first to describe the Basin's human and natural features in terms of distances on an automobile odometer."[24]

Environmental historian Susan Rhoades Neel analyzed the promotional literature of late-nineteenth- and early-twentieth-century Yellowstone to show the remarkable extent to which its promoters were implicitly and sometimes explicitly promising women romantic experiences and men opportunities to establish or reaffirm their manhood.[25]

In the third period, 1941 to 1972, Byrand notes, there was less emphasis on accommodations and creature comforts (though these were still of great importance), and a little more on the wildness of the setting. As Byrand points out, this was due in good part to changes in the management of national parks; the closure of the swimming pools and the public bear-viewing areas at park dumps reflected the trend away from recreational activities that either had gone out of fashion or were increasingly recognized as inappropriate in national parks.

The new emphasis on nature appreciation on nature's terms, that is, without so much human interference or manipulation, was continued and heightened in the fourth period, 1973 to 1990. In this period, according to Byrand, "The NPS had reevaluated the purpose of the parks, focusing more on their ecological values and less on their recreational ones. As such, the NPS sold the parks as places to partake in more nature-oriented, environmentally friendly activities." [26]

"Sold" is probably a poor word choice for what the National Park Service was doing by 1972. After World War II park managers were less and less interested in attracting larger crowds, and by the 1970s were doing relatively little publicizing or encouraging of tourism. But selling of one sort or another was going on by many commercial interests in and around Yellowstone.

The park was and is a kind of nature show with a series of acts, some performed by scenery, some by biology. The rangers act as masters of ceremonies, and many bus drivers, commentators, and other park staff act as supporting hosts. There has always been considerable emphasis on the weirdness of the setting, and perhaps just as much on nature as spectacle, but thanks to the efforts of the early ranger-naturalists, an attempt was made to integrate all these wonders, so that visitors would appreciate the whole process of nature as much as its most striking scenes and most glamorous animal species.

The impetus for the park's creation, the geothermal activity, was most heavily exploited and abused in the first half-century. In almost all of the other places on the planet where tourists went to hot springs, the waters were used for "medicinal" or "therapeutic" bathing, and such was the intent of the early primitive hotels run by McCartney and McGuirk near Mammoth. In 1891 the Fountain Hotel opened just northeast of the Lower Geyser Basin, complete with two plumbing systems, one for "normal" water and one for hot water piped from nearby springs.[27] A number of other enterprises using hot-spring water were launched in the park in the late 1800s and early 1900s, but Yellowstone never suffered the kind of wholesale destruction and alteration visited upon other geothermal areas, probably because park managers had already developed a sense of the worth of the unhindered expression of nature in at least this one respect.

This is not to say that Yellowstone's springs and geysers were not abused; uncounted thousands of Wister's "silly asses" continued not only to scrawl their names in the delicate minerals but also to

Tourists viewing the captive bison at Mammoth Hot Springs, 1922. *NPS photo*

scramble atop them, hack at them, and try various means to force eruptions. Even today a hot-spring runoff channel near any park boardwalk seems an almost irresistible lure to many visitors, who hastily sign their names or leave some other banal message.

Far more than the geological wonders of the park, the biological ones were subjected to what we now would regard as unforgivable indignities. Though some people might consider the bear-feeding grounds the most egregious example of an artificial wildlife show, that show actually had other acts. There was probably not a time between 1890 and 1940 when there wasn't at least one captive bear cub available for public entertainment somewhere in the park. From 1902 into the 1950s, one could always see some semidomesticated bison, either at Mammoth or out at the Buffalo Ranch in the relatively little traveled Lamar Valley.

But the ranger-naturalists sponsored more diverse collections in the interest of public education. In February 1926, *Yellowstone Nature Notes,* the wonderfully informative monthly newsletter put out by the chief park naturalist for more than forty years, included a report titled "The Captive Animals," which described the latest doings of the black bears Juno and Pard (sluggishly active rather than asleep in the unseasonably warm weather). The report went on to explain that the male badger was "apparently quite contented with his winter quarters," and a bald eagle, recuperating after being found in a coyote trap, was "doing well and bids fair to be one of the attractions in the coming tourist season." And the buffalo calf was quite friendly, "insisting on close and very personal and direct attention on the part of anyone who chances near her corral."[28]

Parts of the animal show were intentionally deceptive. In the 1920s Superintendent Albright arranged for the construction of several miles of carefully placed corral in the Antelope Creek drainage on the lower north slopes of Mount Washburn. Much of the fencing was obscured by trees, giving an effect of open range.[29] Every year some bison were turned out in this enclosure, to graze in the creek's bottomlands and be "sighted" by motorists, most of whom had no idea that the encounter had been carefully staged.

But no mammal was so popular or so successfully presented as the bears. The informal bear-feeding sites whose beginnings were described in Chapter 5 quickly became a primary visitor attraction. Very early, probably sometime around 1900, the bear replaced Old Faithful as the most recognizable symbol of the park. This tourist attraction grew and spread as more visitors arrived. Shortly after 1900 black bears began to be seen along the roads, "begging" for food from passing visitors. The arrival of automobiles and buses and the ensuing increase in traffic hastened the institutionalization of roadside bear feeding. Though a violation of park regulations as early as 1902, feeding the bears was an important pastime along the park's roads until the early 1970s, introducing millions of Americans (and thousands of bears) to a "cheap-thrill" approach to enjoying wildlife. From 1930 to 1970 this close contact between black bears and humans cost the lives of an average of twenty-four bears a year, victims of human enjoyment just as surely as they were victims of management's traps and guns. Some were hit by cars, and many more were killed by rangers, to protect visitors and maintain some peace and safety on the roadsides. The viewing of bears at dumps came to focus on one site, south of the Grand Canyon, by the late 1930s. There, under the watchful and interpretive eye of an armed ranger, hundreds of visitors nightly watched crowds of grizzly bears paw through piles of hotel garbage, with the occasional added treat of a loud, spectacular fight to add a thrill to the evening.[30]

Most of the conservation community now recognizes that the open garbage dumps of Yellowstone, with grizzly bears wading through piles of junk in search of food, were an awful thing to allow in a national park, but we must not underestimate the power of the show that went on for all those years. Many local people recall watching grizzly bears at dumps in or near the park, and though we may agree or (in my case at least) even strongly insist that it was ugly or wildly inappropriate, we also still shake our heads in wonder at the memory, and we unhesitatingly admit to ourselves how lucky we feel to have seen it. A grizzly bear is an impressive animal, whether you see it backlighted at dusk in an alpine meadow or wallowing in rotting trash. It is no wonder that Yellowstone came to mean bear country.

At Yellowstone between the wars, wildlife was viewed condescendingly, even paternalistically. Wild animals were cute, lovable, and great fun — in their place. The bear was transformed "into a kind of national toy, from wilderness personified to wilderness enfeebled."[31] Cubby knew the ranger was his friend. We had also perceptually domesticated the other mammals that we tolerated; those we didn't tolerate, we shot.

This was no little progress, however, in the few decades since the park's establishment. The protection of wildlife *solely for people to watch and enjoy them* became an important goal and an important aspect of the visitor experience very quickly after the prohibition of hunting in 1883. By the 1920s wildlife watching was a Yellowstone tradition. If we tended to idealize the animals — constructing the image of a peaceable kingdom where predators were either eliminated or did their nasty work out of sight — we were at the same time falling deeply in love with these animals. Because of that love, they would never lack for a very protective constituency.

There are many other animals besides mammals, and people love wild things in many ways, not all as passive as watching bison graze in a meadow. Few people love fish more than the fishermen who annoy them without end in hopes of hooking or killing a few. As mentioned in Chapter 5, when Yellowstone was created about 40 percent of the park's area was barren of fish. It seemed only sensible to stock those waters with sport fish, often with nonnative species, just as it seemed sensible to develop hatcheries to replenish fish populations in other waters. Starting with the work of the U.S. Fish Commission in 1889, Yellowstone became the world's foremost exporter of cutthroat trout eggs, with a system of hatcheries that would produce more than 800 million eggs before the hatcheries were finally shut down in the late 1950s.[32] Perhaps more important, the park became a fisherman's paradise.

Early Yellowstone has left us many accounts and photographs of merry tourists with strings of dead trout, catches we now would consider almost obscenely large. Despite efforts in the late 1800s by a number of sportsmen-conservationists to convince fishermen and hunters to moderate their kill, a big take was still widely regarded as proof of success, prowess, or manhood, and many people could not resist excess killing. One of this century's most famous fly-fishing writers, Edward Ringwood Hewitt, wrote about a visit to the park in 1914 during which the commercial fisherman who supplied the hotel restaurants challenged him to see who could kill the most fish in a day. Fishing either the Firehole or the Madison (Hewitt's account is very confused), the commercial fisherman killed 165 to Hewitt's 162.[33] Having read a lot of Hewitt's self-promotional writing, I'm not sure I believe those numbers, but they are suggestive of common public attitudes and also of the availability of fish.

Most fishermen in the 1920s and 1930s were less athletic, renting a boat for the day to explore the shores and islands of Yellowstone Lake or strolling out from their hotel to fish the nearest stream. They could bring the catch back to the restaurant for preparation or save the fish for the bears in the campground, or simply throw them away after they were photographed. Other well-known accounts of fishing in the park between the wars, as in Howard Back's *The Waters of Yellowstone with Rod and Fly* and Ray Bergman's *Trout*, portray a time of quiet, uncrowded waters and a mood of discovery and adventure.[34] The park's waters, especially those that had had no trout only a few decades earlier, were coming into their own as a special recreational mecca, and before long there would be a whole subset of American recreationists for whom Yellowstone did not mean geysers, scenery, bears, or great old hotels so much as it meant the trout of the Wild West.

All these enthusiasts and pilgrims, bear feeders and fishermen, were the temporary wards of the rangers. Judging from the many surviving memoirs and recollections of those early rangers, whether seasonal "ninety-day-wonders" or permanent year-round staff, between the wars was a wonderful time to be a ranger in Yellowstone. Albright's "outdoor activity amid forests and a fine invigorating atmosphere" seemed to more than make up for the low pay and long hours (today this is known as "getting paid in sunsets"). The rangers expressed few regrets about the time they had to spend shepherding tourists around, separating them from bears and other attractants, and otherwise overseeing the joys of Wonderland. Each generation succumbs to nostalgia for the time of its ancestors, and just as the tourists of the 1920s and 1930s, hosted by earnest young rangers, yearned for the stagecoach days, we now are seduced by the attractions of a time that on the one hand enjoyed cars and many other comforts but on the other hand offered uncrowded roads, empty trails, and long, dream-perfect reaches of trout stream without another fly rod in sight.

9 | REASONABLE ILLUSIONS

I T IS ONE of the great peculiarities of the national parks — one of their most distinctive and also difficult characteristics — that they often operate with considerable independence of one another and of the agency's leadership in Washington, D.C. Unlike the national forests and wildlife refuges and the various orphaned lands managed by the Bureau of Land Management, the four hundred or so areas managed by the National Park Service were not created to be easily managed from a central office. Remember that Yellowstone was forty-four years old and had been joined by thirty other areas before there even *was* a central office. National forests, for all their ecological diversity, were long thought to be easy to manage, in terms of logging prescriptions, mining claims, and so on; there would always be disputes over which use should be given preference, but there was relatively little disagreement over the way a specific use should be handled. After all, we thought, a forest is a forest is a forest.

But the parks, whether archeological, historic, geologic, or ecological in their emphasis, were not intended to produce a crop of this or a carload of that. They were intended for a different, complicated, and uncomfortably intangible use; the enabling legislation of each unit suggests how many variants there really are on the national park idea. Perhaps even more important, by definition there was nothing standard about them. As the park system grew and firmed up the goal of preserving representative samples of landscape and key sites in our cultural heritage, it became ever more obvious that each chosen site must be unique to be worthy of national park status in the first place. That uniqueness, more than anything else, may be why National Park Service policy has so often been generated from the bottom up. An issue surfaces in one park, eventually gets the attention of the national leadership, and sometimes becomes an example of how we should handle a similar issue in the future. Because each park's problems are unique or at least unusual, local managers must have a fair amount of creative leeway in dealing with them.

This looseness of administrative structure gives many critics the fits. The "balkanization" of the national parks, which have sometimes been characterized as hundreds of independent fiefdoms, has been blamed for all manner of ills, real or alleged — but it has also been credited with much that is good in evolving policy.[1] This system of fiefdoms has certainly been seen as a blessing by park managers who treasure their freedom.

Yellowstone has long provided both opponents and proponents of park management's independence with ammunition, especially in the ecological controversies, such as wildlife management. Though other wildlife issues have at times proven more appealing to the media or more likely to briefly dominate public attention, no single issue has so engaged Yellowstone's managers and constituencies as the "elk problem," and no other issue is more likely to shape future attempts to manage the park with concern for ecological processes. Since the 1890s, when the acting superintendent reported surprise bordering on alarm at how well the elk were prospering, we have struggled with the amazing ability of these beautiful, romantic, marketable, and problematic animals to flood across a landscape, affecting vegetation, soils, property rights, value systems, policies, careers, and everything else in their path.

It is the northern herd, the park's largest, upon which we have lavished most of our confusion. Spending their summers scattered over half the park and much surrounding land, every fall these animals drain from the high ranges downslope into the Lamar River and Yellowstone River valleys in the park. Many then migrate down the Yellowstone Valley outside of the park. On these lowlands they occupy a winter range that was vacant of wild grazers through the spring and summer growing season. Thus, after grazing on lush, succulent summer grasses in the higher country, they spend the winter in lower country, eating dried grasses, aspen, willow, and a variety of other foods (including any unprotected shrubbery, Christmas trees, and flower gardens in Mammoth and Gardiner), until spring returns and they again head upcountry. As Yellowstone's resource interpreter Norm Bishop puts it, "All summer they eat the cereal, and all winter they eat the box."[2] In varying numbers and patterns of migration, these elk have been doing much the same thing for thousands of years.

The conviction that the northern herd was growing much too large emerged early in the century. The story of Yellowstone elk management at that time is a colorful saga of youthful institutions coming to terms with their missions and responsibilities. As park leaders awakened to the challenges of managing a huge herd of continually puzzling wild animals, the community of early ecologists and range scientists was beginning, often unconsciously, to think in terms of ecosystems; at the same time an embryonic and fragmented conservation movement was seeking a way to protect this nationally treasured wildlife resource, and a concerned public, though new to such issues, was paying close attention.

Between the time the army left Yellowstone in 1918 and the mid-1930s, a series of opinions about the northern herd became almost certainties. Some of these beliefs were based on observation, some were just presumptions based on local "common knowledge."[3]

First, and essential to all that followed, was the conviction that before the park was established, elk did not winter in the park area. There were, however, variations on this view. As already mentioned, many people now believed that elk did not live in the park winter *or* summer. Others allowed that the elk probably did spend summers in the park but vacated it wholesale when the snows came.

The second belief, a historical consequence of the first, was that the elk (assuming that they did summer in the park) once migrated much farther down the Yellowstone River Valley to the north. Some believed that they migrated as far as the present site of Livingston and beyond, as much as seventy miles from the present park boundary. There was not a shred of written evidence to support this belief, but it was not inherently impossible; elk herds are known to move a long way if circumstances justify it. Some elk that summer in Yellowstone now winter on the National Elk Refuge near Jackson, Wyoming, a similar distance.

The third belief was that when the Yellowstone River Valley was settled in the late 1800s, the elk migration route was cut off by a combination of settlement and hunters' rifles. This was a kind of latter-day variant on the old "pushed back up into the mountains" theory of wildlife distribution. It proposed that the elk wintering in Yellowstone's northern valleys in the late 1800s and early 1900s were only there because they had nowhere to go. This was usually seen as the primary reason for the great "increase" in elk numbers reported by the army acting superintendents between 1890 and 1910.

From this conceptual foundation, observers developed a perspective on the consequences of what was happening. Aided by the young but rapidly developing science of range management, which by 1920 was able to measure the condition of commercial livestock ranges, park staff and others made several determinations that, though occasionally challenged even then, ruled most management decisions until well into the 1960s.

The first and most often heard statement was that the winter range grasses and some woody vegetation (willow, for example) were being badly overgrazed and overbrowsed. There were too many elk for the vegetation to support, in this view, so the elk, like poorly managed cattle or sheep, were simply eating themselves out of house and home (a phrase used relentlessly). The resulting range deterioration would eventually mean a greatly reduced carrying capacity for elk and a great many other animals. At its worst, this deterioration could cause soil erosion — long recognized as one of the great evils of any agricultural region. Researchers and less formal observers identified areas with what they considered serious erosion problems on the northern winter range, and concern grew as the years passed.

Range deterioration and overpopulation of elk had other perceived consequences, which were expressed at various times. Park

Park workers loading elk carcasses from a sled onto a truck at Slough Creek, February 14, 1935, during an early elk reduction program. The meat was usually given to charitable organizations or Indian reservations. *NPS photo*

naturalist Milton Skinner reported in the 1920s that white-tailed deer had declined; this assumed that white-tails had been more numerous in the park before its establishment, though they were rare before Skinner began observing them, except for a brief increase shortly after 1900. Many later writers, citing Skinner rather than historical records, mentioned this decline, attributing it to competition with elk for food. Later, beaver declines were also linked to the large number of elk; both elk and beaver eat aspen, but beaver often depend heavily upon it while it is of only marginal importance in the elk diet.[4] Concerns were often expressed about other species that were not seen as able to compete with the large and very numerous elk.

The response to this set of beliefs was a strong one: it was imperative to reduce the elk herd to save Yellowstone's range from ruin. "A near-agricultural philosophy of stewardship of ungulates prevailed," growing more aggressive from the 1920s until the mid-

1960s.[5] When elk from the northern herd migrated north out of the park in the fall, they were harvested by hunters, but even when hunters were very successful, the elk seemed to have no trouble maintaining their numbers. Even before the turn of the century park officials had sent a few elk to zoos, and in the 1920s and 1930s many were sent to other parts of the country to restore elk to ranges where they had been wiped out by the big-game slaughter of the late 1800s. But park managers themselves gradually killed more and more elk; by the 1960s the kills were large enough (the high year was 1962, when 4,619 elk were taken) to reduce the northern herd to around 4,000 animals for a few years. That was the only time that managers succeeded in reducing the population below 5,000, the number often recommended by range scientists in this era as appropriate for the available forage.

As in the case of big-game ranges elsewhere in the nation, the *public* (as opposed to the professional managers) focused on the well-being of individual animals, not on the herds as a whole. As the animals were studied and their life histories became known, so did their deaths. Even in a herd that is not running out of food, some percentage of the population will reach old age and die each year. If the average life expectancy of a species is, say, ten years, then 10 percent can be expected to die in any given year. Ten percent may seem reasonable, but the real numbers often are alarming to people: if there are 15,000 animals, and 10 percent die, that means 1,500 decaying carcasses on view each spring. Harsh winters reach further into both ends of the age structure, taking more of the youngest and oldest animals than do mild winters. The public does not like to see dead animals, and their distaste for death, combined with the fame of Yellowstone, led to a politically volatile situation and a publicity nightmare for the National Park Service.

Even during the army days, feedlots were established to help some of the elk and deer get through the winters. Such artificial feeding of deer and elk is now judged inappropriate by most wild-life biologists, though it is still practiced in some states to satisfy "humanitarian" sentiments among the public. Winter feeding does little to maintain the long-term health of a herd and has a number of harmful consequences. If it works — and it doesn't always — the population expands beyond its range's carrying capacity. That means more elk to be fed next winter and more impacts on the range. Feeding also increases the likelihood of overgrazing of the existing range near the feed sites, where artificial concentrations of animals chow down on whatever they can find. It also increases the transmission of diseases, some of which reach epidemic magnitude among tightly gathered herds.

But winter feeding reflected attitudes that prevailed around the country at the time. It, like the fish hatcheries that sprang up in the late 1800s, was a product of an aggressive and husbandry-oriented view of wildlife conservation: not only can we save these animals, we can make them better, and we can make sure they serve us efficiently.

Forest Service ecologist Dan Tyers, in the most thorough history of the northern range controversy, pointed out the dilemma faced by managers, who almost always viewed dead elk as a bad thing. Tyers observed that by 1919 "it would seem that the ultimate management goal was to prevent the loss of life by elk by whatever means. Elk taken through hunting were part of population regulation; elk expiring by any other cause were wasted."[6] Tyers was speaking specifically about predator control, which was then cranking along pretty aggressively, but the attitude he described was applied just as energetically to winterkill. No matter what forces had limited the elk herd before 1872 — the availability of winter forage, predators, Indian hunting, disease — now the elk were not supposed to die of anything except bullets. That was asking a lot of the elk, but it was asking even more of their managers.

Other grazing animals were likewise intensively managed. Of course the bison being ranched at Lamar were in good part an artificial population; various culling and reduction programs dramatically affected their numbers, which sometimes exceeded a thousand and sometimes dropped to less than two hundred.[7] Pronghorn, encountered in abundance by travelers in the river valleys near the park before the 1880s, fared poorly as their habitat north of the park was developed. The pronghorn on the northern winter range were reduced to a few hundred by 1930, and were at times fed or fenced to help them through the winter and protect them from hunters. By the late 1960s there were less than 150.[8]

But as managers and biologists sought a better understanding of the northern range in the 1920s and 1930s, nature threw them a curve. Complicating and confounding their interpretations of past range conditions as compared to the present, the extended drought of the 1930s laid an additional level of change on the landscape beyond whatever effects the ungulates were having. From today's longer perspective, it appears that many of the most important change-forcing events of this landscape (indeed, of most landscapes) are episodic, random, and not necessarily aimed at advancing the ecological processes in any specific way. Nature doesn't "manage" landscapes according to especially systematic plans.

This was not a common view of nature in the 1920s and 1930s. Under the influence of a giant of early ecological thinking, Frederic L. Clements, range managers, while recognizing that change was central to ecology, believed that change proceeded at an ordered pace, as through "plant succession," a predictable sequence of vegetation types that occupy a landscape following a disturbance of any sort and tend toward a climax state. Clements made a great contribution to our understanding of ecology, because he recognized that we must think in terms of entire landscapes whose numerous life forms make up a sort of "superorganism" whose parts are fully interrelated and must be managed as such. Perhaps more important, he admitted change as an essential ingredient of life, in a world where most people still treasured stability above all else. But as environmental historian Donald Worster has explained, Clements saw change itself as having a kind of cyclical stability: "Change upon change became the inescapable principle of Clements's science. Yet he also insisted stubbornly and vigorously on the notion that the natural landscape must eventually reach a vaguely final climax stage. Nature's course, he contended, is not aimless wandering to and fro but a steady flow toward stability that can be exactly plotted by the scientist."[9]

More recently, ecologists have tended to see ecological processes as much more unruly, indeed undirected. Rather than humming along at a steady pace, all kinds of paces seem to interact, from the very gradual accumulation of soil (which is itself seasonally episodic) over centuries to the powerful, fast-acting, landscape-rearranging actions of large fires, windstorms, and other forces. Rather like a stream channel that might undergo its most dramatic changes in a two-week period of spring flooding, a wild landscape changes in response to both small forces, like the tilling of the soil by an elk's hooves, and large forces, like a 200,000-acre fire. Even today there is great reluctance to tolerate this irregularity of process, but in the 1930s it was barely even recognized as what kept the landscape wild and vital in the first place.

While ungulate management was dealing with the unappreciated serendipity of Yellowstone ecology and pursuing a determined course of herd reduction, the place of carnivores in a national park was being reconsidered almost decade by decade. As early as 1939 wildlife biologist Victor Cahalane noted that "predator management in the parks followed the general trend and pattern of thought of the times." [10] Yellowstone's history confirms Cahalane's statement, but only if we recognize that the park was usually out toward the front of "the general trend and pattern of thought" at any given time.

The comprehensive predator-control program developed in Yellowstone, summarized in Chapter 7, was in some cases devastatingly effective. Aggressively pursued throughout the West and in the areas around Yellowstone, wolves and mountain lions were both brought near extinction in the park by 1930. Coyotes, on the other hand, were reproductively flexible enough that despite yearly harvests of 100 to 200 for many years, they never seemed even to become scarce; they just cranked up their compensation mechanisms and had more pups.

The institutionalization of bears as managed tourist attractions was complete by the 1920s, as increasing amounts of garbage in the dumps and increasing numbers of motorists along the roads drew more and more bears to those two great opportunities for easy food. Both grizzly and black bears used the dumps, but virtually all roadside and campground feeding was of the slightly more human-tolerant black bear.

It was a time of rapidly changing attitudes about wildlife and of the rapid professionalization of conservation. The National Park Service Act of 1916 had charged the secretary of the interior with conserving "the wild life" in the parks, but it had also given him a good deal of freedom in dealing with unpopular animals, saying that the secretary "may also provide in his discretion for the destruction of such animals and such plant life as may be detrimental to the use of any said parks, monuments, or reservations."[11] Detriments to use included anything that might interfere with public enjoyment of the classic national park scene: motorists looking out across a mountain meadow (whether Half Dome, Mount Washburn, or some eminence along the Blue Ridge) at a herd of peacefully grazing deer or elk.

Even from the leisurely perspective of hindsight, it is amazing how fast traditional predator control was challenged once the National Park Service took charge. We tend to view past massacres of predators with cynicism and resentment, but in fact the parks provided society with a context in which to take a different view of carnivory. The changes in predator policy were all the more remarkable for taking place at the same time that the federal government was for the first time engaging in the industrial-scale killing of predators on many western public lands. Western stockmen, through their congressional representatives, compelled government agents to pursue predators with a very nearly religious intensity. A historian of the destruction of the wolf in Montana has said that starting in about 1915, when funding became available for these programs, the attitude still held by many western stockmen was shaped and hardened: "In their efforts to obtain bounty legislation, stockmen generated a hatred toward the wolf which still remains. The publicity was deliberately exaggerated to obtain favorable bounty legislation to eradicate the wolf. This publicity aggravated the stockmen to such an extent that their animosity toward the wolf became nearly pathological."[12]

It is hard for many of us today to imagine this kind of hate toward an animal that now stares with profound wistfulness at us

Chief Ranger Sam Woodring (left) and companion, November 1925, with the last mountain lion, a large male, killed in the park during the predator-control era. *NPS photo*

from so many T-shirts and posters, but even if the harmfulness of wolves was wildly exaggerated, they, like grizzly bears, coyotes, and other predators, were a real threat to quite a few ranching operations, especially those that were marginally viable to begin with. There weren't all that many wolves left in the West after 1910, but they included some infamous and well-publicized stock killers. It is one measure of the power of the antipredator bias, and its depth in regional rural cultures, that it is held with equal fervor today by people who have had no personal dealings with wolf predation and whose parents, and maybe even grandparents, didn't either.

But the pattern was breaking in Yellowstone. By the late 1920s a number of people within and outside of the National Park Service were speaking out on behalf of predators. Perhaps more important, various scientific societies were now critiquing the management of the parks, which they recognized as both fertile research fields and great testing grounds for new theories. Among those opposing predator control in the parks by 1930 were the American Society of Mammalogists, the Wilson Ornithological Club, the Cooper Ornithological Club, the New York Zoological Society, and even the big-game-oriented Boone and Crockett Club.[13] The ornithological groups were concerned about the terrible nationwide destruction of raptors, and Yellowstone must have seemed like a small bright spot in an otherwise dreary scene for both professionals and amateur bird enthusiasts.

The National Park Service has never been given a firm legislative mandate to do research, yet it has always had a great need for reliable scientific information on its resources. This problem has led to partnerships with numerous universities and other agencies, but it has also led to endless quarrels with scientists from many institutions who have told park administrators how to manage their resources. The managers of the parks have often been put in the awkward and embarrassing position of having someone else know more about the resource they are assigned to manage than they do, while the scientists are regularly put in the equally awkward position of seeming to assume that just because they know a lot about some animal or plant, they therefore also know how best it should be managed in a national park. In the early days of the National Park Service, a superintendent might not have felt any more obligation to follow a scientist's directions than to listen to the local chamber of commerce. These were all special interest groups, and he had to find his way among them by whatever bureaucratic savvy he could muster.

In Yellowstone's case, the pressure to stop killing predators was met by other pressures, some of which seemed incontrovertibly valid to managers even though they had little to do with science. Both Mather and Albright expressed great concern that Yellowstone not become too productive a reservoir or sanctuary for coyotes. They thought the coyotes took a heavy toll on the pronghorn kids (which they no doubt did, and still do), but they also thought it unneighborly, to say nothing of politically disastrous, for the park to be supplying the surrounding ranchlands with so many stock-killing coyotes.[14] (They were, in fact, taking an ecosystem view rather than just a park view.)

In national park controversies, the advocates of change often tend to have a tight focus on one issue, while the managers must envision and face a much wider variety of consequences. About fifteen years ago I had a direct lesson in this phenomenon when I asserted to then-Superintendent John Townsley how urgent it was to get on with wolf recovery. He listened patiently, then responded that he was just getting some of the more traditional stockmen near the park to stop shooting grizzly bears on sight, so it didn't seem an auspicious time to force another predator on them, one they hated even more. It will always be a matter of opinion in each case whether administrative hesitation is wise discretion or merely the easy way out, but there is no question that the manager faces more complexity than does the advocate.

In 1931 Horace Albright, then director of the National Park Service, published a landmark policy statement; significantly, it appeared in the *Journal of Mammalogy*, further legitimizing the role of scientific opinion in park management. Albright announced that "predatory animals are to be considered an integral part of the wild life protected in national parks, and no widespread campaigns of destruction are to be countenanced. The only control practiced is that of shooting coyotes and other predators when they are actually found making inroads upon herds of game or other animals needing special protection."[15]

The first sentence sounds like change; the second sounds like business as usual, and in Yellowstone it was. Coyote control continued to be one of the most "widespread campaigns of destruction" ever conducted against a park predator. "It might not be cynical to say that by 1930 Albright could comfortably order a cessation of killing wolves and mountain lions in Yellowstone because they were already wiped out, or to point out that the year this policy was published, Yellowstone staff killed 145 coyotes in the park. On the one hand, a more enlightened perspective was emerging, but on the other, it had not yet prevailed."[16]

But it soon would. In 1933 a self-funded scientist of true vision, George Wright, and his distinguished scientific colleagues Joseph Dixon and Ben Thompson published a small but far-reaching volume, *A Preliminary Survey of Faunal Relations in National Parks.* It was the first attempt to describe the parks' wildlife resources and their conditions. Among many other things, the authors proposed taking another step toward equal treatment for predators, recommending eloquently "that the rare predators shall be considered the special charges of the national parks in proportion that they are persecuted everywhere else." Concerning the fate of any individual prey species, they maintained that "no native predator shall be destroyed on account of its normal utilization of any other park animal, excepting if that animal is in immediate danger of extermination, and then only if the predator is not itself a vanishing form."[17] This was political dynamite in more conservative circles even in the parks, and of course it was sacrilege out among the predator-hating agricultural community. But by 1936 Wright's view had become National Park Service policy, and even coyote killing generally ceased in Yellowstone. Ecologist Gerald Wright has accurately described this report, known as *Fauna No. 1,* as "the first document that defined a clear rationale for managing wildlife in national parks. It recognized the fallacy of single-species management. More important, it placed recommended actions in an ecosystem framework that recognized the role that natural processes played in achieving management objectives."[18]

In another publication that year, George Wright became one of the first scientists to specifically link predators with the ungulate problem, asserting that "we must arrange for the predators to control the number of elk to the point where the devastation of the range will cease."[19]

Wright, Dixon, and Thompson likewise pushed for changes in bear management. They were especially troubled by the bear shows:

> The bear show has been one of the greatest assets of the national parks. However, it has served its greatest purpose in the period when bringing the people to an appreciation of the

The nightly show of grizzly bears feeding at the dump south of Canyon, a major attraction in the 1930s. Notice the well-worn bear trails approaching the feeding platform from several directions and the many gulls joining in the feast. *NPS photo*

wonderful things to be seen and done in the parks was of prime importance. Now that the popularity of their values is established and their place secure, it may be necessary to modify the old practices in the interests of the welfare of both people and bears. . . . The sight of one bear under natural conditions is more stimulating than close association with dozens of bears.[20]

Besides the obvious advance in the aesthetics of bear watching, there is a suggestion here that a great flexibility is appropriate in park management. Perhaps Wright and his associates were just being polite, not wanting to criticize Albright and others for prostituting wild animals as tourist attractions, but I think Wright actually did believe that the bear show had been all right in its day. He seemed to apply some version of situation ethics here: we are free to compromise a principle now and then if it serves the long-term needs of the system.

In any event, his voice and others were heard. During World War II, when visitation at Yellowstone dropped dramatically, the last public-dump viewing area, near Canyon, was closed. Black bears were still fed by tourists along the roads, and black and grizzly bears still ate garbage at the dumps, but the public was no longer invited to the spectacle. It was still acceptable for bears to eat at garbage dumps in Yellowstone, but it was no longer acceptable for people to watch them do it.

Though there had been occasional brief studies and papers on Yellowstone predators, and though some species had been written about popularly at great length, there was an unfortunate lag between the time that ungulate-range issues came under professional scientific scrutiny and the time predators were first studied. In the spring of 1937 Adolph Murie began a two-year study of the coyotes (published in 1940) that set a standard for many later studies and represented a conclusive vindication of Wright's policy proposals. Murie discovered, among many other fascinating things, that in fact the coyotes were not a major factor in the size of ungulate populations.[21] Murie's monograph remains one of the best books ever written about Yellowstone, both for its natural history and its entertainment value, and it may have been one of the factors leading to a general conviction, by the 1960s, that predators were not going to "solve" the elk problem.

For forty years Murie's work remained the only study of a coyote population not being heavily harvested by humans. There have been only two more since then, one of which was conducted in Yellowstone in the 1980s and 1990s.[22] One of the special values of national parks is the opportunity they provide for studies of unmanipulated populations; it is a sad and recurring irony in the park's history that ecological conditions here are often seen as "unnatural," when in fact they are unusual only because most other landscapes are so altered by more intensive human use. Eventually the coyotes of Yellowstone would prove to have lessons for those who must deal with these predators on commercial grazing lands, lessons that could not be learned except in this rare setting.

In 1943 Adolph Murie's brother Olaus, also a distinguished ecologist, contributed a less well known but no less insightful document in Yellowstone predator science, a short paper based on a summer's study of the bears. His findings went against much common knowledge about these animals; he concluded that the bears did not need the garbage dumps to survive, that bears conditioned to human food could not be broken of the habit as long as food was easily acquired, and that bearproofing and improved sanitation were essential if what was now known as the "bear problem" (sister to the "elk problem" and not commonly recognized as a "people problem" until the 1970s) was ever to be solved.[23]

In the first years after World War II, national park managers had less and less time to worry about animals, for traffic snarls and deteriorating buildings and generally collapsing infrastructure held their attention. This was not a time for change in wildlife management policies, unless change be measured in the declining fortunes of the species being managed. As another staggering increase in visitation began, the park's wildlife management program was a peculiar mixture of tradition and forward-looking science. This period was a kind of pause, not so much to take a breath as to look around and gasp at what was coming. For all the recognition of wildlife "problems," there still was an underlying confidence that we understood this place: that by killing enough elk, we could straighten out the northern range situation; that given some more rangers and a little public cooperation, we could get the bear problem under control.

The best symbol of that confidence is a letter from Yellowstone superintendent Edmund Rogers to his supervisor in July 1943, explaining why he was not interested in hiring Aldo Leopold to study the northern Yellowstone elk. Leopold, who is now thought of as the father of modern wildlife management, was one of the most influential thinkers in the history of the American conservation movement. In 1943, late in his career, Leopold had seen many ranges and questioned many traditional views; he was still a man of his time, but he might have been just the person to break through to some higher appreciation of the complexity of the wildlife situation in Yellowstone. But here is what Rogers said:

> It is noted that the purpose of a study by Mr. Leopold would be to assist in arriving at conclusions regarding the current management program and to establish greater confidence in management measures. While an investigation by Mr. Leopold would be helpful it is our opinion that the first step in the current management of the northern herd is to have a meeting of the three interested agencies at which time the director or the Regional Director can make an authoritative statement as to what the National Park Service proposes in the way of future elk reduction. When such a statement is made it should automatically take care of confidence in the program by interested agencies and the general public.[24]

Rogers concluded that "the proposed study would cost approximately $500 and we do not believe that this amount of money should be diverted from essential work to research at this time."[25] The war years were a time of dire funding shortages, so Rogers did have a point, but it is sad to think that but for $500, Yellowstone, perhaps the leading North American laboratory of wildlife management experimentation, would have come under the brilliant scrutiny of the foremost pioneer in that field. Only a year later, in 1944, Leopold recommended restoring wolves to Yellowstone; surely a mind that open and inquiring would have come to interesting conclusions about the elk. Rogers was convinced that the problem was simply one of deciding how many elk to kill; he could not conceive of its being more complicated. Whether or not Leopold would have helped, we are all still waiting for something that will "take care of confidence in the program by interested agencies and the general public."

While Yellowstone struggled to define its responsibility for native species, it was facing difficult challenges from nonnative species. Considering the eagerness with which most North American land managers were introducing new species to the continent in the early 1900s, concerns over nonnative species surfaced surprisingly early in the park's history. In a variety of instances, Yellowstone managers resisted adding new plant or animal (especially fish) species to the park even before the National Park Service was created.[26] By the 1920s, when both the American Association for the Advancement of Science and the Ecological Society of America passed resolutions opposing introductions of nonnative species to national parks, Yellowstone had already largely accepted that position, which was reaffirmed by Wright and others later.[27] But in many ways the damage had already been done. Not only had numerous native fishes and fishless waters been subjected to destructive invasions of new species (or of native species that had not occupied that drainage before), but a growing number of nonnative plants were appearing in the park. Some arrived uninvited, some were intentionally cultivated to feed the captive bison herd, but all were complicating the ecological setting; the problems persist today, with at least 170 known nonnative plant species in the park.[28] The "Johnny Appleseed" mentality of many land users, whether managers or the public, has done irreparable harm to native landscapes. Aquatic ecosystems are exceptionally vulnerable to invasions of nonnative species, and the recent discovery of illegally introduced lake trout in Yellowstone Lake is just one example of a problem of epidemic and sometimes catastrophic proportions in public waters throughout the United States. All too many individuals believe they have the knowledge and wisdom to decide how a certain ecosystem should be altered.

Despite the National Park Service's resistance to the introduction of additional exotic species, managers were guilty of what we would now consider appalling discrimination against certain native species, perhaps even more outrageous to modern sensibilities than the killing of wolves and other mammalian predators. Sport fishing and commercial fishing began to affect trout populations in the park quite early, though Yellowstone's fishing continued to be world-famous and aggressively promoted by regional businesses even through the 1960s, when it was obvious that fish populations were in wretched condition. As early as 1917 it was recognized that the cut-throat trout were declining in parts of Yellowstone Lake.

Based on informal observations, the managers eventually con-cluded that the only way to make sure the tourists continued to get their fair share of the trout was to reduce predation by pelicans. These birds were also suspected of being the alternate host for one of the common native trout parasites that human fishermen found so distasteful. In 1926 park personnel visited the Molly Islands, the pelicans' nesting area in the Southeast Arm of Yellowstone Lake, and crushed the 200 pelican eggs they found there. In 1927 and 1928 they visited the islands a little later in the season and killed more than 200 baby pelicans. In response to sharp and highly publicized criticism from conservation groups, the killing stopped in 1932, but the epi-sode remains one of the most bald-faced instances of favoring tour-ists over wildlife in the history of the national parks. It seems all the more egregious because of the good work that National Park Service staff were doing right then in protecting other bird species, such as the trumpeter swan.[29]

In the late 1940s and 1950s ecological thinking and the conserva-tion movement were expanding in exciting ways, and the national parks were under growing scrutiny. The view of ecology champi-oned by Frederic Clements was being challenged in academic circles, and a new mood was emerging among people concerned with the protection of national park resources. The defeat by conservationists of the proposed Echo Park Dam, which would have flooded por-tions of Dinosaur National Monument, likewise signaled a new era for conservation groups, whose growing political influence showed great promise for park protection.

It is perhaps too easy to view Yellowstone history in a framework of important legislation and policy milestones; typically such bu-reaucratic developments are only the visible published moments in a very tangled, even chaotic, flow of events. One cannot use them as a full reflection of what is going on in the professional or public mind any more than one can really understand the tourists of early Yellowstone by reading only the travel writers of that time. But occasionally an event or a statement becomes the story, and thus also a prominent milestone, upon which we tend to hang all sorts of later ideas and developments. The foremost of these in Yellowstone wildlife management history, certainly much more influential and more frequently invoked in all subsequent management dialogues even than the organic act or the National Park Service Act, is the Leopold Report, written by Aldo Leopold's eldest son, A. Starker Leopold, for many years a professor of ecology at the University of California at Berkeley. By the 1960s Leopold had established himself as a leading thinker in the field who had a gift for transforming ecological principles into practical directions for resource management. Like his father, he wrote clearly, powerfully, and persuasively. In the early 1960s, because of the escalating controversy surrounding the elk reductions in both Yellowstone and Rocky Mountain national parks, the secretary of the interior invited Leopold to chair a committee of prominent scientists and conservationists, including Stanley Cain, Clarence Cottam, Ira Gabrielson, and Thomas Kimball. Their mission would be to address several wildlife-related issues in the United States. The most famous of their products was the 1963 report "Wildlife Management in the National Parks," now universally known as the Leopold Report, for its primary author.[30]

The report has taken on an almost scriptural aura in recent years. Scholars return to it for new interpretations and even inspiration regularly, speakers invoke it on all occasions, and it is trotted out to prove almost every perspective in debates about modern park management. One set of scholars described it as highly traditional and conservative, "to a considerable degree a reaffirmation of the existing NPS general policy to engage in active natural resources management in the parks," but another scholar considered the report anything but practical, representing a "philosophical idealism rather than sound scientific sense," because it proposed restoring "the ideal pristine wilderness of the frontier," an "impossible goal."[31] Like other great, far-reaching statements of principle, part of the beauty of the Leopold Report may be its susceptibility to so many interpretations. Leopold, who died in 1983, was fond of saying that if he had known so many people would spend so much time dissecting it, teasing new meanings and nuances from each paragraph, he probably would have been a little more careful in how he said things.

For all the spins that people have put on the Leopold document, they have not blunted its main messages. These include several statements that have become almost gospel in modern park management circles:

> As a primary goal, we would recommend that the biotic associations within each park be maintained, or where necessary recreated, as nearly as possible in the condition that prevailed when the area was first visited by white man. A national park should represent a vignette of primitive America. . . .
>
> Yet if the goal cannot be fully achieved it can be approached. A reasonable illusion of primitive America could be recreated, using the utmost in skill, judgment, and ecologic sensitivity. This in our opinion should be the objective of every national park and monument. . . .
>
> The major policy change which we would recommend to the National Park Service is that it recognize the enormous complexity of ecologic communities and the diversity of management procedures required to preserve them.[32]

As my earlier discussions of the effects of American Indians and Euramericans on the Yellowstone landscape suggest, much of what Leopold and his colleagues recommended here was indeed unachievable. They acknowledged this, both in the report and later; Leopold himself was eminently practical about park management. Even they, however, did not realize how difficult it would be to approximate some of the conditions they wanted the parks to display. Their recommendation to maintain parks as they were when first seen by white men was their way of saying "prior to the influences of white men," but as I have suggested, the influences of white men often arrived before the people themselves.

The report was not unrealistic or impractical for its time, however. It seems clear, for example, that by "vignette of primitive America," the committee meant not a frozen snapshot but a dynamic ecological community whose ecological and geophysical processes operated as they had before whites arrived. Leopold and his colleagues wrote well before the nonequilibrial nature of ecosystems had been much discussed, so they did not appreciate just how variable such systems can be, but they favored letting the ecosystem handle its own internal "management" whenever possible. One of the areas in which they reached beyond previous policy makers, in fact, was in their view that predators should be protected "in and around the parks."[33] The increasing understanding of ecosystems led them to realize that the parks alone were not enough and that predators had a place beyond those boundaries.

Yet though they obviously hoped for the minimum of interference, they saw a national park system overwhelmed by the need for manipulation, whether it be by allowing natural fires to burn, controlling exotic plants, reintroducing lost native plants, or controlling ungulate populations. More than anything else, it was the elk controversies in Yellowstone and Rocky Mountain national parks that led to the formation of the Leopold Committee in the first place, and elk were the primary focus of the report's comments on Yellowstone. The committee accepted the "common knowledge" interpretations of the northern Yellowstone elk herd's history: that it grew to 35,000 by 1914, then crashed in 1919–1920 and that the range "continued to deteriorate" in the 1930s and 1940s. The very large reductions of the early 1960s were reviewed with apparent approval, and future annual removals of 1,000 to 1,800 seemed also acceptable to the committee. Like most scientific observers, they seem to have accepted the necessity of elk control.

The Leopold Report, like a series of other reports from that year to the present, emphasized a great need in the parks for both research and experimental management. "In essence, we are calling for a set of ecologic skills unknown in this country today. Americans have shown a great capacity for degrading and fragmenting native biotas. So far we have not exercised much imagination or ingenuity in rebuilding damaged biotas. It will not be done by passive protection alone."[34]

Even though the report by Wright, Dixon, and Thompson thirty years earlier had foreshadowed many of the points made in the

In 1964, at the height of the elk reduction program, a helicopter (lower left) drives a herd of elk into corrals for processing. *NPS photo*

Leopold Report, the National Park Service leadership took several more years to embrace this complex and in many ways controversial view. Yes, the report did look back to existing policies, just as it relied on a variety of existing information (some good, some poor), but it also reached forward to a far more ecosystem-oriented time, admitting that the parks needed a great deal more knowledge than existed.

Meanwhile in Yellowstone, elk continued to dominate policy dialogues (even as Yellowstone's management would spend the next thirty years becoming accustomed to the language of ecosystems, the issues surrounding individual species would continue to absorb most of their attention). The shooting of thousands of elk in the park by rangers stirred up what was Yellowstone's most volatile and nationally publicized controversy yet. In 1967 the coverage by network television and the print media of the elk slaughter resulted in enough public opposition that congressional hearings were held, and the National Park Service, cast in the unfamiliar role of villain, announced that it would stop killing elk.[35]

The public and political outcry was a mixture of many sentiments. Some people were simply disturbed over the "waste" of elk, others considered the killing cruel or inhumane, and others wished to open the park to sport hunting so that the public could benefit more directly from the elk killing (the carcasses were sent to Indian reservations). But with television now playing a role in the intensifying public attention on environmental issues, it was no longer possible to kill thousands of elk without a powerful public reaction.

It did not matter that the scientific community and the professional wildlife management community largely agreed that the killing of all those elk was necessary. Here, the search for Yellowstone was not a matter of ecology *and* wonder so much as ecology *versus* wonder. The best ecological understanding of the day indicated that we needed to kill lots of Yellowstone elk. The prevailing public wonder over the elk didn't allow room for what the best knowledge of ecology might say.

The late 1960s were transitional in many ways besides the forced change in elk management. The cutthroat trout of Yellowstone Lake had been so brutally overfished that the population was in a state of collapse. Grizzly bears, which owed their existence in the region primarily to the protection of the park, were finally gaining the attention of an awed and admiring public, which sensed that all was not well for this great predator. Experiments with fire as a management tool, conducted for many years in the national forests and more recently in other national parks, were getting the attention of Yellowstone managers, who had a better understanding of the ecology of lodgepole pines. Some people in the conservation community and in the National Park Service were beginning to wonder about the park's other present and former predators and about the damage done to ecological processes by past predator policies.

The end of elk control came at a time when a few ecologists were beginning to wonder whether the Yellowstone elk really were overpopulated; the often predicted collapse of the herd never seemed to happen.[36]

If this range had been in such poor condition all these years, how did the elk herd continue to produce such a huge crop of healthy elk calves and trophy bulls year after year? And why, even when the elk were reduced to a few thousand, didn't the aspen and willows that they were accused of overbrowsing recover and grow the way they should? Exactly why *did* these elk keep increasing? Were we sure we understood what was "right" for this place, when the elk kept disagreeing with us? What was reasonable here, and what was the illusion? The forced cessation of elk killing resulted in a fortuitous combination of political expediency and scientific curiosity; ultimately not only would our understanding of the elk change, but so would our approach to managing the park itself. The search for Yellowstone was about to enter uncharted and often very hostile territory.

10 THE HIGH PRICE OF SUCCESS

IN OCTOBER 1953 *Harper's Magazine* ran an editorial by Bernard DeVoto entitled "Let's Close the National Parks." DeVoto, a long-time park enthusiast and conservationist, described his previous summer's tour of fifteen parks. He concluded that even though congressional parsimony was starving them out, the park staffs were working heroically to keep the parks running and that their "success at improvising and patching up is just short of miraculous. But it stops there, just short of the necessary miracle. Congress did not provide money to rehabilitate the parks at the end of the war, it has not provided money to meet the enormously increased demand. So much of the priceless heritage which the Service must safeguard for the United States is beginning to go to hell." Running through a long list of reduced staffs and funding, he came to Yellowstone: "In 1932, when 200,000 people visited it, its uniformed staff was large enough to perform just over 6,000 man-hours of work per week: last year, with one and one-third million visitors, the shrunken staff performed just over 4,000 man-hours per week."[1]

Complaining about parks with "true slum districts" and "hot dog stand budgets," DeVoto stated that only a massive infusion of congressional funding would save the parks. But, he predicted, "no such sums will be appropriated. Therefore only one course seems possible. The national park system must be temporarily reduced to a size for which Congress is willing to pay. Let us, as a beginning, close Yellowstone, Yosemite, Rocky Mountain, and Grand Canyon Na-

Long after the collapse of this bridge over the Lamar River in 1932, many park roads continued to be regarded as substandard. *NPS photo*

tional Parks — close and seal them, assign the Army to patrol them, and so hold them secure till they can be reopened."[2]

More parks could be closed, DeVoto proposed, if these were not enough to bring action. The result he hoped for, of course, was that "letters from constituents unable to visit Old Faithful, Half Dome, The Great White Throne, and Bright Angel Trail would bring a nationally disgraceful situation to the really serious attention of the Congress which is responsible for it."[3]

In Yellowstone's case this all sounds more than vaguely familiar, right down to the spooky déjà vu of bringing in the army. But what Yellowstone needed saving from was something quite different from the problems of its early days, when cries to save the park were aimed at a largely uninterested and almost totally uninformed public. Now it was the public from which the park most needed saving. DeVoto's voice was just one in a chorus, with even agency bureaucrats speaking quite openly (DeVoto's sympathetic assertion to the contrary that the typical park superintendent "is withheld from saying what would count, 'Build a fire under your Congressmen'").[4] In

1955 National Park Service Director Conrad Wirth helped build such a fire when he was quoted in *Reader's Digest:*

> It is not possible to provide essential services. Visitor concentration points can't be kept in sanitary condition. Comfort stations can't be kept clean and serviced. Water, sewer and electrical systems are taxed to the utmost. Protective services to safeguard the public and preserve park values are far short of requirements. Physical facilities are deteriorating or inadequate to meet public needs. Some of the camps are approaching rural slums. We actually get scared when we think of the bad health conditions.[5]

It is revealing how often the humble comfort station has been invoked to demonstrate the problems of the parks. The mundane is essential to the appreciation of the sublime. In the 1950s and 1960s, one of the most effective photographic appeals for funding showed national park visitors standing in line to use an outhouse. Such pictures evoke an immediate and personal sympathy in almost all viewers. But sometimes the comfort station had a more villainous symbolic role. In 1963 a special commission was "shocked to learn that the research staff (including the chief naturalist and field men in natural history) was limited to ten people and that the Service budget for natural history research was $28,000 — the cost of one campground comfort station."[6] Edward Abbey, in his inspired and grouchy masterpiece, *Desert Solitaire,* described national park rangers "going quietly nuts answering the same three basic questions five hundred times a day: (1) Where's the john? (2) How long's it take to see this place? (3) Where's the Coke machine?"[7] The john comes first, and actually I'm surprised he put the Coke machine third.

I mention this not so much to speak ill of the average park visitor (though Abbey usually did) but to recognize fundamental human needs, whether those humans are in a cathedral, a shopping mall, or a visitor center. It is an often neglected reality of the conservation debates — and, thus, of the search for Yellowstone — that all the time we are arguing over aesthetic sensitivities, carrying capacities, and complex demands on even more complex resources, most visitors will ask comfort-station-level questions first — and they may ask no others. If the ranger doesn't have satisfactory answers, or if for some other reason comfort is not forthcoming, the park has already failed.

Yellowstone managers had been adjusting their policies in response to increased numbers of visitors at least since the prohibition of public hunting in 1883. The individual visitor's use of Yellowstone's features has become gradually less consumptive ever since: fishing bag limits have been repeatedly reduced (and may eventually vanish entirely); the hot-spring and geyser formations were made off-limits for climbing and unavailable for bathhouse and greenhouse plumbing; flower picking and specimen collecting (rocks, antlers, driftwood, and so on) were outlawed except under permit; camping and fires were ever more tightly regulated and contained; and in many other ways a more gentle approach to the park experience has been encouraged. There have been very few serious objections to most of those restrictions. But the explosion of visitors after World War II abruptly outran the managers' ability to adjust. It was no longer possible to fine-tune regulations to take up the slack, and in reality it probably hadn't been possible for quite a while.

One of modern environmental journalism's favorite chestnuts is that the national parks have always been managed to favor tourism and increasing development. There is certainly evidence to suggest this, if one compares costs of comfort stations with science budgets, for example. I hope, however, that I have shown that this accusation is not fairly applied to all earlier generations, which lacked the apparently delicate and sophisticated tastes of us modern enthusiasts of wild ecosystems. Roads, bridges, and a system of comfortable accommodations were universally regarded as great triumphs in the early years of Yellowstone and are still heartily admired and insisted upon by most modern visitors. (There was much ironic comment among National Park Service personnel a few years ago when the Greater Yellowstone Coalition, a regional conservation group that has attacked park managers for allowing so much development, chose to hold their annual membership meeting in the cavernous, landscape-gobbling facilities of the Old Faithful Lodge.)

The development of the great resort hotels exemplifies precisely what the park's early supporters had in mind. While smaller hotels, lodges, and chalets would come and go over the years at numerous locations — Mammoth, Tower Junction, Norris, Canyon, Old Faithful, Sylvan Pass — the park became known for its grand structures: the National Hotel (1883), the Fountain Hotel (1891), the Lake Hotel (1891), the Old Faithful Inn (1904), and the Canyon Hotel (1910). All of these were either extensively modified or replaced over time, but each developed its own constituency of visitors who would return again and again and who complained bitterly if their beloved hotel was modified, much less removed.[8] A number of park visitors I met in the 1970s still talked about the demolition of the structurally compromised Canyon Hotel in 1959 as if it were an assassination rather than a condemnation. Such huge buildings may seem jarring to the modern eye (Richard Bartlett, a thorough and thoughtful historian of the Yellowstone concessions, described the Lake Hotel as "beautiful but architecturally misplaced"),[9] but their devotees are as avid as those who focus their passion on the geysers or the wildlife.

The most famous Yellowstone hotel is the Old Faithful Inn. Architect Robert Reamer's original log structure was augmented by additional (and rather less attractive) wings in 1913 and 1928 and soon became a Yellowstone landmark almost on a par with Old Faithful itself. The cavernous lobby, the massive fireplace, and the rustic interior balconies and stairs still awe visitors today, and many of us find it hard to imagine the Upper Geyser Basin without that gigantic gabled roofline.

Many of the smaller vintage structures, especially the stores and the older National Park Service museums, present the same homey yet primitive aspect — a beautifully cultivated, freely idealized image of human habitation in a wild place. Together with the hotels, this system of structures offered earlier visitors what most apparently considered just the right combination of comfort and exoticism for a foray into the "wilderness." But by the 1940s, perhaps earlier in a few cases, the buildings were wearing out, though their charms were getting better known by the year. It is a very short slide from rustic to tacky.

The great proliferation of leaseholders in the army days was rapidly streamlined when the National Park Service came in, under what was rather awkwardly termed a "regulated monopoly."[10] (The Northern Pacific Railroad remained a forceful presence in these operations long after it had lost almost all of the transportation trade to the park.) Directors Mather and Albright much preferred large companies to small, and convoluted relationships developed between the National Park Service and its commercial partners, who grew accustomed to having to renew their leases only every twenty years or so and being subjected to only the most cursory inspections and regulations.[11]

Some concessioners became multigeneration institutions, their employees part of the Yellowstone family. The most notable, perhaps, was the Haynes photo shops, which were established by pioneer park photographer F. J. Haynes in the 1880s and thrived under family ownership until bought out by the equally venerable Hamilton Stores in 1968. Marriages between the children of concession executives and National Park Service officials suggest a kind of "administrative inbreeding" that may not have been desirable from a regulatory standpoint but that were all but unavoidable in a place like Yellowstone. Socializing between these groups is more than acceptable; it is essential. Besides being a national park, an international symbol, and a great regional cash factory, Yellowstone has also long been a very small, very isolated human community.

Haynes provided outstanding service to the public for many decades, but not all concessioners did as good a job or made as good an impression on the public. Often, especially in the 1920s, the profits of Yellowstone concessioners were quite large, even unseemly, but nobody seemed to find that embarrassing; the period from 1892 to 1929 has been called the "golden age of park concessionaires."[12]

The consolidation begun under Mather and Albright reached a new level in 1936, when four companies, the Yellowstone Park Hotel Company, the Yellowstone Park Transportation Company, the

Yellowstone Park Lodge and Camps Company, and the Yellowstone Park Company, already under the management of one person, were merged into the Yellowstone Park Company. That company, which shared ownership of the Yellowstone Park service stations with the Hamilton Stores (two monopolies owning a third), was given a twenty-year contract that year, and facilities began a long downward slide that would continue, quite painfully for all concerned, through a second twenty-year contract and a two-year extension beyond that.

Though in principle the idea of the regulated monopoly was and is a workable one — several national park concessioners, including the company that now operates Yellowstone's hotels, T. W. Recreational Services, prove this — the disastrous career of Y. P. Co. demonstrated just how wrong it could be. I doubt that the company's legend of disservice will ever equal that of the short-lived Yellowstone Park Improvement Company, described in Chapter 6, but Y. P. Co. lasted a lot longer and affected millions of visitors rather than a few thousand. Despite periods of widely publicized scandalous service, the company survived past the park's centennial in 1972; it was finally sent on its way in 1977, with a generous buyout of its facilities to ease the pain. In 1979 T. W. Recreational Services took over, with much more frequent contract reviews.

Against this background we can consider the earlier-mentioned chestnut that the parks favor tourism and increasing development. The gradual reversal of Mather's promotional policies took hold firmly in the 1960s, and by the 1970s much of the old National Park Service promotional rhetoric was gone. What remained (slogans such as "Parks Are for the People" and "Yellowstone: A World Apart," which were embedded in the jargon of both the National Park Service and the concessioners) had a hollow ring for park employees who saw the harm "the people" could do when too numerous, and who knew that Yellowstone was, for better or worse, not apart from the rest of the world. National Park Service staff members have put progressively less time into encouraging visitation to Yellowstone in the past twenty years and have spent a great deal of time trying to find polite ways to explain the crisis of overcrowding to the public.

The idea that Yellowstone is overrun with development, more all the time, seems firmly entrenched in the folklore of conservationists, who are surprised to hear that development of the Yellowstone landscape, in terms of acreage of land under human use, peaked several decades ago and has been declining ever since. One advantage of the consolidation of services undertaken in the 1920s and 1930s was the eventual elimination of a lot of small ground-disturbing sites and a surprising number of large ones. A quick run around the Grand Loop Road reveals some of these (of course not all of these were in place at one time, but there were always more of them in the early 1900s than there are now).[13]

I will start at Mammoth and travel clockwise. The Mammoth Lodge and associated developments (cabins, swimming pool, service roads, and so on) that sprawled just opposite the hot springs are gone, and most of the ground has been reclaimed at least in part. The Lava Creek Campground is gone. The Wylie Permanent Camp at Tower Junction is gone. The Wylie Camp and the Shaw and Powell Camp at Canyon are gone, and at the Upper Falls the huge Canyon Hotel and the smaller hotel and store, along with almost all of their related facilities, have been replaced by one (albeit less attractive) Canyon Village. The marina at Fishing Bridge is gone. The Wylie Camp at Lake is gone. The Shaw and Powell Camp at Bridge Bay is gone. At Old Faithful the Wylie and the Shaw and Powell camps are gone, as is the National Park Service campground. Just north of the Lower Geyser Basin, the Fountain Hotel (capacity 350) is gone. The Norris Hotel and Lunch Station are gone. So are the Shaw and Powell Camp at Willow Park and the Wylie Camp at Swan Lake. The removal of the many permanent camps run by Wylie or Shaw and Powell, with their hundreds of tent-cabins and support facilities, is a remarkable gain in ground; at most of these sites only archeologists and a few knowledgeable locals even notice evidence of what once were big, active villages.

On the other hand, there have been losses of unoccupied landscape, the most notorious being the Grant Village development, with its accommodations, campground, marina, and associated facilities, which has been roundly vilified by environmental groups. But in all there has been a substantial net gain of acreage once covered by major developments in the past sixty years; most of the "new buildings" that make headlines in the regional papers are actually on the sites of old buildings.

The overall reduction in acreage of major developments may not be the most significant gains. Along the park's roads large and small maintenance camps, woodcutters' cabins, lunch stands, dairy operations, horse pastures, random junk piles near construction sites, slaughterhouses, dump sites (both for garbage from hotels and camps and for other kinds of refuse), sawmills, and other intrusions almost beyond counting proliferated in the first fifty years. In the weeks following the 1988 fire season, it seemed that anywhere I left the road and walked back fifty yards, I would find freshly exposed and badly charred refuse heaps — artifacts of the sagebrusher era, when a family could pull its wagon off into the woods, string a clothesline between two trees, and set up housekeeping for a week or so. The arrival of motorized transportation in Yellowstone and the preference of early National Park Service leaders for monopolistic concessions meant consolidation of facilities, to the immediate advantage of the landscape.

But the removal of all of these developments may not have opened up as much acreage as did changes in the roads themselves. In the 1930s there were often two or even three different routes between the major developments; the alternate roads and "cutoffs" weren't usually shown on the tourist brochures of that time. Known locally as "Model T roads" because the old cars were able to handle their rutted, high-centered grades, these were older sections of park roadway that had been replaced by better-engineered routes, but they were still open to anyone willing to try them (and willing to get themselves out if they got stuck).[14] Today's 3 million visitors have significantly fewer road miles available than did the 317,000 visitors of 1935. More important, human disturbance of the landscape is now more concentrated.

Some people believe that the park is overdeveloped, others wish it was more developed, but the *extent* of current development — the acreage occupied by human structures and therefore more or less divorced from the ecological setting — isn't the real problem. It appears that the resources of the park, especially those considered most vulnerable to competition for space, such as the grizzly bears, can handle the current level of disturbed landscape. What the resources are less able to handle is the number of people who, using those developments as bases of operation, spread out through the park in spatial and temporal patterns that cause all manner of complications. It appears, in fact, that the people raising alarms about overcrowding in the 1950s were right; they were only faintly aware of what the crowding could do.

In 1955 the National Park Service launched a broad, ambitious program, called Mission 66, to upgrade facilities, improve the roads and trails, and in other ways solve the problems of overcrowding by 1966. In Yellowstone, specifically, the agency aimed to achieve not only these goals but also "effective presentation, interpretation, and protection of the resources in Yellowstone by a management staff."[15] Mission 66 has left a complex legacy in Yellowstone. It did, indeed, upgrade many roads, bridges, and facilities, and no doubt visitors are now better served, but the program is routinely criticized for simply accommodating more traffic rather than trying to control or limit it. The biggest monuments of Mission 66, Canyon Village and Grant Village, are unpopular with environmentalists, although most visitors using these facilities are more than satisfied. Short of telling people "No, you can't come in today," the National Park Service had no choice but to create and improve accommodations, and they did succeed at that.

Canyon Village consists of a large, rectangular parking lot surrounded on three sides by stores, dining facilities, and a National Park Service visitor center. A campground stretches out to the north and northeast of this rectangle, and cabins and larger accommodation structures spread out to the east and south. The complex sits well back from the rim of the Grand Canyon of the Yellowstone, correcting one objection to earlier facilities, that they were too close.

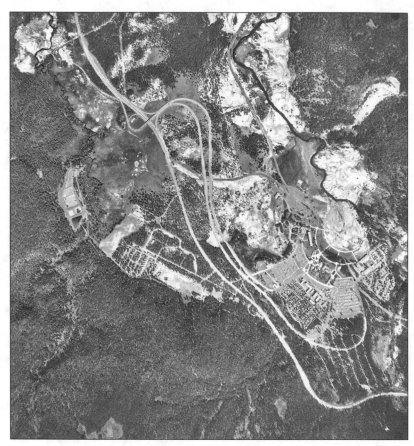

The Grand Loop Road runs just west of the Upper Geyser Basin. In this 1976 aerial photograph the famous and controversial highway overpass, the "Old Faithful exit," is at the upper center. Prior to the 1970s the road went through the geyser basin, but because of the growing crowds it was moved. Many people objected to the perceived suburban appearance of the overpass. Old Faithful geyser is at the center of the crescent of facilities on the right; the campground, whose narrow avenues are barely visible through the forest canopy at lower right, has since been removed. In the center of the photo the development to the left of the Grand Loop Road is employee housing, maintenance buildings, and a sewage treatment facility. The Firehole River winds through the geyser basin at the right. *NPS photo*

But by the 1980s Canyon Village was already out of fashion among many who toil in the troubled fields of national park aesthetics: it was too "suburban," architecturally inappropriate in a national park. Tastes change fast, leaving the parks in odd dilemmas. In the 1990s there was already talk among cultural resource specialists in the National Park Service Regional Office in Denver of recognizing that Canyon Village, like the Old Faithful Inn before it, should be *preserved* because it represents a certain era in Yellowstone's history. Mission 66 became History very fast.

Mission 66 reveals some fascinating aspects of the process by which Yellowstone's mission has become more complicated over time. The National Park Service is required by law to protect natural and cultural resources; these are defined in a raft of legislation and policy, much of which tends to increase the number of things to be protected. The things now recognized as needing protection in Yellowstone but not envisioned as part of the park's mission by its founders range from ecological process, biological diversity, and endangered species to hundreds of archeological sites and hundreds of historic structures.

The buildings make the point very well. It is transparently obvious that as these cultural artifacts of our use of Yellowstone get older, their upkeep will become more and more expensive, especially considering the stringent federal regulations concerning their care and maintenance. Only half in jest, using the working title "Random Acts of Senseless Preservation," I have spoken about these policies, wondering if it isn't time for the national parks to develop some exemptive procedure by which new structures would be forbidden any future protective classification. But our societal and legislatively mandated urge to protect many aspects of our heritage is quite strong and is guarded by a competent and energetic bureaucracy of state and federal agencies and an ardent community of public preservationists.

The recent emphasis on historic preservation represents as big a change in Yellowstone's original management direction as did the formal recognition of the park as a wildlife reserve, and it is representative of trends in the entire national park system. The National

Park Service is now charged with broader responsibilities than the founders of Yellowstone ever would have imagined. As the park system grew, it absorbed not only other great so-called natural sites but also a host of historic or cultural sites, from the Statue of Liberty to Anasazi ruins at Hovenweep. The number of sites will continue to grow in response to our continuing actions as a nation and our changing perceptions of ourselves. The system is a source of great national pride; what began as an effort to save one extraordinary place has become an effort to celebrate the heritage of a multi-regional, multicultural nation. As national parks tend more and more to memorialize structures no longer common elsewhere — from winding, low-speed auto trails to romanticized rustic architecture — they add yet another significant, costly, and complicated element to their missions: they become in effect museums for really big objects. This new emphasis promises to occupy a growing percentage of the time and the budgets of managers.

A popular arguing point among historic preservationists in recent years has been that Yellowstone National Park is really just a very large cultural site; proponents of this view usually pronounce it with smugness, even defiance, as if they would like nothing better than to fight about it. This argument has it that we humans decided to set Yellowstone apart because it was valuable to our culture; we would establish human boundaries on it and manage it for our benefit and enjoyment. There is a sound principle here — only recently, for example, have park managers recognized the extent to which North American landscapes were affected by humans prior to 1492 — but this fundamentally sound argument represents a crossroads in the search for Yellowstone. While some hold that even the architectural and engineering legacy of the National Park Service itself must be preserved and protected in the parks, others worry that we risk turning too much of Yellowstone into sites for stockpiling neat old buildings, bridges, culverts, and other human constructions that were created in the first place only to enable us to enjoy other resources here. The buildings in Yellowstone are both interesting and historic, but they were a side effect of the park's purpose. Now they have become a purpose in themselves, and one of the great challenges facing future managers will be coming to terms with that purpose. A recent example is Grant Village.

This development has been much more troubled than Canyon Village. In addition to complaints of compromised aesthetic integrity (it is routinely likened to a standard condominium community), critics have raised a variety of other political and ecological issues. Located on the shore of Yellowstone Lake's West Thumb, Grant Village was developed much more slowly than Canyon, in good part because the expense of the earlier development almost did in the Y. P. Co.[16] By the late 1960s Grant Village featured a campground, a marina (later closed because of engineering insufficiencies and now a largely deserted eyesore on the lakeshore), and some related facilities. Growth stopped for a few years, and in the meantime the planning plot thickened considerably. It was Grant Village's administrative entanglements with other developed areas, as much as its own character, that caused it to eventually become such an issue in the conservation of park resources.

Over the course of half a century and more, a development known as Fishing Bridge had grown up around the outlet of Yellowstone Lake. The park's 1974 "Master Plan," however, stated that this area was simply too valuable as "critical wildlife habitat" to be compromised by a development.[17] As early as 1968 park biologist William Barmore had pointed out that "the merging of lake, river and terrestrial ecosystems creates a complex of environmental conditions and habitats that supports a great diversity of plant and animal life." He concluded, "If we had it to do all over again, it seems unlikely that we would create an extensive development at Fishing Bridge."[18] By the early 1970s other park biologists were also noting how many grizzly bear problems had been concentrated in the Fishing Bridge area over time (more than half of the thirty-three grizzly bears killed in the park between 1943 and 1959 died within three or four miles of the bridge). The concentration couldn't be attributed solely to tourists' ice chests; the unavoidable conclusion was that bears really wanted to use this area, whether burgers and Twinkies were available or not.[19]

With this additional information, National Park Service plan-

As the Yellowstone River leaves Yellowstone Lake, it passes under the famous Fishing Bridge. In this 1976 aerial photograph, north is at the top. The Fishing Bridge development is to the immediate right of the bridge. The group of cabins just north of the road near the river has since been removed, as has the large NPS campground farther east, between the road and the lake. The long oval clearings on the far right are the concession-operated recreational-vehicle campground, which remains today, as do a few other facilities. On the left is the Lake Area, a separate development with cabins, lodge, and hotel. *NPS photo*

ners began the long, arduous process of removing the Fishing Bridge development and relocating its facilities to an enlarged Grant Village, which at the time was seen as a less ecologically sensitive or important area. The grizzly bear, in 1975 classified as threatened under the terms of the Endangered Species Act, took center stage in this issue, and in 1979 the U.S. Fish and Wildlife Service issued an opinion that Grant Village could be enlarged without jeopardizing the bears, *if* the Fishing Bridge development was removed.[20]

But in 1984 the community of Cody, Wyoming, about fifty miles outside the east entrance of Yellowstone, expressed their fears that the reduction of facilities on their side of the park (Fishing Bridge is closest to the east entrance) would cause visitors to enter the park through other gates. The Wyoming congressional delegation stepped in and, in the restrained language of one planning document, "requested that NPS reevaluate the decision to relocate facilities from Fishing Bridge to other in-park locations."[21] The following year a regional travel study conducted by the University of Wyoming indicated that visitors coming from long distances simply entered the park on the side from which they approached it without concern for the location of facilities in the park. But local certainty about what visitors did ruled the day in this matter, and to a great extent still does.

Further objections to the removal of the Fishing Bridge development came from historic preservationists; the federal oversight agency that monitors the care of historic structures, the Advisory Council on Historic Preservation, and the Wyoming State Historic Preservation Commission both voiced concerns about the removal of these facilities, pointing out that Fishing Bridge was historically significant in part because it was one of the first examples of strip development in the state of Wyoming.[22]

When the National Park Service leaders, bowing to pressure from the Wyoming congressional delegation, announced that they would prepare an environmental impact statement (EIS) for the Fishing Bridge plan, it became clear that though the construction of Grant Village was moving along, Fishing Bridge would not be demolished right away. Conservationists were outraged, and the ensuing media, political, and legal battles have been described as a "five-year bloodbath."[23] When the Fishing Bridge EIS was completed in 1988, changes were made in the plan: the government campground (310 sites) and some other facilities would be removed, but the concessioner-run RV campground (360 sites), general store, other smaller facilities, and the National Park Service visitor center-museum would stay. It was also decided that when "visitor demand warranted," the removed campsites would be "replaced" at other locations throughout the park.[24] Visitor demand was defined as "95% occupancy at the remaining 12 campgrounds in Yellowstone during the peak summer season . . . for three years out of any five-year period," and that percentage was quickly met.[25] Since then planning has begun to find suitable locations for these new sites at other park campgrounds.

Meanwhile our understanding of what constituted an ecologically sensitive site was changing. The new, more restrictive fishing regulations resulted in tremendous increases in spawning runs of cutthroat trout into streams around Yellowstone Lake, which brought impressive gatherings of grizzly bears to most of these streams. Suddenly the "sterile" lodgepole pine areas around the Lake and Grant Village developments, so attractive to the threatened grizzly bears, no longer seemed like promising spots for extensive new development.[26] The campground replacement process may ultimately result in some net loss of undisturbed landscape, as sites are added to the Norris, Canyon, and Grant Village campgrounds (on a more modest scale than originally planned).

The effects of Mission 66, like those of the great wildlife slaughter of the 1870s and the resort-era hotel building of the park's first half-century, will ripple down the decades, affecting subsequent management directions and decisions in ways we cannot imagine. Besides the big developments at Canyon and Grant (a third, "Firehole Village," was planned but never developed in the Lower Geyser Basin),[27] Mission 66's facility upgrades resulted in employee housing so standardized that National Park Service employees could follow their careers through several different parks without having to buy new curtains. It also led to the construction of the tradition-defying Old Faithful interchange, with an actual highway overpass that has irked countless people.[28] Mission 66 represented the National Park Service's acceptance of one reality: that the parks had to be prepared to handle more people.

But even in the 1960s there may have been more public support for controlling visitor numbers than most park managers or conservationists realized. In the spring and summer of 1968, journalist Robert Cahn published a fifteen-part series of articles in the *Christian Science Monitor* entitled "Will Success Spoil the National Parks?"[29] A probing study based on Cahn's 20,000-mile tour of the parks, the series showed great sympathy for park resources, the people who manage and use them, and the many people who depend upon them for a living. It also earned Cahn a Pulitzer Prize and still is instructive reading today.

Written at the close of the Mission 66 era, when visitor services had been much improved, Cahn's articles devoted much less attention to facilities and more to the bigger problem of crowds. It contained what may have been the first idealized fictional portrayal of a better-run future (1984) Yellowstone. Cahn's visitors, the Norton family from New Jersey, began their trip with a visit to a regional visitor center in Philadelphia, where they learned about making advance reservations at campgrounds or motels. You can almost hear the romance in Cahn's voice as he wrote that they could make reservations "by computer" and could also rent "home-play television tapes describing several parks." As they approached the park, they tuned in to a "special wave length" on their car radio to hear a voice describing their surroundings and what the park held in store for them. Having chosen not to make reservations in the park, they could not drive in; they rode in an "electric-powered minibus," walking "the final quarter mile to Old Faithful Geyser because all roads and parking areas were moved away from the fringes of the geyser back in 1971."[30] (This last part actually has happened, but the effect is probably not as delightful as Cahn imagined.)

Some of the most intriguing passages in this series of articles were written not by Cahn but by his readers. At the conclusion of the series, the *Christian Science Monitor* published a survey questionnaire entitled "How Would You Run the National Parks?" More than 2,000 readers filled out and returned the forms. When asked about overcrowding, 402 people agreed that the National Park Service should "build more campgrounds, lodges, and roads to take care of more people," but 950 said the agency should "limit the stay in a campground to the number of days it takes to see the major attractions, with a maximum of three days," and 801 supported establishing "a limit for entrance to each park, much as you would for a theater. When a certain capacity is reached, a park would be closed and reopened only to fill vacancies."[31] An amazing 759 — almost twice as many as wanted more campgrounds — agreed that all campgrounds should be taken out of the park in favor of developments elsewhere.

When asked about the balance of nature, 1,878 people, that is, almost all who answered, agreed that we should "determine what human influences are causing wildlife problems, and develop park-management programs designed to offset man's adverse impact." Last, and perhaps most eye-opening, 708 people supported an option to "restore wolves, cougars, bears, and coyotes to park areas where they once were native."[32]

"However," the paper's editors concluded, "some readers objected specifically to reinstating wolves."[33]

11 | GREATER YELLOWSTONE

I N 1959 JOHN AND FRANK CRAIGHEAD, ecologists already prominent for their milestone studies of raptor populations, initiated a long-term ecological study of the grizzly bears of Yellowstone. Probably in part because of their background in studying bird populations, the Craigheads focused on understanding the bears' population dynamics. This was in contrast to earlier carnivore studies in Yellowstone by the Muries, who had emphasized observation of individual animals to determine the behavior patterns of coyotes preying on ungulates and of bears using natural and human-provided foods.[1] The Craigheads' study focus was also an expression of changes in wildlife ecology and management, as the importance of understanding whole populations was becoming more and more evident.

By 1967 the two men had become the world's leading authorities on grizzly bears — not merely on their population dynamics and ecology but on their capture, handling, and all other aspects of studying these grand and elusive animals.[2] That year, in a preliminary report entitled "Management of Bears in Yellowstone National Park," the Craigheads expressed alarm over the National Park Service's plan to comply with recent environmental regulations by closing the garbage dumps.[3] The grizzly bears, for better or worse, were accustomed to feeding at these sites, as they had done for decades. As the dumps were closed in the late 1960s and early 1970s, and as dramatically increasing numbers of grizzlies were killed or otherwise removed from the Yellowstone ecosystem as a result of this and other management changes, what had begun as a fairly restrained

Grizzly bears greeting the garbage truck at the Trout Creek dump in central Hayden Valley in the 1960s. The dumps provided impetus both for a milestone scientific study and for a controversy about grizzly bear management, which continues today. *NPS photo*

dialogue erupted into a bitter debate that quickly spread to the media and has never really ended.

This was much more than a quarrel over garbage management. The Craigheads disagreed with the park's newly arrived managers on many issues, and the dump debate, for all the attention it was given in the press (to the exclusion of almost everything else), was really not the heart of the struggle; the two sides had a fundamental philosophical disagreement over how a national park should be managed. Ironically the Craigheads held very close to the traditional management approach of the National Park Service, believing that the various wildlife resources had to be manipulated in many ways. They argued that the dumps should be maintained so that the bears were concentrated and kept away from people during peak visitor season, that "surplus" elk and bison could be killed to help feed the bears if need be, and that the feeding of black bears along the roads should continue and could be acceptably maintained with an annual loss (from accidents and management kills) of twenty-eight black bears. They proposed an ambitious "zoning" plan for management of park wildlife, including areas of little or no management activity and areas where intensive manipulation of wildlife would occur. Citing the widespread belief that past mismanagement of elk and bison had resulted not only in overpopulation of those species but also in serious damage to their ranges, the Craigheads argued for a much more systematic, science-based program that would more closely monitor and much more consistently and intensively control the various animal populations. In short, they proposed a professionalized blueprint for doing what park managers had done haphazardly and ineffectively for decades. They repeatedly invoked the pro-manipulation language of the Leopold Report in support of their approach.

But by 1967 the new superintendent, Jack Anderson, and a new chief biologist, Glen Cole, had in mind even more sweeping changes — in the opposite direction. It is safe to assume that, having watched the political damage of the televising of the elk reduction program and the resultant Senate hearings, Anderson and Cole had no interest in pursuing that kind of wildlife management.[4] Just as important, as I mentioned at the close of Chapter 9, there was now reason to wonder if such management was the right approach anyway. Were the elk really producing a "surplus"? Was it appropriate in a national park to pack all the bears into small artificial feeding areas or to sacrifice a couple dozen black bears a year to the roadside feeding circus? And Cole, like the Craigheads, cited the Leopold Report: isn't the real idea of national parks to make the illusion a little more reasonable?

The Craigheads focused on the operational specifics of the Leopold Report, especially its encouragement of aggressive interference with the ecological setting (such as killing "surplus" animals), while Cole and Anderson emphasized its general spirit of experimenting and of stretching traditional ideas. In the first years after the report was published, Leopold continued to believe that Yellowstone's elk were too numerous and must be controlled, but when evidence began to accumulate that traditional elk control may have been misguided, Leopold was an interested (and generally noncritical) observer.[5] He was one of several advisers consulted frequently during this period, for Cole and Anderson reported regularly to the park service's scientific advisory committee to explain and propose changes in policy.

Though park managers took a terrific beating in the popular press (which portrayed the Craigheads as heroic underdogs taking on the bureaucracy), their approach was more in keeping with the general direction of wildland management since then. People may never stop arguing about elk and bears, but the principles of less intrusive management have been applied with considerable success (if no less controversy) to fisheries management and fire policy. The reduction of human intervention in the biological processes of Yellowstone, though constantly under attack from a variety of critics, has come to be recognized as an important principle by almost all of the leading environmental groups. A generation after the end of the Craighead study, John Craighead still maintains that the park should reopen the garbage dumps, but now he and his colleagues stand more or less alone in that position, at least among the now large and experienced community of bear managers and researchers, all of whom agree that artificial feeding on that scale is simply a bad idea.[6]

The philosophical chasm between the Craigheads and the park's new leadership foreshadowed most of Yellowstone's more recent major ecological debates since then, between people inclined to try to stabilize or control the ecological system and those inclined to let the system take its own direction.

But besides the remarkable scientific achievements of the Craigheads, we may owe them a greater debt for doing more than anyone else to call attention to the Greater Yellowstone Ecosystem. Their tracking of the grizzly bears to and beyond the park's boundaries revealed that the bears are a single interacting population whose fate is linked to habitats on a sprawling mosaic of federal, state, and private lands. On most of those lands in the 1960s, the bear's future was at best a low priority; if Yellowstone National Park seemed to be failing to care adequately for the bear, it was still the soul of conservationist virtue compared to everyplace else.

IN 1967, the same year that the Craigheads submitted their preliminary report on grizzly bear management, Princeton University Press published a small volume by Robert Mac Arthur and Edward O. Wilson entitled *The Theory of Island Biogeography.*[7] The authors encouraged ecologists (and thus land managers) to consider "insularity" as a factor in the well-being and prospects of individual species populations and of the communities of species that make up ecosystems. Island biogeography applies to terrestrial "islands" as well, especially isolated tracts of relatively wild land that are cut off from other similar areas not by water but by agricultural and residential lands.[8] Mac Arthur and Wilson brought attention to what now seems to be the great question about all such isolated areas: how big must they be to ensure the survival of the species they protect? The persistence of an area's "biodiversity" has become the primary test of its well-being.

The emergence, especially in the 1970s, of a widespread public consciousness of Yellowstone National Park as part of a greater ecosystem is probably the most important conceptual shift in public understanding of the park since it became a formal wildlife reserve in the late 1800s. However, this view is part of a long tradition of concern about the park's boundaries. In 1880 Superintendent Norris stated that the park's boundaries should be extended, an opinion that would often be echoed later. His goal, and the goal of most others of his era who made similar proposals, was to protect wildlife ranges to the east of the park.[9] But over the next decade other ideas emerged relating to the protection of Yellowstone, revealing that even a century ago some people were thinking in terms of protecting large landscapes.

By the 1880s, for example, conservationists were already sensitive to the need to protect the headwaters of stream systems; in the East many clear-cut drainages had avenged themselves through catastrophic flooding. The foremost impetus behind the creation of

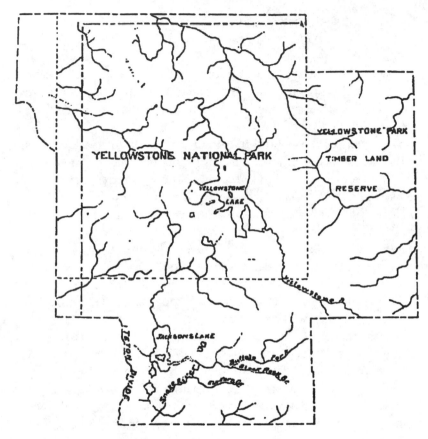

This map, "National Park Boundaries — Present and Proposed," from *Forest and Stream,* January 7, 1899, may represent the most comprehensive early proposal for expansion of Yellowstone. The proposal added the headwaters of the Yellowstone River, extensive game ranges to the east, and additional land in the Gallatin River drainage on the park's northwest boundary. A great variety of expansion proposals appeared between 1882 and 1930, but the adjustments made to the park's boundaries were relatively minor.

the huge Adirondack Park in upstate New York was the recognition that forested headwaters released their waters more gently, to the advantage of downstream navigability, agriculture, and human development in valleys.[10] In his many editorials in the 1880s in *Forest and Stream*, George Bird Grinnell emphasized the importance of watershed protection, which he may have come to regard as more important than wildlife protection (or at least more marketable among the public as a justification for protecting the park):

> The forests of the Park protect the headwaters of two of the most important rivers of North America, one, the Snake, flowing into the Pacific, the other, the Yellowstone, finding its way into the Atlantic. These streams after leaving the mountains flow for long distances through arid regions which are only cultivable by means of irrigation, and should the forests about the heads of these rivers be cleared away, their volume would be so diminished that the farmers, who now and in the future will depend on them for their water supply, would be absolutely unable to raise crops.[11]

But because of this water resource, pressures for expansion of the park were sometimes matched, and nearly overcome, by pressures for shrinkage. Because of this seesaw battle Yellowstone National Park never became significantly larger than its founders made it, and long after the 1880s and the defeat of mining interests that wished to lop off parts of the park, Yellowstone was still at risk of partial disassembly or degrading. The most notable pressures came from parties wishing to take advantage of the park's undammed waterways; the successful incursion of hydroelectric interests into the Hetch Hetchy Valley of Yosemite was a frightening precedent. Defenders of Yellowstone's free-flowing rivers spent much of the 1920s fighting off "reclamation raids," especially in the southwestern corner of the park, where the Bechler River system seemed to have been designed by some engineer deity for a system of impoundments that could feed water to arid Idaho farmlands.[12] Even today a plan occasionally emerges for a dam somewhere in the park.

Though expansion of the park was considered even in the 1920s (by then the emphasis was to the south, to the headwaters of the Yellowstone River and the Teton range), the issue essentially became moot with the establishment of the first forest reserves in the 1890s. The U.S. Forest Service now dates the origin of the national forest system to the creation of the Yellowstone Park Timberland Reserve, east and south of the park, in 1891. The original intention of the creators of this reserve and of the Teton Forest Reserve created south of it in 1897 was to set aside for some distant posterity a great deal of timber. The reserves were also viewed to some extent as de facto extensions of the park (soldiers from the park were assigned to patrol them).[13] For a few years it was unclear whether these areas would become part of the park, but in 1902 both reserves were enlarged and given their own separate administration, setting them on a divergent administrative course from Yellowstone and all the other parks, as formalized by the creation of the U.S. Forest Service a few years later. To a considerable extent the forest reserves accomplished what Norris and others had desired earlier: they gave federal protection to important game ranges beyond the park's boundaries. On the other hand, the creation of the reserves has also resulted in bureaucratic complications in coordinating their management now that the interconnectedness of these lands is more clearly understood.

In the first three quarters of this century, the national parks and national forests established a rivalry of epic proportions. National parks and monuments were occasionally carved from U.S. Forest Service lands, and as both agencies' missions matured, philosophical differences evolved. The agencies became distinctive subcultures of the conservation profession, each with its own jargon and self-image. A segregative language developed, with forest managers aggressively asserting that they practiced "conservation" while park managers were proud to practice "preservation." This artificial distinction among human uses of the land is still common today, though all resources in all parks and forests exist to serve a wide continuum of human needs. One of the original stated aims of conservation, to serve the greatest good of the greatest number of people, can just as easily be applied to the protection of Old Faithful

Geyser for the viewing enjoyment of millions of visitors as to the sustained-yield forestry practiced in national forests. The setting aside from development (in other words, the "preservation") of more than a million acres of land in Shoshone National Forest under the Wilderness Act is as good an example of serving the greatest good for the greatest number of people as is the paving of several acres of land adjoining the Upper Geyser Basin (surely not the "preservation" of that land, but perhaps the result of "conservation") for the parking convenience of visitors. And early park defenders like Grinnell, who saw the park as a reservoir for game that could be hunted when it migrated to surrounding lands and as nature's watershed manager, ensuring reasonable flows in huge areas beyond the park boundaries, were surely practicing a very foresightful conservation.

At its worst, this philosophical rivalry generated a great smugness among personnel of both agencies, who felt that their agency had the "better" goal. In stereotype, the park people perceived themselves as on the aesthetic high road, protecting natural purity from the taint of commerce, while the forest people saw themselves as eminently practical, making essential resources available to a growing nation. In reality, neither mission was that simple.

While Yellowstone's boundaries have not been significantly enlarged, they have been modified. In 1929 most of the east boundary and a small section of the western end of the north boundary were realigned to conform with drainage divides, adding seventy-eight square miles to the park. Superintendent Albright, attributing decided preservationist sentiments to the natural world, said that the lands thus excluded from the park "really were not intended by nature to be a part of the park."[14] Nature's intentions aside, these changes gave the park its only extended boundaries that had anything to do with the geographical character of the land. In 1932, after several years of delay, haggling, and fund-raising, another parcel of land on the west side of the Yellowstone River north and west of Gardiner, Montana, was added to the park as winter range for ungulates. This land, long overgrazed by livestock, would become an important element of later ungulate research.

By the 1960s the park was surrounded by the present administrative units of state and federal lands, including six national forests,
two national wildlife refuges, and Grand Teton National Park (created in 1929 and enlarged to its present size in 1950). Increasing
public use of the region necessitated greater cooperation between
the rival agencies, so in the early 1960s the National Park Service and
the U.S. Forest Service created the Greater Yellowstone Coordinating Committee. This included the six forest supervisors, the two
park superintendents, and the regional bosses of all eight units (the
two park superintendents answered to the same regional director in
the National Park Service, but Greater Yellowstone straddles the
boundaries of three different U.S. Forest Service administrative regions, so three regional foresters were on the committee). The committee's low-profile work dealt with routine administrative matters.[15]

Thus the existence of a "greater Yellowstone" was formally recognized for many years before the modern movement to protect the
Greater Yellowstone Ecosystem. The term "greater Yellowstone" first
appeared in print in 1917, when conservation writer Emerson Hough
(the same man who reported for *Forest and Stream* on the capture of
bison poacher Howell in 1894) was exhorting Wyoming to consider
enlarging the park to include Jackson Hole and the Tetons. "Give her
Greater Yellowstone," Hough said of Wyoming, "and she will inevitably become Greater Wyoming."[16] Wyoming did not see it that way,
and "much effort could have been saved and the general good would
have been better served if more Wyoming citizens had understood
what Hough was trying to tell them."[17]

The idea of a landscape as a community of life forms and
environmental forces was not new even when the term "ecosystem"
was coined in the 1930s. It was a necessary consequence of thinking
broadly about life communities (as, for example, in Frederic Clements's "superorganism").[18] In the language of Yellowstone management "ecosystem" was used first in the late 1970s and in a surprisingly short time became widespread. For quite a while in the 1980s,
federal land managers resisted using it, preferring the more vague
and neutral "Greater Yellowstone Area." By saying "area" instead of

"ecosystem," they could confidently speak only in terms of the federal lands in and around Yellowstone National Park. "Area" was also a lot less politically loaded; for some distrustful members of the general public, "ecology" had the same negative rhetorical force as "environment," as would "ecosystem."[19] These "e-words" apparently all smacked of some radical new way of seeing the region's resources, but by the mid-1980s "Greater Yellowstone Ecosystem" was heard in offices throughout the area.

But the entrenchment of the idea of a Greater Yellowstone Ecosystem (or GYE, often described as the last large intact ecosystem in the earth's temperate zone) was not accompanied by agreement on its size or shape. The interrelatedness that gives the ecosystem concept its power also makes it vulnerable: it is always possible to argue about the edges of any ecosystem. Since the 1970s the definition of the ecosystem that includes Yellowstone has grown from a 4-million-acre circle to a 20-million-acre multilobed amoeboid blob whose vaguely defined boundaries are depicted by bands of progressively lighter shading on the map, a recognition of the difficulty of drawing lines around something so complex.[20]

The problem of definition has not significantly slowed the recognition that the ecosystem concept is a valuable device for regional planning. In 1983 a consortium of conservationists and other special-interest groups created the Greater Yellowstone Coalition, which has since become the region's foremost nongovernment champion of interagency coordination and regional planning. A few years later agricultural interests created the Greater Yellowstone Association of Conservation Districts, also using Greater Yellowstone as the focus of dialogues on land use in the region, but being more concerned with guarding traditional agricultural rights to public lands than with ecosystem values.

If there was any doubt about the permanency of the Greater Yellowstone movement, it must have been dispelled in 1985, when conservationists' concerns led the U.S. Congress's House Subcommittee on National Parks and Recreation to hold hearings on federal land-management practices in the Greater Yellowstone Ecosystem.[21] Though the hearings are recognized as a landmark in the stormy

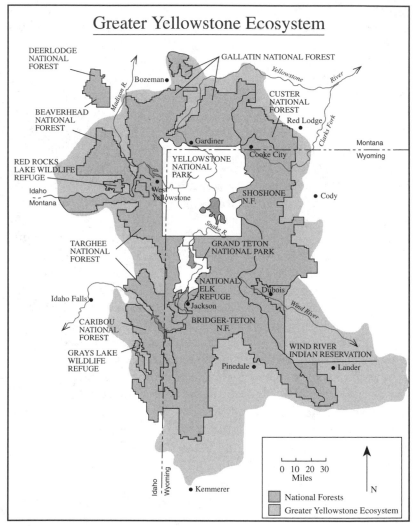

Greater Yellowstone Ecosystem

DEERLODGE
NATIONAL
FOREST

GALLATIN NATIONAL FOREST

Yellowstone   *River*

Bozeman ●

CUSTER
NATIONAL
FOREST

Madison R.

BEAVERHEAD
NATIONAL
FOREST

Red Lodge ●

Clarks Fork

Montana

RED ROCKS
LAKE WILDLIFE
REFUGE

● Gardiner

Cooke City

Wyoming

YELLOWSTONE
NATIONAL
PARK

Idaho
Montana

West
Yellowstone

SHOSHONE
N.F.

● Cody

Snake R.

TARGHEE
NATIONAL
FOREST

GRAND TETON
NATIONAL PARK

NATIONAL
ELK
REFUGE

Dubois

Idaho Falls ●

● Jackson

Wind River

CARIBOU
NATIONAL
FOREST

BRIDGER-TETON
N.F.

GRAYS LAKE
WILDLIFE
REFUGE

WIND RIVER
INDIAN RESERVATION

Pinedale ●

● Lander

0 10 20 30
Miles

Idaho
Wyoming

● Kemmerer

N

National Forests

Greater Yellowstone Ecosystem

Map by Wendy Baylor

history of the GYE, opinions differ on what they achieved. Conservation groups claimed a great victory, but federal managers argued that Congress had found no "smoking gun" to prove that management was failing badly. In 1987 the Congressional Research Service (CRS) published its analysis of the data submitted to the committee by the various agencies relating to their management practices and approach to ecosystem issues; the CRS found much to criticize but did not recommend what the conservation community wanted — overarching management of the GYE that would cut through the thicket of interagency rivalries and conflicting legislative mandates.[22] The CRS described shortages and inconsistencies of data, weak interagency coordination, and the degradation of wildlife habitat due to various developments and road building. The analysis also recognized that the chief economic force in the region was recreation rather than the traditional extractive industries.

The CRS report did include a list of twenty-two coordinating committees and subcommittees that dealt with cross-boundary issues relating to animals such as grizzly bears, trumpeter swans, various ungulate herds, cranes, wolves, falcons, and geese, as well as outfitters, travel and recreation, and sedimentation, indicating that there was considerable interagency coordination, even if not enough[23] This list also revealed, however, that the ecosystem was managed in terms of individual species and issues. While hopeful conservation theorists speak broadly of biodiversity and landscape ecology, the management agencies continue to go about their legislatively mandated tasks in the more traditional way — a species at a time. Advances in management of the GYE have almost without exception been based on concern over individual elements — grizzly bears most often, but also trumpeter swans, bald eagles, or elk — rather than on diffuse characteristics such as ecological integrity or biodiversity.

The spate of federal legislation growing out of the environmental movement of the 1960s gave GYE managers and defenders their best tools for protecting the values of the ecosystem. The Wilderness Act of 1964 led to the setting aside of more than 3 million acres of wilderness in the various national forests around the park;

more than half of the Shoshone National Forest, east of the park, is designated as wilderness. The National Environmental Policy Act of 1969 (NEPA) mandated the preparation of environmental impact statements by any federal land manager whose actions were "significantly affecting the quality of the human environment." NEPA gave conservationists a mechanism for reviewing or objecting to specific management plans on a scale never before possible and gave managers a clear road map for reaching their own goals. The Endangered Species Act of 1973, which prohibited federal agencies from taking any action that would jeopardize a classified species, has strengthened protection for rare plants and animals. The grizzly bear was classified as "threatened" in 1975, and its habitat needs are regularly invoked in objections to intensive development or manipulation of parks and forests. The National Forest Management Act of 1976 directs the U.S. Forest Service to coordinate with other agencies in developing its management plans.[24] These and other acts constituted the formal legal playing field on which the Greater Yellowstone Ecosystem was gradually being defined and directed.

The challenge facing GYE land managers and their many constituencies "is to devise functional policies that protect the region's ecological integrity while also ensuring stable communities and economic opportunities."[25] But there is great disagreement over just what combination of economy and ecology is right for the public lands of the GYE, and management of the GYE's private lands is so volatile an issue that land managers rarely mention it.[26]

In the 1970s and 1980s the park, though it had for many years been recognized as one of the world's premier nature reserves, became the subject of growing celebrity, scrutiny, and interest from the international conservation community. The park's centennial year, 1972, was celebrated during the first world conference on parks, held in Grand Teton and Yellowstone. Yellowstone was the first American natural area to be designated a BioSphere Reserve by the United Nations Educational, Social, and Cultural Organization (UNESCO). Six years later Yellowstone became one of the first American places to be named a World Heritage Site. These high-visibility international honors brought with them few concrete obligations but a great deal of attention to Yellowstone's contributions to world knowledge and culture.

GYE's forest supervisors and park superintendents, buoyed by this interest and spurred by congressional concerns over inadequate coordination, began to advocate ecosystem management more openly. This was a significant change; government land managers did not traditionally look beyond their own boundaries. The change that occurred in the 1980s in that respect was almost spectacular and might be best exemplified by a very public comment made by Yellowstone Superintendent Robert Barbee about the national forests of Greater Yellowstone in the spring of 1989:

> The U.S. Forest Service, through its wilderness system and in many other ways, already has recognized that the forests are not a matched collection; each has its unique qualities. Some forests may be best managed for extractive industry, or recreation, or some other single purpose, to the near exclusion of other purposes. In my opinion, the last option seems best for the national forests in the greater Yellowstone area.
>
> Considering the area's extraordinary values and the public's well-established perception that the area is somehow all "Yellowstone," it appears that the greater Yellowstone can be managed best by not trying to do many things satisfactorily, but by concentrating on doing one thing very well. That one thing is protecting the integrity of the natural systems that are the area's most important resource.[27]

Now, less than a decade later, the National Park Service is routinely involved in regional planning. The park's connections to the rest of the GYE, made clear by the wanderings of grizzly bears, the migrations of elk and bison, and geothermal aquifers that cross park boundaries in many directions, are now seen as giving Yellowstone superintendents a strong mandate to speak out on issues affecting the GYE. Management of the park, for so many decades a fairly contained assignment, now involves paying attention to a minimum of 20 million acres of land, 90 percent of which is beyond the boundaries.

By the late 1980s Yellowstone managers, as well as all the advocates of various management approaches, heard a daily roll call of ecosystem issues. To the time-honored traditional issues, such as logging, mineral exploration and development, livestock grazing, elk, grizzly bears, and human population growth, were added the equally emotional concerns of fire management and development of geothermal resources near the park. There was, justifiably, panic that the development might irreversibly affect the "plumbing" of Yellowstone's unique assembly of world-famous geysers and hot springs.

In 1990, responding to the growing urgency of these issues, as well as to Congress's obvious disapproval of the poor coordination between the National Park Service and the U.S. Forest Service, the two agencies produced a draft document, "Vision for the Future of the Greater Yellowstone Area." An attempt to outline long-term goals for federal lands in the GYE, "Vision" was at least in the short term a political disaster. Conservation biologist Edward Grumbine described the response:

> Few observers anticipated what happened next. A firestorm of controversy exploded at the public hearings on the draft. Agency staff were called communists and Nazis by private landholders who saw "federal takeover" in the public lands document. The misrepresentations of industry groups had influenced them to speak out. The Wyoming Multiple-Use Coalition, for example, demanded that all mention of biodiversity be deleted from the plan because, "left totally unchecked, the ravages of nature would leave far more environmental destruction than management." The commodity-oriented congressional delegations from Wyoming, Montana, and Idaho all criticized the plan. Representative Ron Marlenee's (R-Montana) statement was typical: The document "essentially writes a blank check for a few wilderness advocates within federal agencies and radical environmental groups to impose their narrow ideological agenda on 17 million acres of land."[28]

These claims were all untrue. There were no prescriptions for increased wilderness, no radical environmentalism. There were many wishful descriptions of future regional management and hopes that this document might help guide the way to that end. There were numerous bows to the importance of maintaining the traditional extractive industries in the region — logging, mining, agriculture. The proof of the draft's restrained tone is that it had no meaningful support among the conservation groups, leaving it all the more open to attack. The "Vision" hearings, held over the course of several months after its publication, brought out crowds of people waving American flags and railing against what they had been told was a plot against their freedom to use public lands. As Grumbine wrote, "At one packed hearing in Montana, when an environmentalist asked attendees to raise their hands if they had read the document, virtually no one did."[29] The next year a final document, now called a "framework," was produced.[30] It was only a tenth as long as the draft and was even more vague and unquantified. (Curiously, more than 95 percent of the ideas and proposals deleted from the draft had never been objected to, even by the most outspoken and strident critics.)

The "Vision" battle was instructive. The "e-words" were still poison in many circles, as were a surprising number of others, such as biodiversity. The belief that Yellowstone officials wanted to expand the park's boundaries surfaced constantly; lingering resentment over the small additions of the 1920s and 1930s could hardly account for such a pronounced fear in so many people. The extent to which the park was viewed as a malevolent force in the region would no doubt shock people who know it only as a great nature reserve or vacation paradise.

The message and intent of the "Vision" document itself did not disappear. Many of its specific recommendations were already a part of the National Park Service's consciousness. And in 1994 the Greater Yellowstone Coalition produced its own "blueprint for the future," a far more ambitious and aggressive statement of the need to protect the region's resources. The Coalition, through its increasing involvement in regional planning, has continued to heighten public awareness of the issues involved in thinking that crosses many traditional boundaries.[31] Greater Yellowstone is changing, economically and socially, and what has been described as "a new regional economy" will eventually force some adjustments in direction that the agencies cannot make alone.[32]

The economics that have driven so much of the Greater Yellowstone debates in recent years are nothing like traditional perceptions of the western way of life. Historian Samuel P. Hays has argued that the American West's defining characteristic grows from those changes:

> For most of the nation's media and for many of its specialists in environmental policy, western controversies are thought of as a conflict between those within the region who seek to develop its minerals, timber, water, and grazing lands and those in the East who wish to restrict such activities in favor of environmental objectives. Such a view was fostered by leaders of the Sagebrush Rebellion, by Ronald Reagan during the 1980 campaign, and by his Secretary of the Interior, James Watt. The West symbolized those creative entrepreneurial energies that had been thwarted and that the new administration pledged to release.
>
> These assessments are incorrect. Vast changes of quite a different sort have been taking place in the West to create a new indigenous environmental movement that has challenged the old commodity economy in a fierce struggle for western turf. To whom does the West belong — the old or the new? The contest over the answer to that question is now the political drama of the West. One observes a slow and persistent incremental advantage for the newer environmental West and a fierce but slowly losing resistance on the part of the older commodity West.[33]

Nowhere is this struggle, and the economic realities behind it, more evident than in Greater Yellowstone. It has been said that if the Greater Yellowstone Ecosystem were a state, it would have the fastest-growing population of any state in the nation; little of that growth is related to the traditional western industries mentioned by Hays. A review of the economies of counties in or partly in the GYE in 1991 concluded that even though the statistics were biased by extensive extractive-industry activities outside of the GYE, "mineral extraction, agriculture and forestry, and manufacturing (including lumber mills) were responsible for only one out of six dollars of income and one out of eight jobs in 1987."[34] This has been a pretty startling revelation for regional planners and interest groups which, as Hays described, have long tended to accept the received wisdom that the GYE, like the rest of the West, depends primarily on the extractive industries. Indeed the GYE's national forests, which have become the foremost battleground among competing resource users, account for only 5 percent of the employment in the GYE.[35]

Much of the West is federal land, far more so than any of the East.[36] The cinematic image of the westerner blessed with great individual freedom, the conqueror and inhabitant of a wild but beloved land, is still promoted by many politicians, but it is smudged by the irksome detail that much of that land is owned equally by Atlanta suburbanites and Detroit auto workers.

The federal omnipresence in the West, which has led to repeated "sagebrush rebellions" and other bald-faced attempts to grab public lands, is sometimes a serious complication for Yellowstone National Park, whose federal employees are often painted with the same broad brush used on all other "outsiders" perceived to be interfering with local and regional issues. Even the park rangers — the original white hats of the conservation movement — are portrayed as jack-booted thugs. It is no longer enough for the occasional bad ranger or incompetent manager to be merely bad or incompetent; now they are also seen as symbols of great national ills. The concept of ecosystem management in Greater Yellowstone may only stumble forward intermittently, but it would never have been born at all had not 12 million acres of public lands provided it such a firm foothold.

But the interests in the GYE are no longer simply eastern or western. The majority of people living in this region are showing social, economic, or philosophical alignments not unlike those traditionally associated with "easterners." The long-time locals — third-, fourth-, and even fifth-generation people — are confronted with a flood of changing land uses and values, just as the five-hundredth-generation Native Americans of two centuries ago were confronted by a tidal wave of change when the whites arrived. The children of the logger, the environmental activist, and the district ranger are in the same dance class and on the same Little League team. There is no longer a clearly identifiable colonial West whose fate is in the hands of people far away, but there is still just as strong a need to balance local and regional interests with national ones.

The diversified sustainable economy most practical observers aim for in the GYE requires the continuation of traditional land uses; nonextractive does not mean nondamaging. The rapid suburbanization of private lands, the increasing recreational pressures, and many other aspects of the flood of people now moving to the GYE are threats to the very values they are coming here to enjoy. The traditional extractive industries are sometimes viewed by environmental polemicists as inherently evil impediments to Greater Yellowstone's attainment of environmental utopia, but the ranch that fails because of changing beef markets or grazing regulations or other social forces will be sold, subdivided, and developed in some way that will result in increased human occupation, with consequent loss of wildlife habitat and open space. Loggers and miners are quick to point out that merely replacing extractive jobs with more service-oriented jobs is hardly equitable if people have to support a family on a maid's salary instead of a miner's. The idea of "thinking like an ecosystem," as legal scholar Charles Wilkinson has put it, grows from the American West's continuing redefinition of itself, away from a primarily extractive view of the land to a more complex view that may ultimately be just as threatening to western landscapes in other ways.[37]

The economic debates over the future of the GYE have taken some novel turns. Though the recovery of wolves in Yellowstone was long resisted by ranching interests because they were sure that wolves would hurt the regional economy, a University of Montana study estimated that wolves, especially through tourism they would generate, would serve both society and the economy well: "It appears safe to conclude that the net social benefits associated with wolf recovery are positive and on the order of $110 million for a

20-year horizon."[38] Quantification of the economic value of such things as wolves signals another change in the regional decision-making process. If we can value the wolf on this scale, imagine the social and economic value of Old Faithful, or the Grand Canyon of the Yellowstone, or the grizzly bears of the Greater Yellowstone Ecosystem.

ON DECEMBER 5, 1995, the World Heritage Committee, after a stormy visit to Yellowstone National Park, decided to add the park to its list of World Heritage Sites in Danger.[39] The listing caused great embarrassment to the United States; the world was telling us that we were not doing justice to a treasured place. Of the World Heritage Committee's many concerns, the most serious was the proposed New World Mine project, in the heart of the mining district pioneered in the late 1860s near what would become the northeast corner of Yellowstone National Park. This gold mine, once fully operational, would have dramatically altered the social structure of some small communities near the park, and the potential effects on the area's natural resources were regarded as grave both by the environmentalist community and by some agencies, including the National Park Service, whose staff made one of their most determined beyond-the-boundary forays on this issue.[40] (The mine also demonstrated the magnificently urgent hyperbole of Yellowstone debates. It wasn't just another mine; it was the worst mine in the world. Of course it was — no less a threat would be good enough for Yellowstone.)

The long, contentious examination of the mine revealed most of the important elements of the Greater Yellowstone debate, all of which were highlighted by the World Heritage Committee's participation.[41] The committee's redesignation of Yellowstone as a site in danger, which infuriated extractive-industry interests as it was applauded by environmentalists, may have been the event that decidedly turned the tide against a mine many of us thought was sure to be built. In August 1996 President Bill Clinton stood at the base of Baronette Peak in northeast Yellowstone National Park and announced an agreement in principle between the federal government and Crown Butte Mines to exchange the New World site for less notable or sensitive lands. Clinton, whose support had been enlisted by park superintendent Mike Finley and regional conservationists during a visit to the park the previous summer, said, "The agreement that has been reached with Crown Butte to terminate this project altogether proves that everyone can agree that Yellowstone is more precious than gold."[42] The decisive placing of the park's and the GYE's natural values above those of industry calls to mind earlier conservationist victories, such as the defeat forty years earlier of the Echo Park dam, which would have flooded parts of Dinosaur National Monument.

Whether the New World Mine defeat is a milestone that signals a clear shift in the management direction of the GYE or whether it is just another skirmish in a struggle that will never end, it kept the idea of ecosystem management before the public at a time when the meaninglessness of the park's boundaries was becoming ever more obvious. The land trade means only that the mine will not be developed in the GYE; it will now be in someone else's backyard. Conservationists long ago realized that protecting national parks should never be an excuse for treating other lands badly, and most other public lands do not have Yellowstone's advantage of a passionately attentive public to ensure that they are used carefully. Like the park itself, the GYE is not a free-standing entity immune to our actions on the rest of the planet.

The reality of a global ecosystem has dawned on us in the face of human-caused climate change, which, after many years of debate and political discounting, is more and more often pronounced real. Predictions for the eventual effects on Yellowstone of that climate change include among many other things probable losses of some very important grizzly bear habitat as preferred habitats shrink or vanish.[43] But as we have learned more about Yellowstone, we have discovered that it has numerous links to distant places. More than 100 species of the park's summer birds are neotropical migrants that travel each fall to Mexico and Central America.[44] If changes in willows, aspen, and other habitats for these birds in Yellowstone seem troubling, they are nothing compared to the wholesale market hunting, loss of habitat, and other threats these birds face in their wintering areas. The animals and plants of the Western Hemisphere have spent thousands of years developing long, tenuous connections across great intercontinental distances, and now humans are severing those connections, usually without any idea how far-reaching the consequences of each action may be.

Though advocates of protecting ecosystem values have a growing arsenal of such arguments on their side, they still may be at their most effective in regional debates when they rely on broader appeals, especially our sense of legacy. A central pillar of the self-images of the National Park Service and the U.S. Forest Service has been that they save things for future generations. Former Yellowstone superintendent Bob Barbee, who was the GYE's foremost promoter in the agency during the first ten years of its political prominence, laid out the moral obligations of ecosystem management this way:

> It comes down to this: are the immediate, short-term gains of relatively few people near the park worth the price if America loses the grizzly bear in Yellowstone or permits the park's geysers — some 60 percent of the world's geysers — to suffer irreparable harm?
>
> There is little doubt which way future generations would answer, but they don't get to answer. . . . Our job is to cast a vote on behalf of posterity.[45]

Barbee used the most emotion-stirring examples of loss he knew of, those involving unique park resources, but his statement would have been almost as effective if he had invoked instead the GYE's famed quality of life. Historian Dan Flores has characterized both the power and the elusiveness of the attachment many people feel to a landscape or a region in terms of a "spirit of place":

> The defining essence of spirit of place is not just that it occurs on a bioregional level, or that humans ought to stay put and sink roots, or even that spirit of place requires a shared aware-

ness of history to flower fully. The most important thing about spirit of place is that cultural values and human imagination determine it as much as landscape does — and that it exemplifies history's greatest lesson: everything is always changing.[46]

It is hard to imagine a better description of Greater Yellowstone than as a region that has a unique spirit of place even though everything is always changing.

12 | HOLOCENE PARK

T HE SEARCH FOR THE BEST WAY to manage Yellowstone has proceeded mostly through controversy. If anything, we are more at odds, and on more issues, than ever before, and the disagreements seem ever more heated and pronounced. The pro-development moguls of the Yellowstone Park Improvement Company of the 1880s have their modern equivalents in a tourism industry whose most aggressive members see the park as a huge, tree-covered goose that is capable of laying a bigger golden egg every year; these people can think of nothing more pleasing than the prospect of Yellowstone with 4 or 5 million visitors instead of 3 million. At the other extreme the radical environmentalists, opposed to most past development and all future development, didn't even have an equivalent a century ago; the spectrum of viewpoints is not only more intensely active, it is broader than ever before. Pressures are exerted from clear across the opinion spectrum until some form of resolution, truce, or change occurs.

Arguments in the past twenty-five years about the park's geothermal wonders, the original justification for its creation, reveal how far-reaching the changes can be. As geothermal energy development (and other potentially harmful drilling) increased on lands near the park, concern grew that the park's geysers, hot springs, and other thermal features might be at risk if drillers tapped into an aquifer connected to a park geyser basin. This concern led to a whole series of controversies over various geothermal areas beyond the park boundaries. As a consequence of the federal Geothermal

Steam Act of 1970, national parks with such resources were required to legally define them.

What most park managers outside of Yellowstone did was draw lines around the known surface expressions of geothermal activity in their park: a hot spring here, a collection of steam vents there. But geothermal activity at the surface is only the visible sign of a much bigger, more complex, and deeper system, fed by aquifers that move these unusual waters long distances. Yellowstone managers recommended that the only way to encompass such a resource on a map was by drawing a line that conformed exactly with the park boundary. Thus it was that Yellowstone's geothermal resources were defined as broadly as possible, emphasizing their continuity with similar resources beyond the boundaries to strengthen the park's bargaining position in future controversies over threats to its geothermal resources. Just as cultural resource professionals would describe all of Yellowstone as a cultural landscape and therefore a cultural resource, it is now all legally defined as a geothermal resource.[1]

Protecting the geothermal resources, though a complex legal matter, comes down to a fairly simple symbolic mission: no one wants to be known as the person who killed Old Faithful. Of the major geyser areas of the world, only two, Yellowstone and portions of the Kamchatka Peninsula of extreme eastern Russia, have not been massively disrupted by energy development. Practically all of New Zealand's many geysers are dead, as are most or all of those in every other major geothermal area on earth, including the few others in the United States. The goal is to prevent such a fate from happening in Yellowstone, to keep the park's geyser basins flowing, bubbling, erupting, and fuming just as they do now.[2]

But protecting the park's *ecological* resources continues to be a vexing challenge. There may be vague agreement that the park should be kept "wild" or that we must somehow ensure the survival of its plant and animal species. But there is heated debate over everything else.

Ecosystem management has benefited from the rise in the 1980s of a new discipline called conservation biology, which now supports its own journal and a growing number of university departments and is seen as having a broader (and in the long run, more meaning-ful) mission, which is well defined by Edward Grumbine, one of its leading proponents:

> Most traditional resource management is reductionist, mainly concerned with species of direct utilitarian interest: How can humans have bucks to bag, trees to harvest, salmon to catch? Conservation biologists, in contrast, consider the entire bio-diversity hierarchy at diverse scales of space and time and gen-erally "attach less weight to aesthetics, maximum yields, and profitability, and more to the long-range viability of whole systems and species."[3]

There have been many signs of greater concern for "whole sys-tems" in recent years. For example, there has been growing concern for underappreciated wildlife species and communities in the past two decades. Many state fish and game agencies, sensing shifts in their constituencies, have hired "nongame" biologists and empha-sized watchable (as opposed to just huntable) wildlife. Preservation of native species has been emphasized, ranging from intensified efforts to locate and protect relict prairie grasslands to identification of "heritage" strains of genetically pure trout in some states. Some of these initiatives are as reductionist in their way as the old game-oriented management approach — they just focus on different spe-cies. But they do at least broaden the emphasis of management to include more elements of the setting.

Of course, such activities have been going on for much longer than the three decades of the environmental era. Yellowstone alone, with its early decisions not to introduce any more nonnative fish species and to protect predators, provides its share of examples. And since the 1960s Yellowstone has been the site of one of the most im-portant case studies in the perils and controversies of applying con-servation biology to a large, wild, and globally loved landscape. The decision to stop killing elk in the park and the disagreement between the Craigheads and National Park Service managers and biologists were early skirmishes in a very long battle.

When the elk reductions ceased in 1967, the National Park Service leaders considered their options, none of which were too attractive. They could, for example, try to open the park to hunting as a way to control the number of elk, or they could try to find new homes for the "surplus" animals in other parts of the country. However, even had they approved of opening the park to hunting, it would have been a hard sell with a conservation community that considered the park inviolate by that sport, and even had they committed themselves to a massive trap-and-relocate program, other areas were no longer interested in importing elk. Thus Superintendent Jack Anderson and his chief biologist, Glen Cole, after consulting with the appropriate advisers and supervisors, launched what came to be known as the "natural regulation" policy. Cole's experience with wildlife and his reading of new thinking in population biology made him skeptical of the need to kill elk if they could be managed so that their migrations were not stopped at the park boundary. Anderson and Cole decided to find out if it was really necessary to reduce the numbers of elk. The population would be allowed to increase; its growth and the effects of the elk would be monitored to see if nature, rather than humans, would regulate the herd's size and behavior.[4]

Historically the National Park Service was notorious among land-management agencies for its poor commitment to research. The agency still has no legislative mandate that specifically requires research, though many people over the decades — George Wright, Starker Leopold, and others — have intuitively felt that research was essential to carrying out the park's explicit mandate to care for its resources. In fact the National Park Service had invested great sums on research in Yellowstone on several topics, the foremost being the "elk problem."[5] In 1970, as the new policy of natural regulation was taking hold in everything from dump closures to fisheries management, biologist Douglas Houston initiated another study of the northern range. Like the work of Adolph Murie on coyotes and of the Craigheads on grizzly bears, Houston's research, culminating in *The Northern Yellowstone Elk: Ecology and Management* (1982), is one of the milestones in the history of Yellowstone science and management.[6]

His reevaluation of the early historical record (described in Chapter 7) convinced him that elk were native to the park in good numbers and that they had always wintered there.

Among the new approaches that Houston used was a comparison, in collaboration with National Park Service biologist Mary Meagher, of 300 historical photographs of the park with modern retakes. The comparison revealed that many sites now pointed to as eroding due to ungulate overgrazing looked essentially the same in the 1870s and 1880s, well before the supposed population explosion of elk occurred. Other sites considered eroded due to overgrazing had indeed been overgrazed, either by livestock (as in the ranch lands added to the park north of Gardiner in the 1930s) or by the semidomesticated bison herd, whose movements were constrained by humans rather than by any normal migratory patterns.[7]

Houston pointed out that most earlier studies of "overgrazed" grasslands had focused on a small number of sites: "Range sample units and narrative accounts showed that earlier interpretations of deterioration of vegetation on the northern range were based primarily upon the decrease of aspen, the appearance and utilization of herbaceous vegetation on ridgetops and steep slopes characteristic of about 3% of the area, and the decrease of big sagebrush in the 1932 addition."[8] Again referring to the historical photos, he showed that those ridgetops and steep slopes looked the same very early in the park's history, prior to the supposed increase in elk numbers; those spots just weren't all that hospitable to vegetation.

This sort of revisionism was hard for many people to swallow. How could anybody doubt that this range was in terrible shape? Just look at it — a good rancher would be ashamed to let his land get into this condition! And that was Houston's point exactly: a good rancher wouldn't like it, but the goal of a good rancher is different from that of a good wildland manager. Houston pointed out that by the early 1900s North American rangelands had lost their immense herds of wild, free-ranging ungulates:

Unfortunately, all of these "grazing systems" were destroyed before they could be studied; the intensity of the biotic effects on vegetation from native ungulates at K_1 [defined as the range's self-defined carrying capacity] is outside the experience of most North American biologists. In fact, the disciplines of plant ecology and range and wildlife management evolved here in systems that were largely faunally impoverished.[9]

The wonderful irony Houston proposed was that perhaps Yellowstone, rather than being an example of an especially unhealthy landscape, was instead an example of a normal wild landscape; the problem was that such landscapes had become so rare that they seemed to our eyes somehow unnatural or wrong or in need of repair.

Houston and others made a distinction between a range's *economic* carrying capacity, that is, the number of grazers that commercial range managers might regard as the most appropriate, and *ecological* carrying capacity, the number of grazers that a range might support if left alone. Typically, and certainly in Yellowstone's case, the ecological carrying capacity results in more animals on the range than the economic carrying capacity would allow. Nature "manages" a grazing system in dramatically different ways than humans do, not only in terms of the number of animals but also in terms of their seasonal distribution. Accordingly, under natural regulation, the timing of the elk's movements across the range each year was the product of thousands of years of adjustment to the timing of vegetation growth on that range. Humans, for all their understanding of conditions on the land, were unable to allow domestic grazers the freedom of choice and movement required to let the landscape's own pace of change dictate the grazers' use of it.

Arguments over the validity of current interpretations of both economic and ecological carrying capacity continue; the traditional approaches to range management are being evaluated just as natural regulation and other approaches are debated. The Yellowstone debates are part of a much larger reconsideration of the management of livestock and wildlife grazing, with the park as a leading test case. Natural regulation was a perfect magnet for controversy.[10]

It seemed such a simple idea at first: let's see if nature can decide how many elk should live here. But as Houston and many others pointed out, some of the winter range was north of the park, down the Yellowstone River Valley. This elk problem was a Greater Yellowstone problem, in which a variety of agencies and many other interested parties, especially private landowners, would take part. But in addition to the scientific and geographical complications of this new approach, some very stimulating philosophical and semantic issues had to be dealt with.

Houston, for example, provided tests by which natural regulation could be judged. These included seeing if the increasing numbers of elk excluded other ungulates from the northern range or forced any plant species out of existence or otherwise caused demonstrable "range deterioration."[11] But predictably, as natural regulation, sometimes informally called a "great experiment," was discussed and criticized, these criteria were reconsidered.[12] Species had come and gone in Yellowstone for thousands of years before whites arrived; how would the disappearance of a plant species, much less a shift in its abundance, prove that something had gone wrong? And if we couldn't prove that something had gone wrong, how would we know if the "great experiment" was really succeeding? What, exactly, is natural? If we let nature make the decisions on how many elk there should be, how will we know if nature is doing okay? Or do we assume that because it is nature, it *must* be okay?

From 1967, when the elk reductions ceased, to 1979, when Houston's study ended, the herd grew from less than 5,000 to about 12,000. The 5,000 level had been achieved only by the slaughter of many thousands of elk in a herd that was routinely much larger, but what many people heard was simply that the Yellowstone elk herd was growing alarmingly fast. In the 1980s the herd underwent a second growth surge, to nearly 19,000 by 1988. After a 40 percent mortality in the fall and winter following the fires of 1988 (a combination of human hunting north of the park and winterkill inside and outside the park), the population recovered and has since remained close to 20,000.[13]

The herd's growth in the 1980s was the result of a series of wet summers that favored forage and a higher birthrate and a series of mild winters that reduced the typical seasonal mortality. Many other ungulate herds in the Greater Yellowstone Ecosystem increased for the same reasons, but only the northern herd made headlines.

The growth of the herd in the 1970s had made the potential for recreational hunting obvious, and by the 1980s the northern herd was supporting a profitable, commercially successful hunt, with very high success rates and sizable harvests year after year. In the 1980s, through the inspired leadership and fund-raising of the Rocky Mountain Elk Foundation and the cooperation of several state and federal agencies, thousands of acres of additional winter range were acquired north of the park, which encouraged much of the growth in the herd during that decade.

It is impossible to separate ungulate management from other issues. Since the mid-1970s the food habits of Yellowstone's grizzly bears have reflected the growth of three prey species populations — elk, bison, and cutthroat trout — that had been suppressed until the natural regulation policy was initiated. As the years passed, more and more bears ate these animals.[14] By the mid-1980s the Inter-agency Grizzly Bear Study Team emphasized the extreme importance of elk as a grizzly bear food (as carrion and as live prey), saying that the bear, protected under the Endangered Species Act, now depended upon a large elk population.[15]

Also by the 1980s the community of Gardiner, at the park's north entrance, had added an additional season to their tourist trade, because the hunting season for the larger elk herd was so popular and successful. Ecology and economy were providing new incentives to tolerate a large elk population. As the natural regulation policy continued, the stakes became higher for all concerned, whatever the scientific or public mood might be about common perceptions of overgrazing.

There was still a strong certainty in the scientific community and in the region that Yellowstone was terribly overgrazed. Ranchers, under fire from environmentalists for fostering poor grazing practices and for paying such cheap grazing fees on public lands, lashed out at the park's natural regulation policy as an implicit attack on their values. Conservative politicians used the Yellowstone "elk problem" in antifederal rhetoric, and people opposed to the bison hunt or grizzly bear management or any other remotely related issue routinely trotted out overgrazing as a backup proof of the National Park Service's malfeasance. A variety of journalists and other commentators, including Alston Chase in his angrily antienvironmentalist book *Playing God in Yellowstone,* also helped keep the subject before the public.

In 1986 Congress authorized funding to "start a study on Yellowstone to see whether there is evidence of overgrazing" and "what should be done to avoid that."[16] The University of Wyoming–National Park Service Research Center administered the selection of the nonagency researchers to work with a variety of park and forest service scientists in the largest research program ever focused on a Yellowstone wildlife issue. In the first decade of that initiative, more peer-reviewed scientific research findings about the northern range were published, especially in the leading ecological journals, than had appeared in the previous century. More than 90 percent of these publications suggested that the vegetation of the northern range was not overgrazed, that the range's ecological processes seemed to be working, and that traditional definitions of overgrazing did not seem applicable here.

The studies addressed the question of the prehistoric presence of large mammals in Yellowstone. Paleontological research established that the major fauna of the park had indeed been there for thousands of years. Most of the elk bones found in the Lamar Cave site in the lower Lamar River Valley, the heart of the park's northern winter range, were of juveniles, suggesting that in the distant pre-Euramerican past, elk used that site as a calving area, as they do now.[17] Several investigators used archeology to investigate wildlife abundance in pre-1872 Yellowstone, but no agreement was reached. Elaborating on the view that ungulates were rare in the park prehistorically, one ecological investigator pointed out the rarity of elk in regional archeological sites before the past few hundred years and proposed that Indian hunting and predators kept the number of large ungulates extremely low in the park area prehistorically.[18] On the other hand, new archeological investigations in and near the park revealed a previously unreported variety of both ungulate and predator bones (representing most of the species that are common in the park area today).[19] The most thorough review of the early historical record, though it fell short of establishing specific numbers of animals, indicated that in the early and mid-1800s many ungulates and their predators inhabited the park area and the GYE, reinforcing Houston's earlier contentions that elk had wintered and summered in the park area before 1872.[20] And all of these studies of pre-1900 Yellowstone heightened awareness of the complexities of Native American effects on the landscape.

The greatest concentration of research effort was on the grazing issue. By a wide set of criteria the grasslands of the northern range were judged not to be overgrazed. Indeed, as had been demonstrated by studies of other wildland grazing systems in Africa, heavy ungulate use of the grasslands actually stimulated plant growth and enhanced various nutritional qualities of common grasses.[21] Among the most interesting findings was that grazing in some cases *increased* plant diversity. In some fenced exclosures on the northern range, where ungulates were unable to graze, tall-growing plants grew enough to shade out the shorter species. Where plants were grazed, taller species were kept too short to shade out other species.[22] What was popularly viewed as a fairly simple thing — eater and eaten — was in fact elegantly involved.

In fact, what most of these studies indicated, which may be more important than any of the specific findings, was the great inherent complexity and variability of the system. Not only the amount but the timing of spring precipitation was shown to have dramatic effects on forage production. Again and again climatic variation in any given year was found to be central to the fates of the vegetation and the grazers.[23]

Erosion studies further weakened the case that elk were the primary cause of heavy sediment loads in park streams in the spring, which had been a sore point among local fishermen for some years. A major analysis of the erosive lands in the Lamar and Yellowstone river drainages indicated that most of the sediment came from steep, unstable slopes that were not even used as winter range.[24] Studies of erosion rates around ponds across the northern range failed to find any evidence of accelerated erosion after the turn of the century, when elk numbers had supposedly increased and could have contributed more to erosion.[25] Left largely unstudied were the effects of ungulates on riverbank erosion rates, though one unpublished study indicates very high erosion levels along the lower parts of the Lamar River on the elk winter range.[26]

The historical biography of aspen was clarified, but its role in the elk controversy was not resolved. Paleontological studies indicated that aspen has always been relatively rare in the park; in historical times it seems never to have occupied more than 4 percent of the northern range.[27] Yellowstone, it seems, is marginal aspen habitat and will not host the densities of robust aspen found in many locations farther south. The decline of the aspen to half or less of its distribution in the park since the early 1900s has most often been attributed to ungulates overbrowsing new shoots as they emerge from the ground, but it appears that the aspen story is much more complicated than that.

The bark of almost all aspen trees on the northern range is scarred black from the ground to about eight feet up; elk are fond of aspen bark, and their chewing on these trees resulted in this heavy scarring. One researcher pointed out that in photographs of northern range aspen from the 1890s, the trunks of most of the aspen are white all the way to the ground, providing, according to this researcher, evidence that elk were not as abundant on the northern range back then.[28] However, other researchers, as already mentioned, established that by 1883 elk were in fact quite numerous on the northern range, where they wintered by the thousands, so something must have been keeping them from chewing the aspen as energetically then as they would in later years.

Perhaps as important, in those photographs of aspen in the 1890s, practically all of the trees were very young. This went against the unspoken but universal assumption that prior to the park's establishment in 1872, the park area was more or less an aspen farm, with new generations of aspen trees appearing regularly. Tree-ring studies of aspen in the 1990s proved otherwise: practically all of the aspen now growing old and dying on the northern range were "born" in one short period between about 1870 and 1895. This seemed to suggest that some combination of factors, almost certainly including elk browsing, must have prevented aspen from growing to tree height prior to 1872, and it thus provided circumstantial evidence that elk were fairly common in the park area in the early 1800s.

But what changed to make the northern range more hospitable to aspen during that period between 1870 and 1895? Fire history studies revealed that there were large fires in the years just before the park's establishment: fire is an important part of the aspen renewal process. Also, other studies suggested that the climate in Yellowstone was wetter and therefore unusually hospitable to aspen growth in the period between 1870 and 1895. And what a wonderful coincidence it was that, just as aspen found it easier to grow in the first years of the new park, beaver numbers were decimated by trapping. Ecologists recognized that a number of factors must have been working in concert here, just as some other combination of factors today prevents aspen from escaping from its shrub height and growing into trees on the northern range.[29]

We are left to wonder if the beautiful aspen groves scattered so tastefully around the northern range may owe their existence to some combination of ecological and human forces that we may not feel obliged to duplicate if our goal is to preserve ecological processes in the park. That is to say, yes, the aspen are a beautiful and popular element of Yellowstone's landscape aesthetics, but no, their diminished numbers aren't necessarily proof that the elk population is out of control.

Willows provide an even more intriguing puzzle than aspen, partly because there are about twenty-four species of willows in the park and too little is known of their ecology here. The northern range hosts less than one percent of the park's willow communities (most are south of Yellowstone Lake, at higher elevations). But declines in willows on the northern range were noted in the early 1900s, especially during the great drought of the 1930s. As with aspen, these declines were attributed to an elk overpopulation.

In this 1893 photograph, soldiers march through Pleasant Valley, near Tower Junction in northern Yellowstone. Note the large stands of tall willows along the three straight watercourses that were apparently irrigation ditches; this was a hayfield managed by the local hotel keeper. The disappearance of tall willows from northern Yellowstone's ungulate winter range has been cited as "proof" that elk have overpopulated the area. Since wolves were restored to the park in 1995, however, many willow stands have grown tall again, leading some observers to state that wolves have restored a missing "balance" between vegetation and wildlife. Other observers point to a more complex combination of factors, including climate, as causing the resurgence of tall willows. Haynes Foundation Collection, Montana Historical Foundation, Helena, Montana.

Photographs taken from the 1870s to the 1890s showed much heavier willow growth in some northern range locations, and this was seen by some observers as proof that elk became more numerous and overbrowsed the willows. Also as with aspen, however, elk were more than numerous enough to have browsed the willows short in the 1890s, but something prevented them from doing so. Not surprisingly, recent researchers focused on possible changes in climate. They noted that the most dramatic declines in willows occurred during and after the drought of the 1930s, and that no significant additional declines have occurred since the 1950s, despite the higher elk numbers of the most recent decades.[30]

Plants are not defenseless. As gardeners know, many species have evolved with strong mechanisms to protect themselves from grazing or browsing. Both willow and aspen researchers are investigating the possibility that the drying climate of Yellowstone over the past century has made these species less robust and less able to produce the "secondary compounds" of chemicals that reduce their palatability. Predictably, arguments now continue over those compounds, but the credibility of the simplistic old "too many elk killed the willows" argument has been undermined by a far more complex hypothesis that acknowledges more of the forces that were at work in the landscape.[31]

But declines in northern-range willows and aspen pose interesting questions for managers. Willows and aspen may be minority plant communities, but they are disproportionately important to a diversity of animal species (a number of birds and insects, for example) that would not inhabit the northern range at all were it not for these plants. The decline in these plant species gives rise to concerns about reduced biodiversity on the northern range. On the other hand, recent studies of elk carcasses revealed that the presence of a carcass (whether it died of old age, predation, or winterkill) greatly increases the abundance and diversity of the several dozen beetle species that live on such carrion. Even the dung of ungulates hosts surprisingly complex life communities. In our search for Yellowstone, should we prefer pretty aspen or magnificent elk? Should we prefer songbirds or carcass beetles? If we make decisions — that is, if we choose one species or group of species over another — we are deciding on the fate of many other species that are hooked into these ecological communities. Tracking such possible tradeoffs in biodiversity is complex enough; deciding that one set of species is somehow superior to another may prove impossible.[32]

The great challenge facing those concerned with protecting the biodiversity in a reserve like Yellowstone is coming to terms with ecological complexity and the consequences of assuming we can manipulate it with impunity. It seems most probable that what is occurring on the northern range is not the entire disappearance of some species, but a shift in the relative abundance of many species, something that happens constantly in nature. With the present abundance of ungulates on the northern range, aspen and willows may decline from sparse to scarce, just as the beetles and other scavengers may increase. Whether any species will entirely vanish may seem unlikely now, but managers are still left to make value judgments about allowing it to happen, even if it is in some ultimate sense a "natural" disappearance.

The beaver, which still inhabit the park in numerous locations, continue to be a fairly minor but very interesting sideshow in the northern range debates. Some investigators, and many casual observers, continued to point to the decline of beaver from high numbers in the 1920s as proof of elk overpopulation, but others claimed that the beaver story was more complicated. As explained in Chapter 5, the beaver were trapped heavily in the 1870s, and their numbers were suppressed well after that. But around 1900, almost certainly in response to their sudden protection from poaching, and perhaps more in response to the rich crop of young aspen that had grown up in the 1880s and 1890s, the beaver experienced a population irruption. In the early 1920s, at the invitation of the National Park Service, E. R. Warren studied the situation because park managers were afraid that the *beaver* were going to wipe out the aspen (this was before the elk became the usual suspects in aspen declines). The beaver in fact were killing all the aspen within range of their ponds and dens, and that alone could have accounted for the decline of aspen over the next few decades.[33] Then the elk stepped in and clipped the new aspen shoots before they could become trees. Many recent writers have read of Warren's population counts from the 1920s, which occurred at the peak of a human-induced increase in beaver numbers, and naively assumed that his study somehow reveals the "right" numbers of beaver for Yellowstone.[34]

Yellowstone's bison herd, once released from tight control in the 1960s, grew in even greater proportion to its suppressed number than did the elk herd. The 397 bison counted in 1967 became 2,800 by 1988, and in the 1990s has sometimes exceeded 4,000. But long before then their increases had made them a Greater Yellowstone issue.[35] In 1917 it was discovered that some Yellowstone bison were host to a bacterial organism, *Brucella abortus,* which produces the disease commonly known as brucellosis, a cause of spontaneous abortion in cattle.[36] American livestock growers have spent much of this century in a herculean and very expensive campaign to eradicate this disease from all livestock, and the presence of the disease in park bison has always been a source of contention between the park's managers and its neighbors.

The great wildlife slaughter of the 1870s and the continued poaching of the remaining bison into the 1890s had effectively destroyed the animals' earlier migratory patterns and distribution. After several decades of bison husbandry at the Lamar Buffalo Ranch, herds were reestablished in their historical ranges in the park, and as they increased in number in the 1970s, they began to move down park valleys in the winter. If left unobstructed, they might have gradually recolonized their old winter ranges beyond the boundaries.

But some percentage of these traveling animals carried brucellosis, and though it had never been established that wild bison could transmit the disease to domestic livestock, many observers considered it a real threat. The park staff objected to the wholesale slaughter of the bison in an attempt to get rid of brucellosis, so in 1968 the National Park Service adopted a boundary control program that allowed for shooting of bison that migrated beyond the park.[37]

Another serious problem was the bison's tendency to damage property: walking through fences, goring livestock, and otherwise disrupting long-established agricultural practices and property rights. Bison are stolid, determined migrators, and though they may be temporarily "hazed" away from an area, they will return and eventually continue on their way. The park boundary was not of concern to them, except as it seemed to host an unusual number of anxious humans who kept getting in their way.

When bison shooting began on Yellowstone's boundaries, especially outside the north entrance, along the migration corridor that followed the Yellowstone River Valley northward, public reaction was strong and decisively negative. At first only a few animals were killed: three in 1974, one in 1978. But even those modest numbers were worrisome enough that in 1978, Department of the Interior officials in Washington rescinded the park managers' authority to kill bison, apparently in fear of public reaction against the slaughter of this great national symbol. But because the state of Montana had a legal responsibility to livestock owners, who had worked long and hard to have the state declared free of brucellosis, and because even a single bison can do thousands of dollars' worth of property damage very quickly, the park's rangers and the state's wardens tried all sorts of means of keeping the animals in the park.

Montana officials were rightly miffed that the Department of the Interior had more or less abdicated responsibility for the bison by denying Yellowstone staff the freedom to kill the animals before they left the park and became the state's problem. In 1984 state wardens shot eighty-eight bison that left the park, and the controversy boiled over into the national media. In 1985, with little expectation of a public response, the state declared the bison a game animal and found itself with thousands of applications for hunting permits; here was yet another bison constituency, sportsmen who wanted to participate in a rare and (in its more moderate forms, at least) honored tradition of North American hunting.

The winter following the fires of 1988, almost all nine hundred of the park's northern bison herd moved down the Yellowstone River drainage and either left the park or came near leaving. More than five hundred were shot during a theatrical hunting season that subjected the bison, animal rights activists, sportsmen, state and federal employees, and other interested parties to intensive media coverage. The entire herd was now familiar with the road to gentler winter ranges, and unless all of the animals were killed, the herd would retain that memory. Migrations of bison into Montana have continued to occur both to the north and to the west as state and federal agencies have struggled to develop a management plan. In the winter of 1996-97 more than 1,000 were killed in the midst of the most bitter political controversy in the history of Yellowstone bison management. The bison, so long a symbol of a great conservation success in Yellowstone, have presented us with yet another complication in the search for Yellowstone, and in the struggle to manage far-ranging wildlife herds in an ecosystem where the political boundaries have nothing to do with the ecological ones.[38]

Generally lost in the media attention on this controversy is the reality that the elk herds of Greater Yellowstone also carry brucellosis. In the northern herd, there is a low incidence of infection, with a percentage or two thought to have been exposed to the disease, but with twenty or more elk for every bison on the northern range, that is still a lot of animals with the disease. In the southern Yellowstone elk herd, some of which summer on the same park ranges as many bison but winter on the feed grounds of the National Elk Refuge near Jackson, Wyoming, brucellosis is about as common as in the Yellowstone bison. While the state of Montana and Montana's livestock growers see a problem only with Yellowstone bison, ecosystem-minded observers see a much larger problem. Brucellosis in elk is tolerated in good part because the elk are a well-established recreational crop, bringing sportsmen's dollars to the region. A single bison wandering near a ranch brings great cries of alarm, though hundreds of elk migrate by the same spot annually with no comparable alarm; there is no serious talk about trying to test Greater Yellowstone's 90,000 elk for the disease, much less slaughter those that test positive for brucellosis. Indeed, some biologists believe that if the bison were all killed off, the disease would disappear from the elk too — that the bison are responsible for keeping the disease alive throughout Greater Yellowstone. But nobody can prove that without actually wiping out the bison, and the elk that concentrate at the Wyoming feed grounds like the National Elk Refuge each winter seem to have no trouble keeping their infection rates high without much help from bison.

Even if there were a magic, foolproof vaccine that would cure the bison of brucellosis (and no existing vaccine is regarded as trustworthy even at protecting uninfected animals), in time it seems probable that the bison would simply reacquire the disease from the elk, and no real progress would have been made. Until some broader initiative is launched to deal with brucellosis throughout the ecosystem (or to accept its presence and then develop a management plan for keeping livestock separate from the wild ungulates), Yellowstone managers will probably have to "manage" bison — whether that means shipping them to slaughter, shooting them, or trying to keep them in the park when they want to leave — with relatively little reason to think that this problem will be solved. The state of Montana will have to engage in equally unpopular activities: shooting bison that "escape" from the park before they can approach cattle or cause property damage. And a growing portion of the public, with relatively little sympathy for the concerns of livestock growers but with enormous sympathy for the bison, will complain that these wild animals, an especially abused symbol of our North American heritage, should have a place on public lands outside of Yellowstone National Park.

But for all the attention that bison, aspen, beaver, and some other Yellowstone species get, only one animal is consistently on the minds of those concerned about the long term fate of the northern range. Again and again since the initiation of the natural-regulation policy thirty years ago, the same question has been asked: are these elk going to keep increasing in number forever? And now, after all the recent research, the answer is forthcoming, from several quarters, that the elk are about as numerous as they can get, unless life gets easier for them on the existing winter ranges (as might happen if the climate warmed) or additional summer and winter ranges are added (as happened in the 1980s when historic winter ranges north of the park were again made available to them).

In fact, many things control the elk numbers in Yellowstone. Studies have shown that the elk population is "density dependent," meaning that its growth slows as its numbers increase. As population densities increase, fewer cow elk become pregnant, and fewer elk calves (and eventually fewer adults) survive the winter. A variety of these population-controlling mechanisms kick in, population growth slows or stops or is reversed, and the adjustments continue, in response to the ever-changing environmental conditions. What all this means is death, of course: elk growing old and losing their strength, newborn elk being ambushed by late spring blizzards, and many other hard facts of life in the wild. The northern Yellowstone elk herd, like any wildlife population, is composed at any given time of that moment's survivors. The herd size will fluctuate, sometimes dramatically, depending upon winter weather (the foremost control), human hunting north of the park, the timing and amount of precipitation during the critical growing season of summer forage, and other factors.[39]

The most intriguing of these other factors may be predation, which has been of special interest because of the long campaign to save the Yellowstone grizzly bears and the more recent one to restore wolves to the park. One of the tenets of game management philosophy for many years, one that many of us grew up with, was that hunting was necessary to control animal populations because their natural predators had been wiped out. This had a nice ecological wholeness in theory and gave generations of hunters (including me) a warm feeling of usefulness because we were helping to maintain the "balance of nature." This view does appear to be true in some cases, but its application to Yellowstone has always been less than trustworthy. In too many modern accounts, the park is implicitly presented as a predatorless system. It was common knowledge that the elk population was too large because we "wiped out their predators." One of the most popular and unfortunate justifications offered by wolf-restoration advocates in the environmental groups has been that wolves will "help control the burgeoning numbers of elk."

A number of studies, as well as abundant casual observations, have shown that even before the reintroduction of wolves in 1995, Yellowstone's predators were busy and effective. Every year grizzly bears, black bears, and coyotes typically kill a third of the new elk calves before they are a month old.[40] Another 20 percent or more die from predation, exposure, or other causes before they are a year old.[41] Of course adult elk are also preyed upon, by grizzly bears, mountain lions, coyotes, and, when they leave the park, by hunters. Whether the newly restored wolves will add to the total elk mortality or just replace some of the present predation is one of the many interesting questions we are now waiting to have answered.

RESTORATION HAS been an important part of the management of modern Yellowstone, and it has reached well beyond the restoration of native species like wolves, into the restoration of native processes. By the 1970s it was well known that fire was one of the most important forces shaping the life communities of most North American landscapes. If national parks were to represent such landscapes, they would have to find a way to include fire in the reasonable illusion. In 1972, after many years of experimentation with fire as a management tool by national forest silviculturists and a few years of study in some other parks, Yellowstone adopted a policy of allowing lightning-caused fires to burn in about 15 percent of the park's backcountry.[42] This acreage was soon increased to include most of the park, and for sixteen years the program was widely regarded as a success; many small fires and a few larger ones were allowed to burn, and restoration of fire seemed a good thing all around.

Even before the fires of 1988, however, it was recognized that the fire regime did not function quite so benignly in the long haul.[43] Instead of a patchwork of forest being burned here and there, eventually replacing all stands of trees, in many years there was little burning and in occasional years huge areas burned. As with the occasional harsh winter that knocks down an ungulate population or the spring flood that reshapes stream channels or the windstorm that abruptly redesigns the forest canopy, fire was an episodic force, occasionally introducing major jolts to the system. The fire-return interval of the park's lodgepole pine forests, that is, the time between major fires, was estimated at 250 to 400 years. Dendrochronological (tree-ring) studies have shown that Yellowstone last experienced really large burns in the early 1700s, with some fairly good-sized ones in the mid-1800s. In 1988 about a third of the park's lodgepole pines were more than 250 years old.[44]

The fires of 1988 were often blamed on a century of fire suppression, which had allowed natural fuels to build up to an explosive level. Even people who supported letting fires burn in national parks said this; after all, it was a wonderful cautionary tale of the consequences of uninformed human interference with nature. But fire suppression, though it may have had some significant effects on park grasslands, probably didn't affect the forests, because we didn't have the necessary aerial technology to fight forest fires effectively until after World War II. The forty years of suppression was too short a time (in the lodgepole pine forests' 250- to 400-year fire-return interval) to produce such a spectacular fire season.[45] Yellowstone's vast forests seem to burn or not burn depending upon their age and the infrequent occurrence of extreme climatic conditions; the forests were getting old in 1988, and the climatic conditions have rarely been as extreme in the park's written history as they were that summer. A combination of the park's worst drought and a series of dry cold fronts with high winds set the stage for many small fires and seven major fire complexes that would occupy public attention and the waking hours of exhausted firefighters into late summer. On July 21, when the total acreage included only 17,000 acres, park managers went into full suppression mode, meaning that all fires, whether lightning- or human-caused, were fought as hard as the equipment and conditions would allow. The fires ultimately affected 793,000 acres in the park and more than 200,000 acres beyond its boundaries.[46]

More than 25,000 people were involved in fighting the fires, as were dozens of trucks and aircraft, at a total cost of more than $120 million, the largest single firefighting effort in American history. This huge effort probably did not significantly reduce the total acreage burned, but it heroically saved almost every building threatened by fire in or near the park. By September, when rain and snow put the fires down for the winter (a largely true local sarcasm was that "we throw money at the fires until the rain puts them out"), a national uproar was already under way, not only about future fire policy on public lands but also about the whole idea of managing wildlands in the face of such unruly, unpredictable events. The fires of 1988 opened a new round of acrimonious debate in the search for Yellowstone.

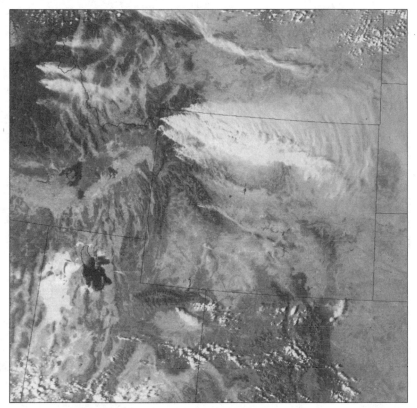

On September 7, 1988, the smoke plume from the Yellowstone fires extended across Wyoming (states are outlined in black) and was beginning to stack up against the Black Hills of western South Dakota. Smoke plumes from other fires in Montana, Idaho, Utah, and Colorado are also visible in this Landsat image. *NASA/Ames Research Center*

Much of what was discussed in the review of the fire season was news rather than history: comparatively minor issues of whether this fire-truck driver really had to go wheeling out across that pristine meadow or whether that ranger facilitated or hindered the use of bulldozers on a certain fire front. But Greater Yellowstone issues were important as well, because the fires roared across the landscape with no regard for agency jurisdiction. In the next few years, as all federal agencies produced new fire-management plans, it did seem that coordination was improving.

Historian Roderick Nash once wrote that the Disney film *Bambi* did "more to shape American attitudes towards fire in wilderness ecosystems than all the scientific papers ever published on the subject," and *Bambi* was also a factor in the public reaction to the fires of 1988.[47] Though Yellowstone's leading fire ecologists could find nothing inherently "wrong" in the effects of the fires on the landscape, and though an amazingly small number of the popular large animals died, National Park Service staff fought hard against the rhetoric of "destruction" — the idea that the fires of 1988 were somehow "bad" or "damaging" to a landscape that had been in good part created by fire.

The fires stirred up all the old debates over what was and was not natural. Some critics trotted out the already discredited idea that the park's forests had been burned extensively by Indians, but other, more interesting questions were raised. For example, were the fires in any practical sense "natural"? On the one hand, three of the seven largest fires, including the very largest, were human-caused, but on the other hand, lightning struck many times within the boundaries of existing burns. To the independent panel of ecologists who reviewed the effects of the fires the following winter, those facts suggested that even if humans hadn't been there in 1988 (or if only American Indians had been there, living as they had a few hundred years earlier), the park area would have experienced fire on a similar scale.[48] The precise boundaries and locations of the burns would have been different, but the overall scale and ecological effects would have been the same.

Another intriguing question had to do with scale as well: even if the fires were "natural," are fires on that scale still appropriate to the GYE? They may have been a fine thing when the entire western United States was totally wild and under the less dramatically intrusive management of the American Indians; a million burned acres here and there in such a huge area was probably not a great calamity. But now that Greater Yellowstone is an isolated wildland, can we afford to have such a high percentage of the remaining wildland burn all at once?[49] The 1988 fire bosses might have answered, well, no, we can't — but we didn't have a lot of choice, either.

Many changes in park management policy were proposed in the aftermath of the fires, but all the traditional position holders in the management debates, recognizing that the fires provided an opportunity, were competing for attention. As a result, opposing pressures were canceled out and the more radical views eliminated (these ranged from "You should never let anything burn" to "You should have let the buildings burn, too"). Eventually the park adopted a new fire-management plan that contained some refinements and corrections but still gave managers latitude to let big fires burn if they had the fortitude to exercise that option. The problem remains, however, that Yellowstone's forest processes have been largely driven by the epic, once-a-century-or-more fires, like the one in 1988. If we want to fully restore fire here, those are the fires we most need. But who is prepared to incorporate fires on that scale into the formal management plan of a national park?[50]

THE RESTORATION of Yellowstone's large carnivores has raised some of the same questions the fires did. The Endangered Species Act requires managing agencies to develop a recovery plan for every listed species, and debates over the grizzly bear plan reveal the same tensions over scale in an ecosystem that seems more and more cramped as we learn more about it. Federal managers point with some pride (and a fair amount of sniping from dissenters) to the recent improvement in the status of the GYE grizzly bears; the population, now generally believed to be between 250 and 350, but perhaps higher, has come a long way from the apparent low numbers following the dump closures. However, there are plenty of reasons for pessimism about the long-term prospects of these bears. Population modelers have argued that to ensure sufficient genetic diversity and to be large enough to handle the occasional random disaster (like a new disease), a grizzly bear population needs to be about 2,000 animals.[51]

No one is proposing to pack that many grizzly bears into the park or even the whole GYE; the park has reached its carrying capacity for grizzly bears, and even the whole GYE probably couldn't contain more than a quarter of that number. Each bear needs a lot of space. The idea is that we must ensure geographical connections via migration corridors between the various grizzly bear populations, especially between Yellowstone's and the populations farther north in Montana and Idaho. If all the bears of the lower forty-eight could be connected to some extent, the population might be of sufficient size. This idea sounds good in principle, but it is theoretical and untested in the field; there is no evidence that the bears will use migration corridors, and there is even question if the risks posed to bears by genetic isolation are as serious as imagined.[52]

In the meantime private land in the GYE is being developed at a fast pace, and demands on its public land resources are ever-increasing. As ecologist William Romme has stated, the grizzly bear has come to epitomize the loss of Greater Yellowstone's wildland values through gradual attrition rather than abrupt violence:

> Erosion of biological diversity, loss of open spaces, diminishment of air quality, and most of the other degradations that we are concerned about usually occur gradually, by small, barely perceptible increments. . . . I think that even the extinction of a charismatic endangered species like the grizzly bear probably would occur over a long enough period of time (a few decades) that most people would get used to it rather than be stimulated to take action. My darkest fear is not that the earth's ecological systems will one day collapse; but that they will be progressively diminished in richness and in beauty, and that the mass of humanity will not even realize what we have lost.[53]

The park's most recent foray into restoration has been the return of gray wolves. In 1995 the first fourteen were brought in, held in acclimation pens for two months to lessen the chance that they would run a long way when freed, then released in northern Yellowstone. The first year of the restoration process was a great success. Two litters were born, and four separate functioning packs emerged.[54]

From left, biologist Mike Phillips, Maintenance Supervisor Jim Evanoff, U.S. Fish and Wildlife Service Director Mollie Beattie, Superintendent Mike Finley, and Interior Secretary Bruce Babbitt carry the first wolf to its acclimation pen, January 1995. *NPS photo by Jim Peaco*

The returned wolves immediately became visitor attractions in the park. These animals are a powerful new presence in the nation's consciousness of nature; they are enormously marketable commodities, and the public is bombarded with prints, sculpture, clothing, and other wolf-related merchandise, especially in regional stores and in park gift shops. A remarkable change in public attitudes either occurred quite recently or occurred some time ago and has suddenly been revealed. Robert Cahn's 1968 survey in the *Christian Science Monitor,* summarized at the end of Chapter 10, revealed that many people supported protection of predators in the parks; that survey may have been telling us that the public's interest in predators had gone beyond the wildlife management profession's. The results of Yellowstone's first wolf-related opinion survey, conducted in 1985, were a shock to biologists and managers, who assumed that the wolf still suffered from its ancient image as a demon among wildlife: visitors favored active efforts to restore wolves by a three-to-one margin. Six of every seven visitors agreed that "a presence of wolves would improve the Yellowstone experience."[55] Since then many more surveys have confirmed that public mood; even in the states around Yellowstone, a majority of people favor wolves, another sign of the slowly fading hold of traditional values on those areas.[56]

ELK, BISON, fire, wolves, grizzly bears, and many other elements of the Yellowstone setting continue to fuel the debate over natural regulation. That term is now so symbolically overloaded by controversy that ecologist Mark Boyce has suggested we replace it with "ecological process management," a term that may more clearly reflect the complexity of what is going on (though it will be no more comprehensible to the public than natural regulation).[57] Those opposed to letting nature have as much freedom as it now has in Yellowstone insist that we need new policies with "standards of naturalness" to tell us just how much freedom the ecological system will be allowed.[58] When such standards are described, however, they sound more like "arbitrary limits on variability," which is to say they sound a lot like Park Superintendent Horace Albright's new predator policy of sixty years ago: we won't kill predators unless we absolutely have to, and oh, by the way, we absolutely had to kill 145 in Yellowstone. We have a very poor track record in our decisions about what is natural and what is not in Yellowstone, and our view of nature's capacity for variation has almost always been too narrow.

And so Yellowstone National Park, like many other nature reserves, is caught in a crossfire. On one side are people convinced that the park is doomed because its current policy relies on a nature that no longer exists as it did before whites arrived in the New World and altered everything. Too much is missing that made prehistoric Yellowstone a vital and durable ecosystem. We simply must step in and take charge or we risk losing much of what we value about Yellowstone.

On the other side are people convinced that "things" should not be what we value most about Yellowstone; rather than focusing on individual species, we should concentrate on the processes that support all species. At first glance this would be judged the riskier course because it surrenders the control that humans have tried to exercise over nature for thousands of years. But these advocates celebrate greater gains: without trying the natural regulation policy for thirty years, we would never have tested so many of the beliefs that guided earlier generations of managers and scientists, beliefs that have now been proven erroneous.

Most of the recent research on the Yellowstone landscape, whether paleontological, archeological, or ecological, challenges the view of the park as a hopelessly damaged natural system. It suggests that "although humans have altered the ecology of the GYE, the ecosystem is nevertheless functioning and worthy of perpetuation."[59] I find this view persuasive. What has Yellowstone lost that cripples it? What was here 200 or 500 or 1,000 years ago that is now gone and that by its absence dooms the park's ecosystem to collapse? Climate still provides the driving force behind annual variation in forage, the pace of erosion, and the return of periodic fire. Once the wolf is fully restored, Yellowstone will be the only large landscape in the lower forty-eight states with its full suite of native predator and prey species, and even without wolves the other predators were hard at work here, with great effect on the prey. Indians are gone, as are their influences on the ecosystem, but Indian fire was not a significant influence in the forests of the park, and suggestions that Indians were a significant control on wildlife populations are still just suggestions, unsupported by convincing evidence. And what proof do we have that the ecosystem cannot function without Indian influences? The place is changing, and many of those changes (such as the decline of willow or the growing press of humanity) demand our attention and study, but nature seems in no danger of self-destructing in Yellowstone.

In a recent essay on the natural regulation policy in Yellowstone, the philosopher Holmes Rolston wrote of seeing the wholeness of an ecosystem not as perfect or imperfect but as a continuum. The goal, he proposed, is not absolute; the goal is the greatest possible level of "spontaneous nature" at work:

> Compared with pristine nature, there is diminished naturalness, but the naturalness that remains is not illusory. Some processes were never tampered with; even restored processes, though minus their original historical genesis, are relatively more natural. A broken arm, reset and healed, is relatively more natural than an artificial limb, though both have been medically manipulated. The arm, decades later, is not a "reasonable illusion" of a pristine arm. Except for hairline bone scars it may be indistinguishable from the arm nature gave. Likewise with a restored forest or range, the historical genesis has been partially interrupted. But henceforth, deliberately put back in place, spontaneous nature takes over as before. Trees blow over in storms, coyotes hunt ground squirrels, lightning causes burns, natural selection resumes.[60]

The history of Yellowstone reveals a recurring mistake of confidence, with each generation imagining itself on the brink of solving the "problem," whether that problem is bears, elk, or any of the park's other perennial mysteries. Superintendent Rogers didn't need to have Aldo Leopold study the elk, because he already knew what the problem was. The regional newspapers' editorials and letters columns are full of offhand assertions by people who are equally sure they can fix Yellowstone. The obvious lesson may be that we are a long way from solving the problem partly because we have failed even to agree on what the problem is. The less obvious lesson may be that the search for solutions is probably more important than the solutions themselves.

The Holocene, a geologically brief but singularly dynamic period, has come rolling down the millennia toward us, busily making and remaking this landscape, fussing with a million details along the way. Early on it picked up humans and bounced them around on its surface until they became part of a mix that was never the same from year to year, much less from century to century. One hundred and twenty-five years ago we inherited this great humming thing, with its sprawling network of habitats and episodes and Little Ice Ages and evolutionary trajectories — its irresistible momentum for change. In 1872 we stepped out in front of all that surging power and announced that we were in charge. Ever since then we have imagined ourselves wise enough to control it and have rushed to judge what is wrong with it. And every time we looked hard enough, we discovered that there was more wrong with our judgment than with Yellowstone.

13 | IMAGINING YELLOWSTONE

I N T H E S U M M E R O F 1996, three modern Yellowstone explorers, Lee Whittlesey, Paul Rubinstein, and Mike Stevens, finished up a remarkable project, the identification and cataloging of Yellowstone's waterfalls. Previous lists of the park's waterfalls totaled 50 or so, but after many years of haunting the park's less-traveled watersheds, these three men catalogued 130. Whittlesey later said, "Any one of these waterfalls, if located anywhere else, would probably be the entire reason for an entire park. But here, 'amidst objects so grand as to strain conception,' most do not even have names."[1] There are hot waterfalls and cold waterfalls, lacy cascades and roaring torrents. Some waterfalls are not seen by people for years at a time. In a remote corner of the Grand Canyon of the Yellowstone River, miles from the nearest trail and not even visible from the air, there is a waterfall that emerges from a cave on the steep canyon wall, drops several stories, and vanishes into the rock below.

Yellowstone has long been described as the home of roughly 200 of the world's 300 active geysers. That seemed distinction enough, but a small cadre of passionate "geyser gazers," in their relentless exploration of the park's dozens of thermal areas, say the total is more like 800.[2]

In these and many other ways we are reminded that the search for Yellowstone is still fresh and vital, still revealing new wonders. Yellowstone exemplifies historian Richard White's description of the American West as "the most strongly *imagined* section of the United States."[3] It seemed perfectly appropriate that the opening scene of Ken Burns's epic 1996 PBS documentary *The West* was of a Yellow-

A portion of the crowd that waits each day for an eruption of Old Faithful. *NPS photo*

stone geyser basin, because this park has caught our imagination in an extraordinary number of ways. Along with individual experiences, there are Yogi Bear, media coverage of the fires of 1988 (and of wolves, grizzly bears, and budget problems), grandpa's 1938 bear story, the postcard of the Grand Canyon of the Yellowstone from Aunt Verna, the poster of the Lake Hotel at the local travel agent's office, the neighbor's home movies of their 1985 visit, and our culture's thousand uses for the name "Old Faithful." All the ways in which Yellowstone intrudes on our consciousness have made the park a cultural icon.

It should be no surprise that visitation increases steadily. Roughly half of Yellowstone's visitors have not been to the park before.[4] One recent survey found that 48 percent stayed one day, 24 percent stayed two days, and 15 percent stayed three days; another study suggested that visits were even shorter. Six states — California, Montana, Utah, Wyoming, Idaho, and Colorado — accounted for the most visitors, though people come from all states and many other countries. Over the course of all seasons, the average age range is thirty to forty-one, but in the fall the percentage of older people (fifty-four to sixty-five) increases substantially. Yellowstone visitors are better educated than national norms.

In 1994, the first year the park had 3 million visitors, the hotel dining rooms (excluding the Hamilton Stores food shops) served 434,400 pounds of potatoes, 8,518,464 scoops of ice cream, 155,520 pounds of prime rib, 86,160 pounds of ground beef, 52,245 pounds of bacon, 98,600 pounds of cheese, 84,790 gallons of coffee, and 37,780 gallons of milk.[5] At the Yellowstone Park service stations, visitors bought 10,004 quarts of oil, used 3,360,000 sheets of toilet paper, and needed a wrecker 1,004 times. They were involved in 603 traffic accidents, 274 court cases, 39 search-and-rescue operations, 63 fishing regulation violations, 182 camping regulation violations, 65 "car clouts" (vehicles broken into), and 25 firearms violations. Fifteen people were convicted of poaching. There were 717 personal injuries, 9 deaths, and property losses totaling $1,755,875.[6]

All of this activity had some direct effects on the park's resources, of course. Perhaps the most startling is in car-killed wildlife; during the busy summer season, motorists cause the death of one large animal every day. In 1994 this alarming total included 51 mule deer, 49 elk, 19 coyotes, 12 moose, 11 bison, and assorted others.[7]

The fires of 1988 raised concerns that people would enjoy the park less, but enjoyment has remained high:

> Most visitors in the summer (94 percent), fall (92 percent), and winter (99 percent) stated that they would like to return to Yellowstone National Park, rating their trip between 7 and 10 on a 1-to-10 scale where 10 was "fantastic." Wildlife viewing was cited as the most enjoyable experience, while viewing fire effects, road conditions, and crowds were stated as the least enjoyable experience.[8]

Though the above-quoted investigator found that "viewing fire effects" was not regarded as enjoyable, he also found that many people were interested in the fires: "Viewing of the fire effects in the park did not reduce overall satisfaction of most visitors. In fact, many visitors came to see the effects, and most visitors hold positive attitudes toward the fires."[9] Visitor approval of the quality of park fishing actually rose following the fires.[10]

One study found that "84% of Yellowstone visitors are clustered in the park campgrounds, thermal and scenic viewing areas, and the developed areas along the park roadways. Only 7% of visitors hike off the main roadways into the park backcountry."[11] According to another study, the two most popular spots in the park are Old Faithful, where 78 percent of all visitors go, and the Grand Canyon, where 70 percent go.[12] By far the most common complaints in recent years are about the poor conditions of the roads. Thirty years into the National Park Service's intensive effort to educate the public about the need for a widely distributed and unmanaged bear population, however, many people are still disappointed that they didn't see bears.[13]

The three most common visitor activities, rated by the percentage of visitors who participated in them, were walking for pleasure (74 percent), going to a visitor center or museum (72 percent), and shopping (70 percent). Forty-one percent picnicked, 18 percent went to a ranger talk or walk, 15 percent fished, 9 percent took a backcountry hike, and smaller percentages boated, swam, bicycled, or rode a horse.[14] The finding that shopping is the third most common activity in Yellowstone National Park, however, tells us much about what the public enjoys in Yellowstone. The National Park Service is managing a large wilderness area, but the concessioners are clearly running a resort complex and running it very successfully. It may come as a surprise to people who think of Yellowstone as a great wilderness reserve that most visitors view it in part as a shopping trip.

According to one survey, visitors ranged across a broad spectrum in their understanding of animals but showed a very high level of concern for the well-being of the wildlife, with many expressing concern about people getting too close to animals. On the other hand, they displayed a perhaps predictable breadth of ideas about what was "too close." While 64 percent knew that bears should be viewed from a distance of 100 yards or more, more than 20 percent believed that 100 feet was enough, and a few regarded 10 feet as sufficient. When asked what large animal causes the most human injuries in Yellowstone, few knew that it was the bison. Most thought it was the bear, and 4 people (out of 252 who were asked) thought that wolves hurt the most people.[15]

When I compare today's visitors to those of earlier times, I see far more similarities than differences. But numbers alone cannot tell us what the visitor experience in Yellowstone is or what it should be. The emergence of an ethic for the enjoyment of national parks has reached its fullest expression so far in legal scholar Joseph Sax's milestone book *Mountains Without Handrails: Reflections on the National Parks* (1980).[16] The book remains the most persuasive single statement of the challenges faced by the parks and the directions they should take. But, though it is easy to form broad, overarching statements of principle and direction for the national parks, it is hard to buttress them with reliable specifics.

For example, Sax bemoaned the mass-ness of the park experience: so many tourists, so little time. Like many other observers, from Edward Abbey to a thousand park interpreters, he wanted visitors to connect more directly with the place than is possible through a windshield or a hotel window. Sax distinguished between the "banality and predictability" of standard tourist activities and the deeper experience that comes from individual initiative. He recommended the wholesale abandonment of standard activities throughout the national park system:

> The drearily routine mule rides at the South Rim of the Grand Canyon for which people line up morning after morning; the one-hour, two-hour, four-hour horseback loops, with a daily breakfast ride or "chuck wagon dinner" thrown in, that are so common a sight; the round-the-lake commercial boat ride that is a standard feature at a number of parks. All these are nothing but amusements, however beautiful the setting, and they seem indistinguishable from the local pony ride. Their capacity to

get visitors deep into the park experience seems minimal, they have a mass production quality about them, and they have considerable capacity to detract attention from the fashioning of a personal agenda. They can be dispensed with.[17]

It appears to be a fundamental tenet of modern environmentalist thinking about national parks that the parks cannot be adequately enjoyed by large groups of people at once, or by people doing something that another group of people did in essentially the same way the day before, or by people under commercial guidance. It does not become clear how these activities that Sax dislikes necessarily prevent the visitor from exercising his or her individual passion for the country. Most of them sound like reasonable opportunities for just such exercise, especially by people without the specialist's equipment and experience in wilderness. I doubt that all the people from Poughkeepsie, Ashtabula, and a thousand other towns who arrive for the first time at Grand Canyon National Park find anything in their day, much less the phenomenal adventure of riding a mule down to the river, "drearily routine." The only ways in which people can get deeper into the Grand Canyon than on the back of the mule is on foot or by boat. These mule riders have abandoned their cars for the day; more power to them.

But then consider fishing, an activity that Sax regarded as especially appropriate in national parks because it (especially fly fishing) engages individuals so intensely in the natural setting. As a former director of the American Museum of Fly Fishing and the owner of an embarrassing number of fly rods, I share Sax's idea of fly fishing as an appropriate park experience. But we have already seen that the desire among early park enthusiasts for recreational fishing resulted in the serious alteration of the fauna of many of Yellowstone's watersheds; the native fish populations were disastrously damaged by overharvest and by the introduction of nonnative species; some native species were extirpated. Even today, when Yellowstone's fishing regulations protect against overharvest and aim especially to protect or restore native species, we still treat fish with less respect than we afford all other park animals except, perhaps, mosquitoes. We fishermen drag them gasping and struggling from their native habitat because we love to connect with the natural world, but also because we find joy in outsmarting them and making them fight; if a similar attack was made on an elk or a raven, the perpetrator would be arrested for harassment of wildlife.

This is shocking talk to most recreationists, for whom fishing is the only way to enjoy fish, but the inconsistency of treatment it represents has not escaped the notice of forward-looking conservationists. It has been thirty years since F. Fraser Darling and Noel Eichhorn, in their important book *Man and Nature in the National Parks,* warned, "Fishing, surely, is one of those outworn privileges in a national park of the later 20th century."[18] The growing emphasis on fish watching in Yellowstone is a modest sign of changing values.

The point is not whether Sax's recommendations for the national parks are in error. In principle I agree with almost every position he takes. It would be wonderful, for example, if every visitor had both the time and the interest to become immersed in the park's wonders for several days, and if there really were enough wilderness land in the national parks to absorb that amount of attention. The point is that we are little closer to agreeing on the right way to enjoy Yellowstone than we were when the park was created.

At the end of his turbulent eleven-year superintendency of Yellowstone, Bob Barbee submitted to an extended interview; he was asked if it wasn't essential that a great deal more sociological surveying be done to understand just what people wanted when they come to Yellowstone and how many visitors the park could successfully handle at once. He replied:

> My opinion is, that's good and I think we ought to do that, but we pretty much know that the public attitudes are going to range clear across the waterfront. Some people think the experience today is an abomination, and other people think it's wonderful. That being the case, how do we decide on the sociological trigger [to determine when the park is overcrowded]?

How do we define the acceptable experience, so we know exactly when to close the gates? . . .

So what are we trying to achieve here with the Yellowstone experience? Some kind of contrast with everyday life? Rediscovery of elemental kinds of things? And why do people come to parks, other than to eat some really nice meals and get some really neat fudge?

Is it our job in the National Park Service to offer a great contrast to the rest of the world, and be exemplars of environmental quality? We think so, and we think that we as an agency should be able to say something about that with relative impunity. But we aren't. At least not yet, not in any precise way.

We know we're advocates and spokespeople for an extremely important good cause; national parks have a central role to play in the future of the global environmental movement. But this is a dangerous area because for all our knowledge and experience we don't dare forget that we're public servants, not oracles. If we try to tell the public what they should like, we're stretching any definition of our authority and getting into the father-knows-best syndrome. We have to be really careful there.[19]

The measure of the appropriateness of a park activity has come to be in good part a measure of its tradition. In the 1970s and 1980s kayaking became more popular around the country, and a few enthusiasts wanted to kayak in some park streams, which, unlike most of the lakes, have long been closed to watercraft. Kayakers from nearby communities began to run Yellowstone's less accessible rivers illegally. They accurately observed that unlike backpackers, kayakers "left no tracks" and touched very little land at all; they just zoomed through the setting with little apparent impact. The decision to ban kayaks on park streams was based on the known ecological effects of watercraft traffic (for example, on nesting waterfowl) as well as on a vague sense that the aesthetic experience of a wild river would be compromised by the presence of bright yellow watercraft. But the decision was also based on a broader concept: that although one use is not necessarily inherently less right than another, the park can accommodate only so many uses at once. Some of the kayakers said they preferred that it be illegal, because when they sneaked in they knew they would be unencumbered by rules, permits, river rangers, schedules, and all the other bureaucratic attachments that form around any visitor activity in a national park.[20]

Where tradition has almost completely failed to help Yellowstone find its way is in something that Barbee alluded to in the interview quoted above: more and more people coming all the time. Yellowstone's crowds, especially at Old Faithful and a few other hot spots, have been legend for many years. Bernard DeVoto in the 1950s and Robert Cahn in the 1960s, complaining of the ruination caused by all these people, have a horde of modern counterparts.

The first kind of ruination we hear of is damage to the park's resources; the park is being loved to death. There is an enormous body of opinion on the overuse of Yellowstone, but there is remarkably little formal proof — of the kind that would hold up in court — that the park resources are declining in some meaningful way because of all that use. The park's developed acreage is less than it was fifty years ago, and though there are more people on the roads and trails, there are fewer miles of roads and no more miles of trails than there were then.

This is not to defend current levels of development; we know better than ever that the park's developments and travel corridors are not without cost to the wildlife; trails and roads displace grizzly bears from substantial acreages. But we have little reason to believe that that displacement has increased in the past thirty years. Indeed, the establishment of a backcountry permit system in the early 1970s essentially put a cap on public overnight use of the backcountry, just as the number of campground sites, hotel beds, and other accommodations has not significantly increased in many years. At the same time, selective backcountry closures, some for only a few days or weeks, others limiting hikers to established trails, have in fact improved grizzly bear access to large chunks of good habitat that was long denied them.

But there is another kind of damage that the park can suffer: a decline in the quality of the visitor experience. Erosion of quality is very difficult to measure, partly because there is so little agreement over what quality means and partly because as ecologists Tim Clark and Steve Minta have written, "People are short-term entities, far more flexible than institutions. When circumstances are perceived by individuals to change slowly enough, history has shown that people will adjust marvelously. Our turn-of-the-century grandparents would be shocked by the GYE of today, yet we are not. Likewise, we would be shocked by the GYE of fifty years hence, but our descendants will not be."[21] Several early visitors to Yellowstone commented on their gratitude at seeing it before the hordes arrived, and one of the reasons we find their descriptions so interesting is the vicarious joy of having the place to ourselves.

But how do we measure quality of experience? And, once we have measured it, how do we enforce its protection? Is there a significant difference between sharing an eruption of Old Faithful with ten, fifty, or one hundred strangers and sharing it with two thousand? Is a day hike less enjoyable when you encounter one hundred other hikers than when you encounter none? Bob Barbee was right when he said that if we ask the public what to do about this, we will get a continuum of responses; also, most of them will probably be in the high middle of the bell curve, reasonably content with the park as they know it and with little awareness of what constituted such contentment fifty or one hundred years ago and no idea what contentment might require fifty years from now.

The dialogue over quality of experience is beginning to change, however, with discussions of the park's carrying capacity and caps on visitation. Yellowstone's current superintendent, Mike Finley, has generated an epidemic of edginess among regional business interests by openly discussing the theoretical limits of the park's capacity to benefit the public while maintaining its legally mandated health.[22] Though eventually such discussions must focus on the overwhelming numbers of summer visitors, the staffs of Yellowstone and Grand Teton national parks have started with the comparatively smaller (though no less contentious) issue of winter use. Only thirty years ago there was virtually no winter visitation, but since the early 1970s the growth in winter use has continued to outrun the most generous predictions.[23] It may seem odd to focus on the 140,000 or so people who use the park in winter rather than the nearly 2,800,000 who use it in summer, but besides the practicality of biting off the smaller piece first, it may be easier to measure or demonstrate that this use is harmful to the resource. If such harm is demonstrated, the political and legal process of doing something about the use, such as redirecting or limiting it, is slightly more straightforward than it would be with just a public survey demonstrating declining visitor satisfaction.

We look back on the promotional efforts of early National Park Service administrators with a mixture of condescension and annoyance; that they could be so naive as not to realize the eventual consequence of inviting sod many people into these fragile places seems retroactively unforgivable. Was it really worth it, we wonder, just to make sure that the new National Park Service and its small collection of landholdings had enough friends? Today's parks, for all the press of humanity lined up to get in, still seem short of friends, or at least lacking in just the right combination of friends to ensure adequate budgets and reasonable protection.

The plight of modern parks, including Yellowstone, is worse than it was when Stephen Mather and Horace Albright were welcoming motorists and transforming the parks into great outdoor hospitality centers. Current complaints about Yellowstone's collapsing infrastructure — wretched roads, overtaxed sewage systems, and so on — are valid, but even if all those things are fixed, the park will still be inadequate to the task we have given it, of preserving an ecological system it never entirely contained in the first place. As the Greater Yellowstone Ecosystem continues to be developed, each acre of the park becomes more important. Tourism and second-home building are growth industries; grizzly bear habitat is not.

Yellowstone is like the Shangri-La of *Lost Horizon*, James Hilton's classic novel of a secret Himalayan paradise. Its residents and visitors knew that Shangri-La was precious, and they knew it contained important treasures, especially in the lessons it held for the rest of the world. But they also knew that it alone could not serve the world's many needs. As the ancient High Lama of Shangri-La ex-plained to the story's adventurer hero, "We are a single lifeboat riding the seas in a gale; we can take a few chance survivors, but if all the shipwrecked were to reach us and clamber aboard we should go down ourselves."[24] Yellowstone is such a lifeboat. For all our in-creased awareness of the vulnerability of this particular lifeboat, we do not seem to have figured out how to prevent it from going down. We are unwilling to come to terms with the reality that the longer we wait, the harder it will be to prevent Yellowstone from finally taking the last of its friends down with it. Everybody loves it, but nobody loves it enough to leave it.

In *Biophilia* (1984), the scientist Edward O. Wilson proposed that humans are driven by an "innate tendency to focus on life and lifelike processes"; he concluded that "our existence depends on this propensity, our spirit is woven from it, hope rises on its current."[25] This seems to me to apply directly to the fate of Yellowstone, which has been a prominent and stormy testing ground for just such notions.

> There is more. Modern biology has produced a genuinely new way of looking at the world that is incidentally congenial to the inner direction of biophilia. In other words, instinct is in this rare instance aligned with reason. The conclusion I draw is optimistic: to the degree that we come to understand other or-ganisms, we will place a greater value on them, and on our-selves.[26]

Greater Yellowstone's great chance, and perhaps the foremost goal toward which the park itself can strive in the future, is to unite our existing management skills with the growing public awareness of the opportunities that this extraordinary region provides for integrating what Wilson called instinct and reason. In Yellowstone's case these may be called just as aptly wonder and ecology. But Wil-son's optimism does not translate into a clear course of action for a place like Yellowstone.

One risk of broadening the way in which we "value" Yellowstone is that even this new, more comprehensive perception falls far short

The grizzly bears of Yellowstone, great stimulators of the imagination, have come to symbolize many things in the modern conservation movement. The attempt to preserve the grizzly bears of Greater Yellowstone is seen as a test of our willingness to share a spectacular and world-famous landscape with its wild native inhabitants. We have the scientific knowledge and the management skills to preserve the bears, but it remains unclear whether we will do so. *NPS photo*

of capturing the fullness of our experience here. Numbers, whether board feet, trends in grizzly bear litter sizes, or any other quantifiable element of resource analysis, are the primary tools of professional managers and of the ecologists, geologists, and others seeking to understand how Yellowstone works. It is wonderful and gratifying to see economists giving solid, numerical weight to things that were long simply ignored because they had no dollar value. But the quantification of ephemeral, emotional things into cash amounts stirs great uneasiness in our souls, because we know that not everything should be reduced to such flatness by a spread-sheet mentality that sees no farther than the cash register. No economist can come up with the true value of a single grizzly bear, much less a whole population of them. While we might be comforted to have the economic playing field leveled a little in the battle between logging and the preservation of old-growth forests, or between mineral development and grizzly bear habitat, we know there is more to it. We cannot fully value the old-growth grove any more than we can fully value the subjective, personal enrichment that the logger gets from his chosen way of life.

Geographer Judith Meyer has written that even the most conscientious and precise numerical efforts leave out much that the world values about Yellowstone:

> The job of defining or describing the enduring and endearing essence of the parks has typically been avoided by scientists — whether their fields are the social or natural sciences — because evolutionary theories are based on recording and interpreting change. The task of describing stasis has been left to the poets, painters, and authors of fiction. As a result, a large portion of the evolution of the parks — each park's sense of place — is missing from scholarly interpretation. And much of the information in historical records is typically discounted as nonscientific, invalid, or too mutable for real scholarly consideration.[27]

Numbers alone will never fully portray Yellowstone's sense of place, but sophisticated scientific analyses have an undeniable beauty of their own, revealing the elegance of nature's complexity. Perhaps by combining that analytical beauty with the work of poets, painters, and fiction writers, we will best advance our search for Yellowstone.

We should be grateful beyond words to the thousands of people who have unraveled Yellowstone's ecological and geophysical mysteries. Ecology and wonder combine to feed our hunger for both knowledge and wisdom. The more we grasp ecological process, the deeper our wonder. But a field sketch by Thomas Moran, a photograph by William Henry Jackson, or a child's drawing of a bison may lead us farther than any scientific monograph. The search for Yellowstone is as much a search for ourselves as it is a search for biological understanding, and these emotional, subjective, and shared portrayals of Yellowstone enable us to communicate that search without so many analytical filters. Again, Edward Wilson:

> Natural philosophy has brought into clear relief the following paradox of human existence. The drive toward perpetual expansion — or personal freedom — is basic to the human spirit. But to sustain it we need the most delicate, knowing stewardship of the living world that can be devised. Expansion and stewardship may appear at first to be conflicting goals, but they are not. The depth of the conservation ethic will be measured by the extent to which each of the two approaches to nature is used to reshape and reinforce the other. The paradox can be resolved by changing its premises into forms more suited to ultimate survival, by which I mean protection of the human spirit.[28]

I can picture many of Yellowstone's founders and protectors — Ferdinand Hayden, George Bird Grinnell, William Hallett Phillips, George Wright, Starker Leopold, and others — nodding their heads enthusiastically at language like this. They also tried, as we do today, to hold true to the park's unique value to the human spirit.

Epilogue

M Y WONDER OVER YELLOWSTONE ranges far. Even after forcing myself through the discipline of organizing so many ideas and chronologies into a book-length sequence, I realize that I — like practically everybody, I suspect — do not really wish to deal with Yellowstone systematically once I put down the scientific publications and walk out the door into the park. The search for Yellowstone seems to be at its best when we find time during the organized tour to look around and do a little exploring on our own. For me, that exploration is always a mixture of wonder and wondering, of awe at the place and excitement about what it has come to mean to us.

I wonder what would happen (what will happen, really, for it someday must) if Old Faithful either stopped erupting entirely or became so infrequent that it lost its power to draw people. Would there be a stage of some years' duration, as happened after the fires, when people would come to see what was now gone, and stand there on the boardwalks as at a wake? Would the huge crescent of pavement and construction that now half-encircles the cone of Old Faithful finally look silly enough to us — permanence of structure surrounding a great monument to the impermanence of nature — that we would dismantle some of it, or would the wonder of the other nearby geysers, so long under the shadow of The Geyser, emerge to compensate for and justify all the architecture? Would the very name "Old Faithful" take on a new meaning in our culture, becoming eventually an ironic sarcasm for something sadly short of fidelity?

In another mood, I wonder what ecologists will know about this place in twenty or even fifty years. Which of our philosophical and ecological hunches, theories, hypotheses, and pronouncements will they regard as prophetic and which as harebrained? Will they see our gropings toward an understanding of the ecosystem's long-term complexity and variability as hopeless, or will they have more of it sorted out, or will they confront it with the same mixture of confusion and confidence that we display today?

We routinely insist that our descendants serve as our consciences. In our attempts to justify our positions in the debates over Yellowstone's management, we invoke the needs of future generations, because we see our care of this place as a great trust. We are saving these things for them, and they'll never forgive us if we mess up. But if we fail, say, to save the grizzly bear, I wonder, considering the shortsighted perspective of each generation so far, what the odds are that our great-grandchildren will assert that our failure is worth any more than a few lingering pangs of cultural guilt — about the same amount of guilt that most of us feel today for the destruction of the bison 120 years ago.

Last, though it often seems only a historian's idle exercise, I wonder about the earlier searchers for Yellowstone, from those long-forgotten generations of miners and traders who haunted Obsidian Cliff through the millennia to the more recent questing hordes of white people who strained their aesthetic sensitivities to come to terms with this landscape. Would trapper-diarist Osborne Russell think that the Lamar Valley is still in pretty good shape, or would the road alone ruin it for him? What would old Philetus Norris, decked out in buckskins and dreaming his buffalo-ranching dreams, make of the current crisis over Yellowstone's luxurious overflow of bison? Would George Wright, remembered for his nearly poetic policy statements on behalf of predators, be surprised by the twenty-year saga of wolf recovery? What would Aldo Leopold make of the natural-regulation debate? These people must have wondered where the search for Yellowstone would lead, and if they could know, I wonder how many of them would be pleased and how many would be grieved.

In writing this book, I have perhaps most often wondered about John Muir, the great wilderness sermonizer of the California mountains, though he visited Yellowstone only twice. In my exploration of the vast literature of this place, I have wondered why Yellowstone does not have its own John Muir and what, if anything, would have changed in the park's history if, one hundred years ago, a voice that powerful and distinctive had emerged here instead of in the Sierras. Does a nation get a voice like that only every so often, and does it sound as strong wherever it surfaces? Or did Yosemite Valley have some spiritual geology lacking in Yellowstone, so that this voice could arise only there, echoing from the mountain walls and ringing across the generations?

I also wonder about Muir because whenever my mind drifted from the ecology side of things to the wonder side, I was reminded of his capacity for evoking all that is important and ultimately unmeasurable about the search for Yellowstone. I was reminded, specifically, of his description of what Yellowstone gives us when we follow our search to its heart:

> Now comes the gloaming. The alpenglow is fading into earthy, murky gloom, but do not let your town habits draw you away to the hotel. Stay on this good fire-mountain and spend the night among the stars. Watch their glorious bloom until the dawn, and get one more baptism of light. Then, with fresh heart, go down to your work, and whatever your fate, under whatever ignorance or knowledge you may afterward chance to suffer, you will remember these fine, wild views, and look back with joy to your wanderings in the blessed old Yellowstone wonderland.[1]

NOTES
ACKNOWLEDGMENTS
INDEX

NOTES

INTRODUCTION: ESTABLISHING YELLOWSTONE

1. Kary Mullis quoted in John D. Varley, "Saving the Parts," *Yellowstone Science* 1, no. 4 (Summer 1993):13.
2. Michael Milstein, "Yellowstone Managers Eye Profits from Hot Microbes," *Science* 264 (April 19, 1994):655; Jim Robbins, "The Microbe Miners," *Audubon* (November–December 1994):90–95.

1. ANCIENT YELLOWSTONE

1. Recent histories of precontact American Indians address this issue of "history" versus "prehistory" directly by the way they approach the subject. I have also been impressed by archeologists' statements on the subject, such as Brian Reeves, "Glacier National Park Precontact Native American Archeological Research Design" (Lincoln, Nebr.: National Park Service Midwest Archeological Center, PX611592069, June 1993), 5, and Kent G. Lightfoot, "Culture Contact Studies: Redefining the Relationship between Prehistoric and Historical Archeology," *American Antiquity* 60, no. 2 (1995):199–217. For a sympathetic and helpful overview of the "New Western History" that seeks to integrate native peoples as well as minorities and women into the story of the American West, see Richard White, "Trashing the Trails," in *Trails: Toward a New Western History*, ed. Patricia Nelson Limerick, Clyde A. Milner II, and Charles E. Rankin (Lawrence: University Press of Kansas, 1991), pp. 26–39.
2. Thomas H. Lewis, "Bears and Bear Hunting in Prehistory: The Rock Art Record on the Yellowstone," *Northwest Anthropological Research Notes* 19 (1985):243.
3. Aubrey Haines, *The Yellowstone Story*, vol. 1 (Boulder, Colo.: Yellowstone Library and Museum Association and Colorado Associated University Press, 1977), p. 16.
4. Kenneth P. Cannon, "Paleoindian Use of Obsidian in the Greater Yellowstone Area," *Yellowstone Science* 1, no. 4 (1993):6–9.
5. Bjorn Kurten and Elaine Anderson, *Pleistocene Mammals of North America* (New York: Columbia University Press, 1980); D. N. Walker, "Late Pleistocene/Holocene Environmental Changes in Wyoming: The Mammalian Record," in

Late Quaternary Mammalian Biogeography and Environments of the Great Plains and Prairies, ed. R. W. Graham, H. A. Semken, Jr., and M. A. Graham (Springfield: Illinois State Museum, 1987), pp. 334–393.

6. Among the most important recent papers on Yellowstone's early postglacial environment are R. G. Baker, *Late Quaternary Vegetation History of the Yellowstone Lake Basin, Wyoming* (Washington: U.S. Geological Survey Professional Paper 729-E, E-1-E48, 1976); Cathy Whitlock and Patrick J. Bartlein, "Spatial Variations of Holocene Climatic Change in the Yellowstone Region," *Quaternary Research* 39 (1993):231–238; and Cathy Whitlock, "Postglacial Vegetation and Climate of Grand Teton and Southern Yellowstone National Parks," *Ecological Monographs* 63, no. 2 (1993):173–198.

7. Haines, *Yellowstone Story,* 1:15–20; Joel Janetski, *The Indians of Yellowstone Park* (Salt Lake City: University of Utah Press, 1987), pp. 3–25.

8. Kenneth P. Cannon, "Blood Residue Analyses of Ancient Stone Tools Reveal Clues to Prehistoric Subsistence Patterns in Yellowstone," *CRM* 2 (1995):14–16; Kenneth P. Cannon and Margaret E. Newman, "Results of Blood Residue Analysis of a Late Paleoindian Projectile Point from Yellowstone National Park, Wyoming," *CRP* 11 (1994):18–20; Paul Schullery, "Blood Residues on Prehistoric Stone Artifacts Reveal Human Hunting Activities and Diversity of Local Fauna," *Yellowstone Science* 3, no. 2 (1995):19.

9. Elizabeth Hadly Barnosky, "Ecosystem Dynamics Through the Past 2,000 Years As Revealed by Fossil Mammals from Lamar Cave in Yellowstone National Park, U.S.A.," *Historical Biology* 8 (1994):71–90.

10. Among the recent investigators who have discussed this apparent increase in large mammals in the past 1,500 years are George Frison, *Prehistoric Hunters of the High Plains* (New York: Academic Press, 1978); Elizabeth Hadly, "Late Holocene Mammalian Fauna of Lamar Cave and Its Implications for Ecosystem Dynamics in Yellowstone National Park, Wyoming" (M.S. thesis, Northern Arizona University, 1990); Charles Kay, "The Northern Yellowstone Elk Herd: A Critical Evaluation of the Natural Regulation Paradigm" (Ph.D. dissertation, University of Utah, 1990); and Kenneth Cannon, "A Review of Archeological and Paleontological Evidence for the Prehistoric Presence of Wolf and Related Prey Species in the Northern and Central Rockies Physiographic Provinces," in *Wolves for Yellowstone: A Report to the United States Congress,* vol. 4, *Research and Analysis,* ed. John D. Varley and Wayne G. Brewster (Yellowstone National Park: National Park Service, 1992), 1.175–1.266. As will be discussed in a later chapter, opinions and interpretations differ on the causes and effects of this change in wildlife numbers. Two summaries of the Little Ice Age are Jean M. Grove, *The Little Ice Age* (London: Methuen, 1988); and E. C. Pielou, *After the Ice Age* (Chicago: University of Chicago Press, 1991), pp. 308–310.

11. The figure of five percent of the park having been surveyed for archeologi-

cal sites is from Kenneth P. Cannon, "A Model for Prehistoric Economies of the Yellowstone Plateau During the Altithermal," in *The Ecological Implications of Fire in Greater Yellowstone: Proceedings, Second Biennial Conference on the Greater Yellowstone Ecosystem,* ed. Jason M. Greenlee (International Association of Wildland Fire, 1996), pp. 1–5. It is important to note, though, that five percent surveyed does not mean five percent investigated. The surveying of a site merely means it has been identified, not excavated.

12. Some overviews of precontact human populations of North America are Karl H. Schlesier, ed., *Plains Indians, A.D. 500–1500* (Norman: University of Oklahoma Press, 1994), pp. xvii–xxvii; William M. Denevan, ed., *The Native Population of the Americas in 1492* (Madison: University of Wisconsin Press, 1992), esp. Denevan's chapter, "Native American Populations in 1492: Recent Research and a Revised Hemispheric Estimate," pp. xvii–xxix; Henry F. Dobyns, *Their Number Become Thinned: Native American Population Dynamics in Eastern North America* (Knoxville: University of Tennessee Press, 1983); and Ann F. Ramenofsky, *Vectors of Death: The Archeology of European Contact* (Albuquerque: University of New Mexico Press).

The idea of American Indians as primitive innocents whose "advance" toward civilization was held up by their character has been endorsed surprisingly recently by a historian of Yellowstone. In 1960 the third edition of Merrill D. Beal, *The Story of Man in Yellowstone* (Yellowstone National Park: Yellowstone Library and Museum Association) was published. (At the time Beal was a history professor at Idaho State College, which is now Idaho State University.) The book featured the mixture of admiration and condescension that has characterized so much of white-Indian relations (and still does in some circles). Referring to the Sheepeaters who inhabited the park area in the early 1800s as "degenerate," he said that all the tribes using the park area "possessed certain racial characteristics of the red race."

"Indians are human beings possessing the sensibilities and emotions of white men. However, their manner of living and conception of life has been relatively low. Even so, it is difficult to generalize upon them as a people. As Chief Washakie once said, "Indians very much like white men — some good, some bad." It is generally conceded that they were proud, so haughty in fact that they lacked that quality of mind so essential to progress or adjustment, humility or teachability. They could not learn because they would not admit that they lacked anything." (p. 59).

Of course, by Beal's view and that of most whites, the Indians most decidedly lacked something, for they were reluctant to abandon their own culture and accept that of the whites.

13. Stephen Pyne, *Fire in America* (Princeton University Press, 1982).

14. This position is more often implied than stated, but the presence of only a few

resident Indians in the park area at the beginning of the nineteenth century seems to have suggested to many observers that the influence of humans on this landscape was relatively slight.

15. Charles Kay, "Aboriginal Overkill: The Role of Native Americans in Structuring Western Ecosystems," *Human Nature* 5, no. 4 (1994):359–398; Charles Kay, "Aboriginal Overkill and Native Burning: Implications for Modern Ecosystem Management," in *Sustainable Society and Protected Areas: Contributed Papers of the Eighth Conference on Research and Resource Management in Parks and on Public Lands, April 17–21, 1995, Portland, Oregon, Sponsored by the George Wright Society,* ed. Robert Linn, pp. 107–118. Kay claims that recent reconsiderations of the population estimates of American Indians in North America prior to 1492 are much higher than formerly believed, on the order of 100 million, but he provides no citation to support that number. Modern scholars of pre-Columbian populations have used that number only as a possible total for all of the Western Hemisphere, with less than 20 percent, perhaps only 10 percent, of that total living in North America. Other writers, notably Frederic H. Wagner et al., *Wildlife Policies in the U.S. National Parks* (Washington: Island Press, 1995), p. 141, have apparently appropriated the number of 100 million from Kay; they use it to support similar arguments about extremely large but now "lost" influences of Indians on the Yellowstone landscape. See Chapter 3 for further consideration of Indian population levels in the Yellowstone area.

16. Philetus W. Norris, *Annual Report of the Superintendent of the Yellowstone National Park to the Secretary of the Interior for the Year 1880* (Washington: U.S. Government Printing Office, 1881), p. 36.

17. Ibid.

18. The literature on the mound-building cultures of eastern North America is quite large; a very nice, accessible (if somewhat dated) introduction is Robert Silverberg, *The Moundbuilders* (Athens: Ohio University Press, 1986).

19. Some of the Hopewell blades from this site were pictured in *Yellowstone Science* 1, no. 4 (1993):7.

20. The literature on obsidian studies in archeology is quite large. A few papers especially relevant to this discussion are I. Friedman and W. Long, "Hydration Rate of Obsidian," *Science* 191 (1976):347–352; James W. Hatch et al., "Hopewell Obsidian Studies: Behavioral Implications of Recent Sourcing and Dating Research," *American Antiquity* 55, no. 3 (1990):461–479; Duane C. Anderson, Joseph A. Tiffany, and Fred W. Nelson, "Recent Research on Obsidian from Iowa Archeological Sites," *American Antiquity* 51, no. 4 (1986):837–852.

21. In addition to the sources cited above, see Cannon, "Paleoindian Use of Obsidian in the Greater Yellowstone Area"; and Leslie B. Davis et al., *The Obsidian Cliff Plateau Prehistoric Lithic Source, Yellowstone National Park, Wyoming,* selections from the Division of Cultural Resources, Rocky Mountain Region, No. 6 (Denver: National Park Service, 1995).

22. Ann Johnson, "The Significance of the Obsidian Cliff Archeological Site, Yellowstone National Park," briefing paper prepared for the regional director, Rocky Mountain Region, National Park Service, July 1993.

23. Hatch et al., "Hopewell Obsidian Studies," p. 483.

24. Ibid., p. 477.

2. THINGS A LITTLE INCREDIBLE

1. William Cronon, "The Trouble with Wilderness; or, Getting Back to the Wrong Nature," in *Uncommon Ground, Toward Reinventing Nature*, ed. William Cronon (New York: Norton, 1995), p. 72. It is worth noting, however, that the idea of wild nature as good or somehow useful and even beautiful was not new with the Transcendentalists of the nineteenth century. For overviews of earlier thinking, see Keith Thomas, *Man and the Natural World: A History of the Modern Sensibility* (New York: Pantheon, 1983); Roderick Nash, *Wilderness and the American Mind*, 3rd ed. (New Haven: Yale University Press, 1982); and Max Oelschlaeger, *The Idea of Wilderness from Prehistory to the Age of Ecology* (New Haven: Yale University Press, 1991). Oelschlaeger rightly points out that since humans first developed a concept of wild nature, "the idea of wilderness has been caught up in a never ending process of change" (p. 347).

For a stimulating set of essays on the values and ethics associated with public lands, see the special issue of *The George Wright Forum* 13, no. 2 (1996).

2. A provocative recent consideration of the perception of primitive man as living in harmony with nature is Martin Lewis, *Green Delusions: An Environmentalist Critique of Radical Environmentalism* (Durham, N.C.: Duke University Press, 1992), especially chap. 2, "Primal Purity and Natural Balance," pp. 43–81.

3. Richard White, "'Are You an Environmentalist or Do You Work for a Living?': Work and Nature," in Cronon, ed., *Uncommon Ground*, p. 175.

4. Two recent overviews of North American Indians prior to 1492 are Lynda Norene Shaffer, *Native Americans before 1492: The Moundbuilding Centers of the Eastern Woodlands* (Armonk, N.Y.: M. E. Sharpe, 1992); and Francis Jennings, *The Founders of America* (New York: Norton, 1993).

5. Alfred Crosby, *Ecological Imperialism: The Biological Expansion of Europe, 900–1900* (New York: Cambridge University Press, 1986).

6. Dobyns, *Their Number Become Thinned*, pp. 8–32.

7. Dean Snow and Kim Lanphear, "European Contact and Indian Depopulation in the Northeast: The Timing of the First Epidemics," *Ethnohistory* 35 (1988):15–33.

8. Ramenofsky, *Vectors of Death*.

9. Dobyns, *Their Number Become Thinned*, p. 25.

10. Richard White, *"It's Your Misfortune and None of My Own": A New History of the American West* (Norman: University of Oklahoma Press, 1991), pp. 18–26, pro-

vides a nice summary of this process. For more on the effects of the various epidemics, besides Dobyns and Ramenofsky, above, see Denevan, *Native Population;* David Stannard, *American Holocaust: Columbus and the Conquest of the New World* (New York: Oxford University Press, 1992); and John Verano and Douglas Ubelaker, eds., *Disease and Demography in the Americas* (Washington, D.C.: Smithsonian Institution Press, 1992).

11. Frederick Hoxie, *The Crow* (New York: Chelsea House Publishers, 1989), p. 52.

12. Janetski, *Indians of Yellowstone Park,* p. 32; Reeves, "Glacier National Park Precontact Native American Archeological Research Design," p. 28.

13. H. K. Buechner, *The Bighorn Sheep in the United States: Its Past, Present and Future.* Wildlife Monograph 4 (Washington, D.C.: Wildlife Society, 1960). George Frison, Charles Reher, and Danny Walker, "Prehistoric Mountain Sheep Hunting in the Central Rocky Mountains of North America," in *Hunters of the Recent Past,* ed. L. B. Davis and R. O. K. Reeves (London: Unwin Hyman, 1990), pp. 208–240, discuss hunting practices in Wyoming, including the eastern side of the Yellowstone area, and suggest that scab, a common livestock disease, was probably responsible for the "near-demise of the mountain sheep in northwest Wyoming" in the late nineteenth century. They also provide fascinating documentation for hunting methods, including a variety of drive sites and catch pens and a juniper-bark net at least 165 feet long, created specifically for catching sheep. For a discussion of the effects of wildlife diseases on human populations (not specific to Yellowstone), see Calvin Martin, "Wildlife Diseases as a Factor in the Depopulation of the North American Indian," *Western Historical Quarterly* 7, no. 1 (January 1976):47–62.

14. Janetski, *Indians of Yellowstone Park,* p. 30. Standard references on the spread of the horse through North America include Francis Haines, "Northward Spread of Horses to the Plains Indians," *American Anthropologist* 40, no. 3 (1938):429–437; and Frank Roe, *The Indian and the Horse* (Norman: University of Oklahoma Press, 1955).

15. Janetski, *Indians of Yellowstone Park,* pp. 57–61; Haines, *Yellowstone Story,* 1:27–29; and Wayne Replogle, *Yellowstone's Bannock Indian Trails* (Yellowstone Park: Yellowstone Library and Museum Association, 1956). Even before the 1870s, bison were in decline on the northern Great Plains. See William A. Dobak, "Killing the Canadian Buffalo, 1821–1881," *Western Historical Quarterly* 27 (Spring 1996):33–52, for an overview of probable declines from human hunting prior to the 1880s.

16. Janetski, *Indians of Yellowstone Park,* p. 28.

17. Dan Flores, "Bison Ecology and Bison Diplomacy: The Southern Plains from 1800 to 1850," *Journal of American History* 78, no. 2 (September 1991):465–485. See also Douglas B. Bamforth, "Historical Documents and Bison Ecology on the Great Plains," *Plains Anthropologist* 32, no. 115 (February 1987):1–16. Richard

White, *The Roots of Dependency* (Lincoln: University of Nebraska Press, 1983), p. 220, discusses the effects of Indian horses on native ranges. He notes that Indian agents among the Navajo of New Mexico, Arizona, and Utah in the late 1800s "complained of an excessive number of 'useless' ponies and of the damage they did to the range." We have no direct evidence that there were large numbers of Indian-owned horses in Yellowstone before the park was created, but we will see later that in the park's early decades, horses were numerous enough to require large quantities of forage.

18. Perhaps not surprisingly, there are great disagreements on the details of how the fur trade affected Indian harvesting of animals. See, for example, Calvin Martin, *Keepers of the Game: Indian-Animal Relationships and the Fur Trade* (Berkeley: University of California Press, 1978); and a book published in response to it, Shepard Krech III, *Indians, Animals, and the Fur Trade: A Critique of "Keepers of the Game"* (Athens: University of Georgia Press, 1981). See also Jeanne Kay, "Native Americans in the Fur Trade and Wildlife Depletion," *Environmental Review* 9, no. 2 (Summer 1985):118–130.

19. Hiram Chittenden, *The Yellowstone National Park, Historical and Descriptive* (Cincinnati: Robert Clarke Co., 1905 ed.), pp. 8–9.

20. Reeves, "Glacier National Park Precontact Native American Archeological Research Design," p. 28.

21. Hoxie, *Crow*, pp. 21–34; Rodney Frey, *The World of the Crow Indians* (Norman: University of Oklahoma Press, 1987), pp. 8–12.

22. Frey, *World of the Crow Indians*, p. 12.

23. Janetski, *Indians of Yellowstone Park*, p. 33.

24. Ibid., p. 36.

25. Osborne Russell, *Journal of a Trapper*, ed. Aubrey Haines (Lincoln: University of Nebraska Press, 1955), p. 26.

26. Besides Janetski, *Indians of Yellowstone Park*, important sources on the Sheepeaters include Haines, *Yellowstone Story*, 1:22–29; Ake Hultkrantz, "The Shoshoni in the Rocky Mountain Area," *Annals of Wyoming* 33 (April 1961):19–41; Ake Hultkrantz, "The Indians in Yellowstone Park," *Annals of Wyoming* 29 (October 1957):124–149; Ake Hultkrantz, "The Source Literature on the 'Tukudika' Indians in Wyoming: Facts and Fancies," in *Languages and Cultures of Western North America*, ed. E. H. Swanson (Pocatello: Idaho State University Press, 1970); and David Dominick, "The Sheepeaters," *Annals of Wyoming* 36 (April 1964):131–168. Larry Loendorf of New Mexico State University confirmed my own feelings about earlier misinterpretations of the Sheepeaters during his talk "Changing Attitudes: Ethnography in Yellowstone National Park" (Mammoth Hot Springs, June 18, 1996). He also informed me of the new estimate of their early arrival in the Yellowstone area. I suspect that descriptions of the Sheepeaters as ragged and starving may have contributed to some of the later

"common knowledge" about game being scarce in the park; Russell's description of the Sheepeater people as well dressed and obviously well supplied with game also suggests that game was not scarce.

27. Norris, *Annual Report . . . 1880*, p. 36.

28. Janetski, *Indians of Yellowstone Park*, p. 37; Haines, *Yellowstone Story*, 1:25. Haines says that George Bird Grinnell, a pioneering western conservationist, naturalist, and anthropologist, also identified the wickiups as Crow.

29. Joseph Weixelman, "The Power to Evoke Wonder: Native Americans & the Geysers of Yellowstone National Park" (M.A. paper, History Department, Montana State University, July 19, 1992), p. 8, summarizes the more distant tribes that knew of or visited the Yellowstone area.

30. An important collection of essays and reviews on American Indians and their place in the environmental movement appeared in Richard White, ed., "Special Issue: American Indian Environmental History," *Environmental Review* 9, no. 2 (Summer 1985).

31. The standard reference work on fire in North America is Stephen Pyne, *Fire in America: A Cultural History of Wildland and Rural Fire* (Princeton: Princeton University Press, 1982).

32. William Cronon, *Changes in the Land: Indians, Colonists, and the Ecology of New England* (New York: Hill and Wang, 1983), pp. 48–51.

33. Emily Russell, "Indian-Set Fires in the Forests of the Northeastern United States," *Ecology* 64, no. 1 (1983):78–88. There seems to have been a tendency to presume that fires seen in early historic Yellowstone were started by Indians. For example, Aubrey Haines describes, in *Yellowstone Story*, 1:343 n. 52, how members of the 1870 Washburn expedition, noticing a fire on Mount Everts, assumed it had been caused by an Indian signal fire, but it is much more likely to have been caused by lightning during a storm the previous two days. For more on the difficulties of determining the patterns or effects of indigenous fire practices in a variety of North American settings, see Henry T. Lewis, "Hunter-Gatherers and Problems for Fire History," in *Proceedings of the Fire History Workshop, October 20–24, 1980, Tucson, Arizona*, General Technical Report RM-81 (Fort Collins, Colo.: U.S.D.A. Forest Service, Rocky Mountain Forest & Range Experimental Station), pp. 115–119.

34. Information on the beginnings of Indian burning in the northwestern United States is presented by Stephen Arno, "Ecological Effects and Management Implications of Indian Fires," in *Proceedings — Symposium and Workshop on Wilderness Fire*, ed. James Lotan, Bruce Kilgore, William Fischer, and Robert Mutch, Missoula, Montana, Nov. 15–18, 1983. Arno cites a variety of evidence suggesting that Indian burning began about 1,000 years ago in northern Idaho, 1,000–2,000 years ago in western Montana, and 1,000 years ago in the Sierra Nevada. Most common forest trees in the West do not live long enough to give us reliable fire history further back than a few centuries, but paleoecologists,

studying charcoal in bogs, pond sediments, and debris flows along stream courses, have been able to reach back much farther into the past.

35. Besides Arno, "Ecological Effects," see George E. Gruell, "Indian Fires in the Interior West: A Widespread Influence," in *Proceedings — Symposium and Workshop on Wilderness Fire* (1983); Stephen Barrett, "Indian Fires in the Pre-Settlement Forests of Western Montana," *Proceedings of the Fire History Workshop;* Clinton B. Phillips, "The Relevance of Past Indian Fires to Current Fire Management Programs," in *Proceedings — Symposium and Workshop on Wilderness Fire.*

36. William Romme and Dennis Knight, "Landscape Diversity: The Concept Applied to Yellowstone Park," *BioScience* 32, no. 8 (September 1982):664–670; William Romme, "Fire and Landscape Diversity in Subalpine Forests of Yellowstone National Park," *Ecological Monographs* 52 (1982):199–221; William Romme and Dennis Knight, "Fire Frequency and Subalpine Forest Succession along a Topographic Gradient in Wyoming," *Ecology* 62 (1981):319–326; William Romme and Don Despain, "Historical Perspective on the Yellowstone Fires of 1988," *BioScience* 39, no. 10 (November 1989):695–699.

But as complex as fire's effects on the landscape are, they too are subject to change over a period of centuries. Sarah Millspaugh and Cathy Whitlock, "A 750-year Fire History Based on Lake Sediment Records in Central Yellowstone National Park, USA," *The Holocene* 5, no. 3 (1995):283–292, suggest that the long-term return interval of fire in Yellowstone lodgepole pine forests has not remained constant over the past millennium. They found that fires on the largest scale (such as occurred in 1988) also occurred in about 1700 and about 1560, but that smaller fires prevailed from about 1220 to 1440 and from about 1700 to 1987. These changes were attributed to changes in climate over time.

37. Critics of the National Park Service's fire policy spoke of Yellowstone's forests having been widely burned by Indians prior to 1872, but no one provided evidence; it was simply a matter of "common knowledge" without real basis. Typical of the comments was a remark by historian Stephen Pyne (*Natural History* [August 1989], p. 49) that determining if the fires of 1988 were "natural" required recognizing that the creation of the park had resulted in "the abolition of ancient practices, including anthropogenic fire, that had occurred for millennia." There is little doubt that these ancient practices had occurred elsewhere for millennia, but Indian fires in Yellowstone are still conjectural.

38. Stephen Barrett and Stephen Arno, "Fire History of the Lamar Drainage Yellowstone National Park," in *University of Wyoming National Park Service Research Center: Fourteenth Annual Report, 1990,* ed. Mark Boyce and Glenn Plumb (Laramie: University of Wyoming, 1991), pp. 131–133.

39. Ibid.

40. Douglas Houston, "Wildfires in Northern Yellowstone National Park," *Ecology* 54, no. 5 (Summer 1973):1111-1117. For more on variations in fire regimes, see

Don Despain, *Yellowstone Vegetation: The Consequences of History and Environment in a Natural Setting* (Boulder, Colo.: Roberts Rinehart, 1990); and Roy Renkin and Don Despain, "Fuel Moisture, Forest Type, and Lightning-Caused Fire in Yellowstone National Park," *Canadian Journal of Forest Research* 22, no. 1 (1992):37–45.

The variations in fire regimes in Yellowstone caused a great deal of confusion among reporters and other commentators on the fires, leading quite a few of them astray as they attempted to advocate some policy or simply criticize the existing one. A representative example of this confusion was provided by *Outside* (December 1988):33–36, in which columnist Alston Chase invoked the common misimpression that Indians had routinely set fires in the park; he then added additional confusion by claiming that the park "was swept with fires every twenty-five years or so." He apparently believed he was demonstrating that the park suffered from extreme fuel buildups because more than a century had passed since the fires were allowed to burn. Evidently Chase misread Houston's (or some other ecologist's) description of the twenty- to twenty-five-year fire-return interval on northern range *grasslands* as somehow applying to the park's lodgepole pine forests, where the fire-return interval was often three hundred to four hundred years.

41. Weixelman, "Power to Evoke Wonder," p. 59.

42. Ibid., pp. 52–59.

43. A. P. Nasatir, *Before Lewis and Clark: Documents Illustrating the History of the Missouri, 1785–1804* (St. Louis: St. Louis Historical Documents Foundation, 1952), p. 381.

44. Clarence Carter, ed., "The Territories of Louisiana-Missouri, 1803–1806," in *The Territorial Papers of the United States,* vol. 13 (Washington: U.S. Government Printing Office, 1948), p. 243.

3. WILD ROMANTIC SPLENDOR

1. Haines, *Yellowstone Story,* 1:4–5. Lee Whittlesey, *Yellowstone Place Names* (Helena: Montana Historical Society, 1988), p. 169.

2. Ibid.

3. The Blackfeet, Shoshone, and less clearly attributed names are from a summary of other known Indian names in Weixelman, "Power to Evoke Wonder," pp. 31–32. The Bannock name is from Maxine Edmo and Velda Auck, Shoshone-Bannock Tribes Tribal Tax Commission, letter to Yellowstone Superintendent Robert Barbee, October 7, 1993, Yellowstone Park files. It is interesting to consider the consequences of one of these other names having been adopted by whites as the "correct" name for Yellowstone and used as the name for the national park.

4. The convoluted proprietorship of the Yellowstone region is thoroughly described, with very helpful maps, in Haines, *Yellowstone Story*, 1:30–33 and 60–65.

5. Bernard De Voto, *The Year of Decision, 1846* (Boston: Houghton Mifflin Company, 1943), p. 54.

6. Haines, *Yellowstone Story*, 1:35–38; Fred Gowans, *A Fur Trade History of Yellowstone Park* (Orem, Utah: Mountain Grizzly Publications, 1989), pp. 98–122 and maps 9 and 10; Merrill J. Mattes, *Colter's Hell and Jackson's Hole* (Yellowstone National Park: Yellowstone Library and Museum Association, 1962), pp. 13–17.

7. For the debunking of the name "Colter's Hell" for Yellowstone National Park, start with Mattes, *Colter's Hell*, pp. 19–24. Gowans, *Fur Trade History*, contains numerous early maps that trace the locating of the true Colter's Hell on the Shoshone River.

8. Theodore Roosevelt, *The Winning of the West*, Part I, *The Spread of English-Speaking Peoples* (New York: G. P. Putnam's Sons, 1889), p. 177.

9. Alexander Ross, *The Fur Hunters of the Far West*, vol. 1 (London: Smith, Elder and Co., 1855), p. 267.

10. I quote here from Potts's original letter, quirky spelling and all, rather than from the version later published in the *Niles Weekly Register*. Both Potts's original letter and the published version are reprinted in Gowans, *Fur Trade History*, pp. 187–190.

11. Lee Whittlesey, "Visitors to Yellowstone Hot Springs before 1870," *GOSA Transactions (Journal of the Geyser Observation and Study Association)* 4 (1993):203–211. This work is one of the foundation references on white activities in the Yellowstone Park area between 1800 and 1872, along with Haines, *Yellowstone Story*, 1; Haines, *Yellowstone National Park: Its Exploration and Establishment* (Washington: U.S. Government Printing Office, 1974); Gowans, *Fur Trade History*; and Paul Schullery and Lee Whittlesey, "The Documentary Record of Wolves and Related Wildlife Species in the Yellowstone National Park Area Prior to 1882," in *Wolves for Yellowstone?* 4:1.4–1.174.

12. Haines, *Yellowstone Story*, 1:53–59.

13. Russell, *Journal of a Trapper*, p. 13.

14. Ibid., p. 14.

15. Haines, *Yellowstone: Exploration and Establishment*, p. 10.

16. A. Bart Henderson, "Journal of the Yellowstone Expedition of 1866 under Captain Jeff Standifer . . . Also the diaries kept by Henderson during his prospecting journeys in the Snake, Wind River and Yellowstone Country during the years 1866–1872," ms. no. 452, Beinecke Library, Yale University; typescript in manuscript collection, Yellowstone National Park Research Library, Yellowstone National Park, p. 44.

17. Ralph Glidden, *Exploring the Yellowstone High Country* (Livingston, Mont.:

Ralph Glidden, 1976); Virginia Hansen and Al Funderbunk, *The Fabulous Past of Cooke City* (Billings, Mont.: Billings Gazette Printing Co., 1962).

18. William F. Raynolds, *The Report of Brevet Brigadier General W. F. Raynolds on the Exploration of the Yellowstone and the Country Drained by That River,* 40th Cong., 1st Sess., S. Exec. Doc. 77 (Washington: U.S. Government Printing Office, 1868), p. 86.

19. Charles Cook, David Folsom, and William Peterson, *The Valley of the Upper Yellowstone: An Exploration of the Headwaters of the Yellowstone River in the Year 1869,* ed. Aubrey Haines (Norman: University of Oklahoma Press, 1965).

20. Schullery and Whittlesey, "Documentary Record of Wolves." I am especially indebted to Lee Whittlesey for his years of tireless searching for the early accounts used in this report. His files contain many collaborating accounts and additional information that add support to our conclusions but were not included in this very large publication.

21. Russell, *Journal of a Trapper,* p. 66.

22. Alston Chase, *Playing God in Yellowstone* (Boston: Atlantic Monthly Press, 1986), p. 15.

23. Lt. J. W. Gunnison, *The Mormons, or Latter-Day Saints* (Philadelphia: Lippincott, Grambo, and Co., 1852), is the source of the Bridger information on Yellowstone-area wildlife. Raynolds, *Report,* pp. 84–87, describes the location and wildlife conditions of the area being traveled.

24. Chase, *Playing God in Yellowstone,* p. 15. Chase's other cited sources are just as inaccurately or incompletely portrayed. What makes Chase's argument so odd is that on the following page he disagrees with himself without breaking stride. One of the many criticisms of his book was its striking inconsistencies, such as that on page 16: having just argued that large animals were rare in Yellowstone, he says that large numbers of these animals were killed by market hunters in the 1870s, "according to the park's first Superintendent, Philetus W. Norris, as many as 7,000 in spring 1875 alone." If the park did not have large numbers of animals, where did all those carcasses come from?

What makes this statement even stranger is that it is in error. Norris (who was the second, not the first, park superintendent) actually said that "probably 7,000, or an annual average of 1,000 of them [elk], and hundreds if not thousands of each of these other animals have been thus killed since its discovery in 1870." Norris did not say that 7,000 elk were killed in the spring of 1875 but that 7,000 were killed from 1870 to 1875.

25. Ferdinand Hayden, *Preliminary Report of the U.S. Geological Survey of Montana and Portions of Adjacent Territories; Being a Fifth Annual Report of Progress* (Washington: U.S. Government Printing Office, 1872), p. 131.

26. J. W. Barlow and D. P. Heap, *Report of Reconnaissance of the Basin of the Upper Yellowstone in 1871,* 42nd Cong., 2nd Sess., S. Exec. Doc. 66, SN-1479, vol. 2 (Washington: U.S. Government Printing Office, 1872), pp. 21, 36, 40.

27. A.   . Peale, "1871 Diary, Typescript from book #1871," U.S.G.S. Field Records, Denver, copy at Yellowstone National Park Research Library.

28. William Blackmore, "Personal Diary #6, #7," Yellowstone National Park Research Library, p. 35; A. C. Peale, "1872 Diary, Typescript from University of Wyoming by Fritiof Fryxell, Jul. 21–Oct. 24, 1872," copy at Yellowstone National Park Research Library.

29. One of the most influential statements of the idea that large game was pushed into less desirable mountain habitats is H. S. Graves and E. W. Nelson, *Our National Elk Herds: A Program for Conserving the Elk on National Forests about the Yellowstone National Park*, U.S. Dept. of Agriculture Circular 51 (Washington: U.S. Government Printing Office, 1919). I discuss the development of these issues in Yellowstone in later chapters.

30. Reynolds, *Report*, pp. 86–87, discusses game in the area and the Indians' use of it.

31. Russell, *Journal of a Trapper*, p. 105.

32. Ibid., p. 27.

33. Ibid., p. 27.

34. Henderson, "Journal of the Yellowstone Expedition of 1866," p. 19. It is worth noting that at the beginning of his description of the large party (172 men) that set out under Captain Jeff Standifer from Reynolds City, Montana, in August of 1866, Henderson said that the group had "the understanding to shoot all the Indians that we should fall in with on the line of our trail, with the exception of the Snakes and Sheepeaters, or Bannacks, which profess friendship" (p. 10). Hostility was deep and institutionalized by the 1860s.

35. Ibid., p. 56.

36. A recent scientific book suggests that Yellowstone-area Indians killed so many animals that they provided scavenging carnivores a significant source of food. John Craighead, Jay Sumner, and John Mitchell, *The Grizzly Bears of Yellowstone: Their Ecology in the Yellowstone Ecosystem, 1959–1992* (Washington: Island Press, 1995), pp. 321–328, in a rather confused discussion of the effects of buffalo jumps on carnivores, seem to be proposing that Yellowstone grizzly bears have always congregated at such sites, though there is little archeological evidence of buffalo jumps in the present park, and only scattered sites elsewhere in Greater Yellowstone. The authors argue for the reopening of garbage dumps in the park, stating that they are essential to the nutritional needs and security of grizzly bears; they cite the archeological evidence from elsewhere in the West in part to justify such dumps, which they term "ecocenters." The authors seem not to understand either that Yellowstone lacks buffalo jumps or that such sites in many other locations were used only intermittently. There is no indication that the hunting practices of Indians in Greater Yellowstone created scavenging opportunities on even a small percentage of the scale of park dumps containing the garbage of 2,000,000 visitors.

4. A PUBLIC PARK

1. Haines, *Yellowstone: Exploration and Establishment,* p. 56.
2. The primary sources for the Washburn expedition are Haines, *Yellowstone Story,* 1:105–140; Haines, *Yellowstone: Exploration and Establishment,* pp. 59–99; and Bartlett, *Nature's Yellowstone* (Norman: University of Oklahoma Press, 1974), pp. 165–187. At least eight members of the party of nineteen left accounts, and some left several, in the form of letters, journals, and articles. Lieutenant Doane's account alone, a lengthy formal government publication, would have served for most purposes, and his is not even the most famous. Suddenly in 1870 we move from fragmented and tantalizing reports of some remote, ru-mored place to a full-blown journalistic treatment, and the reading of the Yellowstone adventure has never been improved on.
3. Lee Whittlesey, ed., *Lost in the Yellowstone: Truman Everts' "Thirty-Seven Days of Peril"* (Salt Lake City: University of Utah Press, 1995).
4. Cornelius Hedges, "Hell-Broth Springs," *Helena Daily Herald,* Oct. 19, 1870, reprinted in Louis Cramton, *Early History of Yellowstone National Park and Its Relation to National Park Policies* (Washington: U.S. Government Printing Of-fice, 1932), pp. 102–103.
5. Cornelius Hedges, "The Great Falls of the Yellowstone: A Graphic Picture of Their Grandeur and Beauty," *Helena Daily Herald,* Oct. 15, 1870, reprinted in Cramton, *Early History,* pp. 99–101.
6. Nathaniel Langford, *The Discovery of Yellowstone Park, Journal of the Washburn Expedition to the Yellowstone and Firehole Rivers in the Year 1870,* ed. Aubrey Haines (Lincoln: University of Nebraska Press, 1972), pp. 106–107.
7. Henry D. Washburn, "The Yellowstone Expedition: Explorations in a New and Wonderful Country — Description of the Great Falls of the Yellowstone — Volcanic Eruptions, Spouting Geysers, Etc.," *Helena Daily Herald,* Sept. 27 and 28, 1870, reprinted in Cramton, *Early History,* pp. 92–96.
8. Hedges, "Hell-Broth Hot Springs," in Cramton, *Early History,* p. 108.
9. Chris Magoc, "The Selling of Yellowstone: Yellowstone National Park, the Northern Pacific Railroad, and the Culture of Consumption, 1872–1903" (Ph.D. dissertation, University of New Mexico, 1992), pp. 228–302, discusses the reac-tions of early visitors to the park's various features, including thermal activity. Other helpful studies of visitors' attitudes and aesthetics include Katherine Early, *"For the Benefit and Enjoyment of the People": Cultural Attitudes and the Establishment of Yellowstone National Park,* Georgetown Monograph in Ameri-can Studies No. 1 (Washington: Georgetown University Press, 1984); Judith Meyer, *The Spirit of Yellowstone* (Lanham, Md.: Rowman & Littlefield, 1996); and Karl Byrand, "The Evolution of the Cultural Landscape in Yellowstone Na-tional Park's Upper Geyser Basin and the Changing Visitor Experience, 1872–1990" (M.S. thesis, Montana State University, 1995).

10. The original telling of this story by a historian was Chittenden, *Yellowstone National Park*, pp. 89–91. I am especially grateful for the assistance of and conversations with P. J. Ryan, Richard Sellars, and Lee Whittlesey, all of whom have given the campfire myth considerable thought. Richard Sellars provided me with a number of important items of correspondence from the discussion within the park service of the campfire myth in 1971 and 1972. I first learned about the historical problems of the story from Aubrey Haines in conversations in Bozeman after he retired in about 1975 and, more recently, during a tour of the park with him and other park staff in the summer of 1993.

11. Hans Huth, "Yosemite: The Story of an Idea," *Sierra Club Bulletin* 33 (March 1948):72; Carl Russell, "Madison Junction Museum Prospectus," typescript dated June 3, 1960, p. 19, quoted in Aubrey Haines's letter to NPS chief historian Robert Utley, Jan. 3, 1972, from Haines's files, p. 2.

12. Aubrey Haines, "Excerpts from the Diary of Cornelius Hedges (July 6, 1870 to January 29, 1871)," transcribed from the original diary in Montana Historical Society Library, Helena; typescript in manuscript collection, Yellowstone Research Library, Yellowstone National Park, p. 12.

13. Cornelius Hedges, "Journal of Judge Cornelius Hedges," *Contributions to the Historical Society of Montana* 5 (1904): 372.

14. Haines, letter to Utley, Jan. 3, 1972.

15. Haines, *Yellowstone Story*, 1:138. Bartlett, *Nature's Yellowstone*, pp. 195–206, does a fine and very readable job of summarizing the whole question of patrimony of Yellowstone National Park, discussing various problems with Langford's and others' claims.

16. Haines, letter to Utley, Jan. 3, 1972, p. 6.

17. On the other hand, I share the opinion of both Haines and Bartlett about Hedges. As Bartlett put it in *Nature's Yellowstone* (p. 181), "Cornelius Hedges was a fine man in every way, sensitive to beauty and with a feeling for his fellow men." As Haines pointed out in his letter to Utley (p. 8), when Hedges wrote in 1904 that "I first suggested uniting all our efforts to get it made a national park" around the campfire at Madison Junction, he was making a true statement. It was the first time *he* had made such a suggestion, though by no means the first time anybody had suggested it. Hedges's own interest in the park area and in the public's future enjoyment of it was also obvious in his first writings. On Nov. 9, 1870, in one of his *Helena Daily Herald* articles, he proposed that the park area should be removed from Wyoming Territory and added to Montana Territory so that Montanans could "secure its future appropriation to public use." His awareness that the public would love Yellowstone is obvious in another comment in the same article, a complaint about the sadness of the party (over the loss of Truman Everts) at Yellowstone Lake: "Future generations may find on this south shore hallowed grounds, but it was soundly and sorely cursed by us." And in his Oct. 15, 1870, article in the same paper, he said that the Lower Falls

was "surely destined at no distant day to become a shrine for a world-wide pilgrimage."

18. Besides Haines, *Yellowstone Story,* vol. 1, and Bartlett, *Nature's Yellowstone,* see also Alfred Runte, *National Parks: The American Experience* (Lincoln: University of Nebraska Press, 1979); Hans Huth, *Nature and the American: Three Centuries of Changing Attitudes* (Berkeley: University of California Press, 1957); and Nash, *Wilderness and the American Mind.*

19. Haines, *Yellowstone: Exploration and Establishment,* p. 45.

20. Cook, Folsom, and Peterson, *Valley of the Upper Yellowstone,* p. 103.

21. Haines, *Yellowstone Story,* 1:105.

22. Ibid., p. 137.

23. Ibid., p. 155.

24. Besides Haines's and Bartlett's treatments of the legislative maneuverings, see especially H. Duane Hampton, *How the U.S. Cavalry Saved Our National Parks* (Bloomington: Indiana University Press, 1971), pp. 20–31.

25. Runte, *National Parks,* pp. 31–32.

26. Ibid., p. 14.

27. Ibid., p. 38.

28. Ibid.

29. *U.S. Statutes at Large,* vol. 17 (Washington: U.S. Government Printing Office, 1872), chap. 24, pp. 32–33.

30. Haines, *Yellowstone: Exploration and Establishment,* p. 123.

31. Runte, *National Parks,* p. 50.

32. Ibid., p. 53.

33. Haines, *Yellowstone Story,* 1:124. See also Early, *"For the Benefit and Enjoyment of the People,"* for another overview of the background of the organic act.

34. Haines, *Yellowstone: Exploration and Establishment,* p. 127.

35. Ibid., p. 126.

5. Ecological Holocaust

1. Tom McHugh, *The Time of the Buffalo* (New York: Alfred A. Knopf, 1972); David Dary, *The Buffalo Book* (Chicago: Swallow Press, 1974).

2. Schullery and Whittlesey, "Documentary Record of Wolves," contains the most complete assemblage of these accounts, in the form of firsthand published descriptions, unpublished reminiscences, and correspondence with government officials.

3. Philetus W. Norris, "Meanderings of a Mountaineer, or the Journals and Musings (or storys) of a Rambler over Prairie (or Mountain) and Plain," manuscript prepared from newspaper clippings (1870–1875) and handwritten additions, annotated by the author about 1885, Huntington Library, San Marino, Calif.

4. William E. Strong, *A Trip to the Yellowstone National Park in July, August, and September, 1875*, ed. Richard Bartlett (Norman: University of Oklahoma Press, 1968), p. 104.

5. George Bird Grinnell, "Zoological Report," in *Report of a Reconnaissance from Carroll, Montana Territory, on the Upper Missouri to the Yellowstone National Park and Return, Made in the Summer of 1875*, ed. William Ludlow (Washington: U.S. Government Printing Office, 1876), p. 66.

6. Ludlow, *Report of a Reconnaissance*, p. 37.

7. Gustavus C. Doane, *Battle Drums and Geysers*, ed. O. and L. Bonney (Chicago: Swallow Press, 1970), pp. 476–477.

8. Schullery and Whittlesey, "Documentary Record of Wolves," reviews these accounts. We have since reviewed an additional fifty or more accounts that buttress our interpretations of this period.

9. Strong, *Trip to the Yellowstone National Park*, pp. 46–106, contains numerous mentions of wildlife conditions. According to their guide, Jack Baronett, in eastern Yellowstone "big game is still so very abundant that he says we will see elk in great bands, containing hundreds, and no end to mountain sheep and deer" (p. 47). Schullery and Whittlesey, "Documentary Record of Wolves," 1.97–1.101, reviews Strong's accounts and interprets them in the light of other accounts from the period. The Norris statement is from "Meanderings of a Mountaineer."

10. Besides Haines, *Yellowstone Story*, vol. 1, and Beal, *Story of Man in Yellowstone*, see Richard Bartlett, *Yellowstone: A Wilderness Besieged* (Tucson: University of Arizona Press); Hampton, *U.S. Cavalry*; and Paul Schullery, *Yellowstone's Ski Pioneers: Peril and Heroism on the Winter Trail* (Worland, Wyo.: High Plains Publishing, 1995).

11. Theodore Geikie, *Geological Sketches at Home and Abroad* (London: Macmillan, 1882), pp. 227–228.

12. Philetus Norris, *Report upon the Yellowstone National Park to the Secretary of the Interior* (Washington: U.S. Government Printing Office, 1880), p. 27.

13. John Reiger, *American Sportsmen and the Origins of Conservation* (New York: Winchester Press, 1975), reviews Grinnell's writings. *Forest and Stream* is in some ways a neglected resource, for it tracked the political machinations of park supporters, enemies, and users and also contained, in its more than five hundred Yellowstone-related articles, letters, and notes, a wealth of specific natural-resource information that is only now being fully appreciated.

14. For the development of European attitudes toward wildlife, see Thomas, *Man and the Natural World*. For the humane movement and related issues in the nineteenth century, see Harriet Ritvo, *The Animal Estate: The English and Other Creatures in the Victorian Age* (Cambridge: Harvard University Press, 1987). For two views of the American wildlife conservation movement in the late nineteenth century, see Reiger, *American Sportsmen*; and Thomas R. Dunlap,

Saving America's Wildlife: Ecology and the American Mind, 1850–1990 (Princeton: Princeton University Press, 1988).

15. Secretary of the Interior H. M. Teller, letter to the superintendent, Yellowstone National Park, Jan. 15, 1883, Incoming Correspondence, document 162, Yellowstone Archives. The letter was printed in a variety of periodicals, including the Bozeman *Avant Courier*, Feb. 22, 1883, so local distribution was ensured.

16. See, for example, Grinnell's editorial in *Forest and Stream*, Jan. 18, 1883, p. 481, which reprints the Teller memorandum and states that the hunting prohibition ensures "good hunting for all who may desire to have the satisfaction of killing in moderation these noble species." The Grinnell quotation is from a front-page editorial, "Game in the Great West," *Forest and Stream*, July 8, 1890. Many of the accounts of Yellowstone in the 1870s, including some of those quoted here, obviously saw the park as a potential game reserve. Reiger, *American Sportsmen*, pp. 99–100, also has pointed out that the idea of Yellowstone as a game reserve actually surfaced quite early in the park's history. He cites Theodore Comstock, a scientist who wrote several impassioned articles on behalf of park protection, in 1874 proposing the park as a refuge for the fast-vanishing bison. He also cites Grinnell emphasizing in 1877 the need for better protection of the bison in Yellowstone. There was a chorus of support for protecting park wildlife through the 1870s, but the idea of a game *reservoir* apparently did not arise until the early 1880s, that is, the idea of a reserve in which the animals were entirely protected from public shooting or trapping.

17. Philetus Norris, *Report on the Yellowstone National Park to the Secretary of the Interior* (Washington: U.S. Government Printing Office, 1877), p. 843.

18. Ibid.

19. Norris, *Report upon the Yellowstone* (1880), pp. 43–44.

20. E. R. Warren, "A Study of the Beaver of the Yancey Region of Yellowstone National Park," *Roosevelt Wildlife Annals* 1, nos. 1–2 (1926):12–191. Warren confirmed that the beaver were indeed quite numerous. It appears that their population peaked in the 1920s; by the 1950s, when they were again studied, their numbers were quite low, though they continue to be widely distributed in the park.

21. A typical portrayal of the beaver population of the 1920s as a "natural" population size appeared in D. Glick, M. Carr, and B. Harting, *An Environmental Profile of the Greater Yellowstone Ecosystem* (Bozeman, Mont.: Greater Yellowstone Ecosystem, 1991).

22. James Peek, *A Review of Wildlife Management* (Englewood Cliffs, N.J.: Prentice Hall, 1986), p. 224.

23. Dunlap, *Saving America's Wildlife*, p. 16.

24. Norris, *Report upon the Yellowstone* (1880), p. 42.

25. Schullery and Whittlesey, "Documentary Record of Wolves," pp. 1.1–1.147.

26. For a summary of some of the complexities of wildlife communities, see Peek,

Review of Wildlife Management; and Graeme Caughley and Anthony R. E. Sinclair, *Wildlife Ecology and Management* (Boston: Blackwell Scientific Publications, 1994).

27. Recent computer modeling work includes John A. Mack and Francis J. Singer, "Population Models for Elk, Mule Deer, and Moose on Yellowstone's Northern Range," in *Wolves for Yellowstone?* pp. 4.3–4.42; John A. Mack and Francis J. Singer, "Predicted Effects of Wolf Predation on Northern Range Elk, Mule Deer, and Moose Using POP-II Models," in *Wolves for Yellowstone?* pp. 4.43–4.70; Mark S. Boyce and Jean-Michel Gaillard, "Wolves in Yellowstone, Jackson Hole, and the North Fork of the Shoshone River: Simulating Ungulate Consequences of Wolf Recovery," in *Wolves for Yellowstone?* pp. 4.71–4.116; and Edward O. Garton et al., "Potential Impacts of Yellowstone Wolves on Clarks Fork Elk Herd," in *Wolves for Yellowstone?* pp. 4.131–4.136.

28. William Romme et al., "Aspen, Elk and Fire in Northern Yellowstone National Park," *Ecology* 76, no. 7 (1995):2097–2106.

29. "Murder or Suicide at Mammoth Hot Springs," Bozeman *Avant Courier,* Mar. 14, 1873.

30. Paul Shepard, *The Others: How Animals Made Us Human* (Washington: Island Press, 1996), p. 167.

31. Paul Schullery, *The Bears of Yellowstone* (Worland, Wyo.: High Plains Publishing Co., 1992); Paul Schullery, *Yellowstone Bear Tales* (Niwot, Colo.: Roberts Rinehart Publishing, 1991).

32. A review of the evolution of fisheries management in Yellowstone appears in John D. Varley and Paul Schullery, *Freshwater Wilderness: Yellowstone Fishes and Their World* (Yellowstone National Park: Yellowstone Library and Museum Association, 1983), pp. 100–107.

33. Ibid., p. 21.

34. Rudyard Kipling, *American Notes* (1891; reprint, New York: Arcadia House, 1950), p. 142.

35. Reiger, *American Sportsmen,* p. 106.

6. PRIVATIONS AND INCONVENIENCES

1. Haines, *Yellowstone Story,* 1:354, attributes the source of the name "Wonderland" to imitation of Lewis Carroll, *Alice's Adventures in Wonderland* (1866). He further notes that "the little girl Dodgson [Carroll] wrote his story for visited Yellowstone National Park as a grownup and seemed almost as thrilled as if she had really gotten into that peculiar place through the rabbit hole." Whittlesey, *Yellowstone Place Names,* p. 166, cites A. Bart Henderson's diary for July 24, 1871, as the earliest known use of "Wonderland" in reference to the park. Some parts of Henderson's diary were clearly written after the date given, and I have wondered if this use of "Wonderland" might have been a retrospective addition.

2. Haines, *Yellowstone Story,* 2:31.
3. Nathaniel Langford, *A Report of the Superintendent of the Yellowstone National Park for the Year 1872* (Washington: U.S. Government Printing Office, 1873), p. 2.
4. Carrie Strahorn, *Fifteen Thousand Miles by Stage* (New York: G. P. Putnam's Sons, 1911), p. 268. The best and most detailed summary of the early visitor's experience in Yellowstone is Lee Whittlesey, "Yellowstone's Horse-and-Buggy Tour Guides: Interpreting the Grand Old Park, 1872–1920," manuscript, February 1996. See Haines, *Yellowstone Story,* vol. 2; and Bartlett, *Yellowstone: A Wilderness Besieged,* for more on the early tourist experience. See also Bartlett's excellent overview of the park's first decade of tourism in "Will Anyone Come Here for Pleasure?" *American West* 6, no. 5 (September 1969):10–16.
5. Concerning the issue of value judgments of early park opponents and threats, I am especially indebted to H. Duane Hampton, "Opposition to National Parks," *Journal of Forest History* 25, no. 1 (1981):36–45.
6. Haines, *Yellowstone Story,* 1:196–198; and Bartlett, *Yellowstone: A Wilderness Besieged,* pp. 116–117.
7. Bartlett, who described Waters as "probably the most difficult concessioner who ever operated in Yellowstone Park," told his story superbly in *Yellowstone: A Wilderness Besieged,* pp. 189–193. For a well-researched and entertaining account of the park interior's first hotel keeper, George Marshall, see Lee Whittlesey, "Marshall's Hotel in the National Park," *Montana: The Magazine of Western History* 30 (Fall 1980):42–51. Marshall started his hotel service on Fountain Flats near the junction of Nez Perce Creek and the Firehole River in 1880.
8. Along with the detailed treatment of the YPIC by Haines and Bartlett, see also Magoc, "Selling of Wonderland."
9. Hampton, *U.S. Cavalry,* pp. 53–80.
10. Haines, *Yellowstone Story,* 1:200.
11. Owen Wister, as reprinted in Paul Schullery, ed., *Old Yellowstone Days* (Boulder: Colorado Associated University Press, 1979), p. 74.
12. Ibid., pp. 75–76.
13. Magoc, "Selling of Wonderland," p. 4.
14. Eric Leed, *The Mind of the Traveler: From Gilgamesh to Global Tourism* (New York: Basic Books, 1991), p. 286.
15. Magoc, "Selling of Wonderland," p. 5.
16. John Sears, *Sacred Places: American Tourist Attractions in the Nineteenth Century* (New York: Oxford University Press, 1989), p. 181.
17. Rudyard Kipling, as quoted in Schullery, *Old Yellowstone Days,* p. 87.
18. Frederic Remington, as quoted in Schullery, *Old Yellowstone Days,* p. 119.
19. Yellowstone superintendent Robert Barbee and I, in a presentation given by him to the Arts for the Parks annual awards meeting in Jackson, Wyoming, Sept. 26, 1992, suggested that in fact works of art may have been the most important influence on public impressions of the park at a time when very few Americans

had actually seen it; just as important, they led the way in establishing the aesthetic standard by which later visitors viewed the park:

> In Yellowstone, of course, the name we all think of first is Moran. His field sketches helped Congress to create Yellowstone National Park; when in recent times has an artist wielded that kind of power in the real world of legislative negotiation? And yet, what may be most impressive about Thomas Moran, and about William Henry Jackson, the pioneering photographer who traveled Yellowstone with him in 1871, is not what they achieved politically, but what they achieved aesthetically. What impresses me is how often they got it right — how often they established the standard for the rest of us. They had the vision needed to take a whole new world and define its artistic possibilities for all the generations that followed. There were no signs or boardwalks leading them to the best vistas; they just knew them when they saw them. And we, standing figuratively on the aesthetic shoulders of these giants, look from the same vistas and find all the wonder they did so long ago.

Historian Judith Meyer, in her fascinating study *The Spirit of Yellowstone*, has made a point similar to mine regarding the visitor experience, emphasizing that standardization of the basic trip did not necessarily equate with uniformity of experience: "People have always come — and probably always will come — to Yellowstone 'preprogrammed' to encounter, interpret, and describe the park in particular ways. However, such expectations do not preclude fascination and surprise. Even today, when so much has been written, painted, photographed, even filmed about the park, most tourists still find something about the Yellowstone that is a surprise" (p. 74).

Charles Dudley Warner's statement about the park being well reported is quoted in Schullery, *Old Yellowstone Days*, p. 160. Whittlesey, "Yellowstone's Horse-and-Buggy Tour Guides," points out that "by 1895, there were numerous national, regional, and local lecturers" on Yellowstone Park and provides abundant evidence of their extraordinary reach in American culture.

The importance of art, folk art, and such commercial combinations of art and photography as postcards, is apparent in Richard Saunders, "Graphic Images and Publisher Exploitation of Yellowstone Park in Postcards: 'Viewing the Marvelous Scenes in Wonderland,'" *Popular Culture in Libraries* 3 no. 2 (1995):121–139. As Saunders points out in describing the postcard industry of Niagara Falls, Washington, D.C., and Yellowstone National Park, "There are hundreds of images from each place and even before mid-century literally tens of millions of cards were produced and sold." Imagine the reach of millions of small images of Yellowstone coming into the homes of Americans.

20. Unfortunately, like all those who have positions on this issue, I am unable to provide quantification for my view in terms of undeniable proof of the degra-

dation of the experience. It is almost as difficult to provide incontrovertible proof that the Yellowstone resource has been degraded by the heavy visitation, though it seems obvious that the *Greater* Yellowstone resource is losing ground steadily. See further discussion of this subject in Chapters 11 and 12.

21. Haines, "On the Grand Tour," *Yellowstone Story,* 2:100–159, fully describes the variety and process of the early tourist experience in Yellowstone.

22. Sears, *Sacred Places,* p. 123.

23. A very helpful case study of changing attitudes among managers, concessioners, and visitors in one portion of Yellowstone is Byrand, "Evolution of the Cultural Landscape."

24. Janetski, *Indians of Yellowstone Park.*

25. Haines, *Yellowstone Story,* 1:216–239.

26. See especially Janetski, *Indians of Yellowstone Park,* pp. 77–83, and Weixelman, "Power to Evoke Wonder."

27. John Muir, as quoted in Schullery, *Old Yellowstone Days,* p. 50.

7. A SINGLE ROCK

1. Haines, *Yellowstone Story,* 1:450–453.

2. Lee Whittlesey, "The First National Park Interpreter," *Montana: The Magazine of Western History* 46, no. 1 (1996):26–41.

3. Quoted in Hampton, *U.S. Cavalry,* p. 71.

4. William Hallett Phillips, "Report of W. H. Phillips on the Yellowstone Park," in H. L. Muldrow, "Letter from the Acting Secretary of the Interior, Transmitting, in Response to Senate Resolution January 12, 1886, Report of W. H. Phillips on the Yellowstone Park," 49th Cong., 1st Sess., Ex. Doc. No. 51, p. 8. It is a special joy to do research in the park's research library; the copy of this report that I used was inscribed "Captain Harris with compliments of W. Hallett Phillips." The privy offenses were reported to Phillips in a letter from a New York man, B. P. Lincoln. Phillips appended the letter to his report, pp. 28–29.

5. Phillips, "A Report," p. 6.

6. Ibid., p. 8.

7. Ibid., p. 7.

8. See especially Haines, *Yellowstone Story,* 2:94–95. Haines makes the point that this was the first official expression of the need to extend the park's boundaries and that the primary impetus was game preservation.

9. George Bird Grinnell, "Their Last Refuge," *Forest and Stream,* Dec. 14, 1882, p. 383. This article also reviews earlier recommendations for the expansion or military protection of the park, especially Sheridan's that same year.

10. The essential sources on the military contribution to Yellowstone are Hampton, *U.S. Cavalry;* Haines, *Yellowstone Story,* 2:3–275; and Bartlett, *Yellowstone: A Wilderness Besieged,* pp. 257–279.

11. As quoted in Schullery, *Old Yellowstone Days*, p. 127.

12. The essential sources for the history of the Corps in Yellowstone are Mary Shivers Culpin, *The History of the Construction of the Road System in Yellowstone National Park, 1872–1966*, Vol. 1: *Historic Resource Study* (Denver: Rocky Mountain Region, National Park Service, 1994); and Haines, *Yellowstone Story*, 2:209–255.

13. As quoted in Culpin, *Construction of the Road System*, p. 43.

14. Ibid.

15. Culpen, *Construction of the Road System*, throughout reviews the challenges of this philosophy. Another superb example of the tension between modern standards and traditional values is Going-to-the-Sun Road through Glacier National Park, a classic auto trail that cannot be used by the full range of modern commercial vehicles.

16. A review of the effects of park developments on bears is David Mattson, "Human Impacts on Bear Habitat Use," in *Bears — Their Biology and Management*, ed. Laura Darling and W. Ralph Archibald (International Association for Bear Research and Management, 1990), pp. 33–56. For a study of the effects of human use of trails on grizzly bears, see Kerry A. Gunther, "Visitor Impact on Grizzly Bear Activity in Pelican Valley, Yellowstone National Park," *International Conference on Bear Research and Management* 8 (1990):73–78.

17. The authoritative source on the history of management of Yellowstone bison is Mary Meagher, *The Bison of Yellowstone National Park* (Washington: U.S. Government Printing Office, 1973). See also Paul Schullery, "'Buffalo' Jones and the Bison Herd in Yellowstone: Another Look," *Montana: The Magazine of Western History* (Summer 1976):40–50; and David Price and Paul Schullery, "The Bison of Yellowstone: The Challenge of Conservation," *Bison World* (November–December 1993):18–23.

18. For the capture of Howell, see Schullery, *Yellowstone's Ski Pioneers*, pp. 98–115.

19. My discussion of elk numbers is based primarily on Douglas Houston, *The Northern Yellowstone Elk: Ecology and Management* (New York: Macmillan, 1982), especially pp. 11–25 and 204–237.

20. Houston, *Northern Yellowstone Elk*, pp. 212–229, summarizes army reports on elk.

21. Ibid., p. 15.

22. Paul Schullery and Lee Whittlesey, "Greater Yellowstone Predators: A History of Changing Attitudes," in *Greater Yellowstone Predators*, ed. Tim Clark et al. (in press).

23. Ibid.

24. Theodore Roosevelt, letter to Gen. S. B. M. Young, Jan. 22, 1908, Manuscript File 92–36, Yellowstone National Park Research Library.

25. Secretary of the Interior, *Rules, Regulations and Instructions for the Information and Guidance of Officers and Enlisted Men of the United States Army and of the*

Scouts Doing Duty in the Yellowstone National Park (Washington: U.S. Government Printing Office, 1907).

26. Adolph Murie, *Ecology of the Coyote in Yellowstone* (Washington: U.S. Government Printing Office, 1940), p. 15.

27. Early, *"For the Benefit and Enjoyment,"* p. 6.

8. BIG MEN WITH FINE PERSONALITIES

1. This statement was made by the president of the American Civic Association, J. Horace McFarland. I quote it from Paul Schullery, ed., *Theodore Roosevelt: Wilderness Writings* (Layton, Utah: Peregrine Smith Books, 1986), p. 143. McFarland has until recently been a neglected figure in American conservation history, but a new biography should help place him in context. See Ernest Morrison, *J. Horace McFarland: A Thorn for Beauty* (Harrisburg: Pennsylvania Historical and Museum Commission, 1995).

2. "An Act to Establish a National Park Service, and for Other Purposes," 64th Cong., 1st Sess., H.R. 15522. A good short overview of the evolution of the guiding principles of National Park Service management is Richard W. Sellars, "The Roots of National Park Management," *Journal of Forestry* 90, no. 1 (January 1992):16–19.

Not long after the fires of 1988, a conference was held at Snowbird, Utah, to consider National Park Service fire policy. The park service was not the sponsor, and in fact not all that many of us from the agency were there; at first glance it appeared to be a sort of setup for representatives of other agencies and universities to give us the benefit of their wisdom and bash us into line. But it didn't turn out that way. All the expected opinions were represented, but the most impassioned defense of the park service fire policy was made by a U.S. Forest Service biologist, and the most heated criticisms came from a group that I did not expect (though I should have) to feel so strongly about it: landscape architects. Landscape architecture is an especially important discipline in parks; the professionals in this field help decide many subtle issues, such as the least intrusive way to alter the vegetation at pullouts along park roads, and they deal regularly in such pressing matters as the best ways to restore native soils and vegetation after they have been disturbed because of park development. But some landscape architects from the university community had a larger mission in mind: to reassert the traditional primacy of scenery in the national parks. They invoked the National Park Service Act of 1916, correctly pointing out that it said "conserve the scenery" before anything else.

Here was a constituency I had not even thought about that was outraged at the direction of Yellowstone management. Arguments that ecological realities have forced us to reconsider the whole idea of scenery, or that the scenery before the 1988 fires was itself the product of huge fires, were ineffective against their indignation. For them Yellowstone was legally beautiful and scenically successful only in green. Others at the conference (and not part of the National Park Service, I was relieved to notice) accused the landscape architects of being "scenery engineers" who were missing the point of protecting wildlands and were trying to suppress process, which ought to be viewed as beautiful in a deeper way than any merely pretty scene can be, in favor of an almost theatrical photogenic quality. (This reminded me of a hearsay quotation by an unnamed fire information staffer during the fires of 1988, that she liked driving through the burns in the park because they "broke up the monotony of the beauty.")

3. Anon., "Legacy: The Way We Were," informal note circulated in the National Park Service (n.d.) quoting 1926 letter from Yellowstone superintendent Horace Albright to seasonal applicants, author's files.

4. For more on the modern ranger, see Paul Schullery, *Mountain Time* (New York: Schocken/Nick Lyons, 1984), pp. 141–154; Robert Cahn, "Low Pay and Changing Roles Thin Ranks of Park Rangers," *Christian Science Monitor*, May 30, 1991, pp. 12–13; and Robert Clay Cunningham, "National Park Rangers: Challenges for the Next 25 Years," *Earth Work* (July 1991):29–31.

But the ranger's story is only one aspect of Yellowstone's social history that begs for attention from scholars. There is a world of unwritten social history in the park. Historian Lee Whittlesey recently pointed out that when the first large hotel in the park was completed in 1883, a largely black staff abruptly materialized to tend it (Lee Whittlesey, "A History of Black Americans in Yellowstone National Park," manuscript). Where did they come from, and how and when were they replaced by today's seasonal employees — and who are they?

What other issues of race and gender are revealed in Yellowstone's history? For many years the preferred "big men with fine personalities" weren't even allowed to bring their spouses with them or were not provided with family housing. The first book-length scholarly attempt to consider the role of women in the National Park Service is Polly Welts Kaufman, *National Parks and the Woman's Voice: A History* (Albuquerque: University of New Mexico Press, 1996). Kaufman discusses the barriers that for many years kept women from holding professional positions in the national parks and provides numerous anecdotes of women's experiences visiting and working in Yellowstone.

5. Schullery, *Mountain Time*, p. 14.

6. Frances Joyce Farnsworth, *Cubby in Wonderland* (Albuquerque: University of New Mexico Press, 1932), p. 31.

7. Haines, *Yellowstone Story*, 2:289–291.

8. I am grateful to Susan Neel, Montana State University Library, for reminding me of the idea of Yellowstone as theatre expressed in Sears, *Sacred Places*.

9. Joe Mitchell Chapple, *A'Top o' the World* (Boston: Chapple Publishing Co., 1922), p. 16.

10. Haines, *Yellowstone Story*, 2:263–265.

11. A fine review of early autos in Yellowstone is Bartlett, *Yellowstone: A Wilderness Besieged*, pp. 82–110.

12. Lee Whittlesey, "Yellowstone's Horse-and-Buggy Tour Guides," p. 25; Haines, *Yellowstone Story*, 2:273.

13. Visitation statistics are from Yellowstone National Park records, annually updated by the public affairs office. Railroad statistics are from Kirby Lambert, "The Lure of the Parks," *Montana: The Magazine of Western History* 46, no. 1 (Spring 1996):54.

14. James E. Vance, Jr., *Capturing the Horizon: The Historical Geography of Transportation Since the Transportation Revolution of the Sixteenth Century* (New York: Harper & Row, 1986), pp. 494–499.

15. A contemporary description of the Park-to-Park Highway is "Seeing the Western National Parks by Motor," *American Forests* 35, no. 8 (August 1929), pp. 508–509. A little-known but powerful and fascinating account of a trip to all the western parks in June and July of 1938 is Thomas Wolfe, *A Western Journal: A Daily Log of the Great Parks Trip* (Pittsburgh: University of Pittsburgh Press, 1951). This unedited edition of Wolfe's journal is a continuous sentence of thoughts and impressions, which he intended to develop into a book but was not able to before his death that same year.

16. Eric Sandeen, "Yellowstone Roads," *Yellowstone Science* 4, no. 2 (Spring 1996):12.

17. See, for example, Rose Houk, *Going-to-the-Sun: The Story of the Highway across Glacier National Park* (Englewood, Calif.: Woodlands Press and Glacier Natural History Association, 1984), for an overview of one of the most spectacular road-building achievements, and perhaps the single major visitor attraction, in Glacier National Park.

18. Richard Russell, National Park Service archivist, Harpers Ferry Center, W.V., personal communication, 1977.

19. Horace Albright, Preface, *Ranger Naturalists Manual of Yellowstone National Park* (Yellowstone National Park: National Park Service, 1927), p. ii.

20. *Nature* magazine editorial, quoted in *Yellowstone Nature Notes* 11 (nos. 5 and 6) (May–June 1934):24. A good overview of the development of interpretation under the National Park Service is "Park Naturalists and the Evolution of National Park Service Interpretation Through World War II," *Journal of Forestry* (January 1978):24–43.

21. Whittlesey, "Yellowstone's Horse-and-Buggy Tour Guides." See also Lee Whittlesey, "The First National Park Interpreter," *Montana: The Magazine of Western History* 46, no. 1 (Spring 1996):26–41.

22. Bartlett, *Yellowstone: A Wilderness Besieged*, p. 309.

23. Byrand, "Evolution of the Cultural Landscape," p. 233.

24. Ibid., p. 255.

25. Susan Neel, "All These Things Through the Eyes of Love: Nature, Romance, and

Tourism in Yellowstone," paper presented at Montana State University, Mountain Research Center lunch lecture series, Apr. 10, 1996.

26. Byrand, "Evolution of the Cultural Landscape," p. 270.
27. Haines, *Yellowstone Story*, 2:116.
28. Edmund Sawyer, "The Captive Animals," *Yellowstone Nature Notes* 3, no. 2 (February 1926):6.
29. Aubrey Haines, personal communications, summer 1993.
30. Schullery, *Bears of Yellowstone*, pp. 102–108.
31. Ibid., p. 254. We now know that bears are effective elk predators, taking a significant number each year. The extent to which they were viewed as benign is revealed by Marguerite Lindsley, "Predatory Animals of Yellowstone National Park," in *Ranger Naturalists Manual*, pp. 80–81, in which she declared that "none of the bears are considered predacious." Schullery, *Yellowstone Bear Tales*, provides several firsthand accounts from before 1940 of bears preying upon ungulates, but at the time these acts were apparently regarded as untypical behavior for Yellowstone bears.
32. Varley and Schullery, *Freshwater Wilderness* (Yellowstone Park: Yellowstone Library and Museum Association, 1983), pp. 100–107.
33. Edward Hewitt, *A Trout and Salmon Fisherman for Seventy-Five Years* (Croton-on-Hudson, N.Y.: Van Cortlandt Press, 1972), pp. 16–17.
34. Howard Back, *The Waters of Yellowstone with Rod and Fly* (New York: Dodd, Mead, 1938); Ray Bergman, *Trout* (New York: Alfred A. Knopf, 1938), pp. 227–242.

9. Reasonable Illusions

1. A recent and quite energetic (if one-sided) consideration of balkanization is Frederic H. Wagner et al., *Wildlife Policies in the U.S. National Parks* (Washington: Island Press, 1995), pp. 160–161. Another complaint about this localized authority in the national parks is Stephen J. Pyne, "Burning Questions and False Alarms about Wildfires in Yellowstone," *Forum for Applied Research and Public Policy* (Summer 1989):37: "As a political entity, the National Park Service is feudalistic, with Yellowstone its chief barony. The agency has inadequate control at the national level over programs sponsored by individual parks. Until the agency can enforce conformity to its policies, little will be gained by reforming these policies."
2. Norm Bishop sometimes used this analogy in a slide presentation about the northern range given to a variety of audiences in the 1990s.
3. Major sources for the following discussion of elk management and research history between 1910 and 1960 are Houston, *Northern Yellowstone Elk;* Daniel Tyers, "The Condition of the Northern Winter Range in Yellowstone National

Park — A Discussion of the Controversy" (M.S. professional paper, Montana State University, 1981); and Don Despain, Douglas Houston, Mary Meagher, and Paul Schullery, *Wildlife in Transition: Man and Nature on Yellowstone's Northern Range* (Boulder, Colo: Roberts Rinehart, 1986).

4. The myth that the number of white-tailed deer declined was established by Milton Skinner, "White-Tailed Deer Formerly in the Yellowstone National Park," *Journal of Mammalogy* 10 (1929):101–115. Schullery and Whittlesey, "Documentary Record of Wolves," p. 1.155, reviewed 168 pre-1882 accounts of the park area and concluded that white-tails were quite rare in the park, if resident at all, in the early historical period. Robert Jonas, "A Population and Ecological Study of the Beaver *(Castor canadensis)* of Yellowstone National Park" (M.S. thesis, University of Idaho, 1955), listed several reasons for the decline of beaver between 1920 and 1950; one of his listed reasons, but not the first, was competition with elk. One of the many confused retellings of the supposed "disappearance" of the beaver from Yellowstone is "Jonas and the Beaver," from Chase, *Playing God in Yellowstone,* pp. 11–13, 28, and 85–87; Chase portrays the beaver population of the teens and twenties (actually an unusual irruption) as the appropriate level for the park, and blames the subsequent decline of beaver entirely on an overpopulation of elk.

5. Houston, *Northern Yellowstone Elk,* p. 15.

6. Tyers, "Condition of the Northern Winter Range," p. 18.

7. Meagher, *Bison of Yellowstone,* contains the most extended and thoroughly researched collection of bison population estimates and counts through the history of the park up until 1970.

8. Houston, *Northern Yellowstone Elk,* pp. 167–169.

9. Donald Worster, *Nature's Economy: A History of Ecological Ideas* (New York: Cambridge University Press, 1977), p. 210. For recent considerations of the changing views of ecology beginning with Clements, see Norman Christensen, "Succession and Natural Disturbance: Paradigms, Problems, and Preservation of Natural Ecosystems," in *Ecosystem Management for Parks and Wilderness,* ed. James K. Agee and Darryll R. Johnson (Seattle: University of Washington Press, 1988), pp. 63–86, and Donald Worster, "The Ecology of Order and Chaos," pp. 156–170 in his book *The Wealth of Nature* (New York: Oxford University Press, 1993). For a thorough and thoughtful history of ecological thinking in Yellowstone National Park, see James A. Pritchard, "Preserving Natural Conditions: Science and the Perception of Nature in Yellowstone National Park" (Ph.D. dissertation, University of Kansas, 1996).

10. Victor Cahalane, "The Evolution of Predator Control in the National Parks," *Journal of Wildlife Management* 3 (1939):235.

11. "An Act to Establish a National Park Service."

12. E. Curnow, "The History of the Eradication of the Wolf in Montana" (M.S. thesis, University of Montana, 1969), p. 88.

13. For more on this era and the growing opposition to the killing of predators, see Cahalane, "Evolution of Predator Control," and R. Gerald Wright, *Wildlife Research and Management in the National Parks* (Urbana: University of Illinois Press, 1992), pp. 38–40, 59–68.
14. Stephen Mather, "Remarks to the Tenth Superintendents' Conference, Washington, D.C.," mimeo, Yellowstone Research Library, p. 3.
15. Horace Albright, "National Parks Predator Policy," *Journal of Mammalogy* 12 (1931):186.
16. Paul Schullery and Lee Whittlesey, "Greater Yellowstone Predators."
17. George M. Wright, Joseph Dixon, and Ben Thompson, *A Preliminary Survey of Faunal Relations in National Parks*, National Park Service Fauna Series No. 1 (Washington: U.S. Government Printing Office, 1933), p. 147. For additional background on Wright and the development of his viewpoint, see Lowell Sumner, "Biological Research and Management in the National Park Service: A History," *George Wright Forum* (Autumn 1983):3–27.
18. Wright, *Wildlife Research and Management*, p. 40.
19. Wright quote is from U.S. National Park Service, "Exhibit A: Condensed Chronology and Discussion of National Park Service Predatory Policy, from Policy on Predators and Notes on Predators," typescript, RG 79, Central Classified File, copy in National Park Service Regional Office, Santa Fe, N.M., p. 715.
20. Wright, Dixon, and Thompson, *Preliminary Survey*, p. 84.
21. Murie, *Ecology of the Coyote*.
22. Robert Crabtree's study of the coyote in Yellowstone, initiated in the late 1980s, is now producing a great variety of publications. Crabtree's previous coyote research project, conducted at the Hanford Nuclear Reservation in Washington, was the only other study of an unexploited population.
23. Olaus Murie, 1944, "Progress Report on the Yellowstone Bear Study," typescript, Yellowstone Park Research Library.
24. Edmund B. Rogers, memorandum for the regional director, region two, July 8, 1943, photocopy in author's possession. Copies of this document have circulated through the National Park Service in recent years, but I have not determined its precise archival location. It was published, with commentary, under the title "Historical Vignettes: Lost Opportunities Department," *Yellowstone Science* 3, no. 2 (1993):19.
25. Ibid.
26. Varley and Schullery, *Freshwater Wilderness*, p. 103.
27. See Wright, *Wildlife Research and Management*, pp. 36–38, and 91–110.
28. National Park Service, "Resource Management Plan, Yellowstone National Park" (Yellowstone National Park: National Park Service, 1995), YELL-N-019.000, PS p. 0001. "Plants," *Buffalo Chip: Resource Management Newsletter*, Yellowstone National Park, April/May/June 1996, p. 12.
29. Pritchard, "Preserving Natural Conditions," pp. 121–167; Wright, *Wildlife Re-*

search and Management, pp. 67–68; Varley and Schullery, *Freshwater Wilderness,* p. 103.

30. A. Starker Leopold, Stanley A. Cain, Clarence M. Cottam, Ira N. Gabrielson, and Thomas L. Kimball, "Wildlife Management in the National Parks," *Transactions of the North American Wildlife and Natural Resources Conference* 28 (1963):28–45.

31. Wagner et al., *Wildlife Policies,* p. 29; Bartlett, *Yellowstone: A Wilderness Besieged,* p. 388.

32. Leopold et al., "Wildlife Management," pp. 32, 34.

33. Ibid., p. 38.

34. Ibid., pp. 37–38.

35. Wright, *Wildlife Research and Management,* pp. 78–79. Pritchard, "Preserving Natural Conditions," contains a fresh and very helpful analysis of the competing ideas and personalities in the National Park Service and in Yellowstone at the time of the elk reductions and afterward. Some revealing contemporary accounts of the elk slaughter and perceptions of elk management and ecology include Congressman Arnold Olsen, "Yellowstone's Great Elk Slaughter," *Sports Afield,* October 1962, pp. 40–41, and 87–88; Ted Trueblood, "Too Many Elk," *Field and Stream,* July 1963, pp. 36–39, 72–74; Leslie Pengelly, "Thunder on the Yellowstone," *Naturalist* 14 (1963):18–25; and Alan Woolf, "The Yellowstone Elk Controversy" (research paper, Colorado State University, May 1, 1967). Woolf reprinted several contemporary newspaper editorials as well. See also "Historical Information, Northern Elk Herd," National Park Service mimeographed information report, Yellowstone National Park Research Library (1967), a compendium of papers and reports from 1963 to 1967, including the Leopold Report and several biologists' reports on elk population, aspen, and other aspects of the range issue.

36. Tyers, "Condition of the Northern Winter Range," p. 154.

10. THE HIGH PRICE OF SUCCESS

1. Bernard DeVoto, "The Easy Chair: Let's Close the National Parks," *Harper's Magazine,* October 1953, pp. 51, 52.

2. Ibid., p. 52.

3. Ibid.

4. Ibid., p. 49.

5. Conrad L. Wirth, *Parks, Politics, and the People* (Norman: University of Oklahoma Press, 1980), p. 237.

6. W. Robbins et al., *A Report by the Advisory Committee to the National Park Service on Research of the National Academy of Sciences–National Research Council* (Washington: National Academy of Sciences, 1963), p. 32.

7. Edward Abbey, *Desert Solitaire: A Season in the Wilderness* (New York: Ballantine Books, 1971), pp. 51–52.

8. The era of the great hotels in Yellowstone is described in entertaining detail in both Haines, *Yellowstone Story,* vol. 2; and Bartlett, *Yellowstone: A Wilderness Besieged.*

9. Bartlett, *Yellowstone: A Wilderness Besieged,* opposite p. 177.

10. Ibid., p. 288.

11. Ibid., pp. 365–379.

12. Ibid., p. 169.

13. The establishment of the various structures and facilities described below is well documented in Haines, *Yellowstone Story,* vol. 2. Park historian Lee Whittlesey, in an undated note to me in August 1996, said that building in the park reached its peak at the very beginning of the century. As one of the foremost historians of development and construction in the park, he speaks with an authority beyond mine on this subject: "I feel very safe in saying that there are far fewer buildings in Yellowstone today than anytime since at least 1915 and probably since 1905. The number today may be as little as HALF as many as in the past. While many older buildings were razed in the 1920s and 1930s, many new ones went up during those decades as well. It staggers me to imagine the numbers of buildings that were here in, say, 1930."

For more on the modern dilemma of balancing cultural and natural resource management needs in national parks and other protected areas, see the special issue of the *George Wright Forum* 13, no. 1 (1996).

14. "Transcript of Aubrey L. Haines' Forty-Hour Tour of Yellowstone National Park, August 9–13, 1993," computer file and transcript in manuscript files, Yellowstone Park Research Library.

15. Haines, *Yellowstone Story,* 2:373.

16. Ibid., pp. 376–377. For additional information on Grant Village, see National Park Service, "Environmental Assessment and Preferred Alternative, Development Concept Plan, Yellowstone, Grant Village" (Yellowstone National Park: National Park Service, 1979).

17. "Master Plan, Yellowstone National Park/Wyoming-Montana-Idaho" (Yellowstone National Park: National Park Service, 1974), p. 18.

18. William Barmore, "Proposed Fishing Bridge Bypass Road," memorandum to superintendent, Yellowstone National Park, Nov. 25, 1968.

19. "Fishing Bridge and the Yellowstone Ecosystem: A Report to the Director, November, 1984" (Yellowstone National Park: National Park Service, 1984), pp. 14–15.

20. "Environmental Impact Statement, Fishing Bridge Campsite Replacement, Yellowstone National Park, Wyoming/Montana/Idaho" (Yellowstone National Park: National Park Service, 1994), pp. 6–9.

21. Ibid., p. 8.

22. Ibid. See also Congressional Research Service, *Greater Yellowstone Ecosystem: An Analysis of Data Submitted by Federal and State Agencies* (Washington: U.S. Government Printing Office, 1987), pp. 132–133.

23. "A Bee in Every Bouquet: The Administration of Science in Yellowstone," interview with Bob Barbee, *Yellowstone Science* 3, no. 1 (Winter 1995):14.

24. "Fishing Bridge Campsite Replacement," p. 10.   .

25. Ibid.

26. Ibid., pp. 10–12.

27. Haines, *Yellowstone Story*, 2:375.

28. Culpin, "Construction of the Road System," p. 179.

29. Robert Cahn, *Will Success Spoil the National Parks?* (Boston: Christian Science Publishing, 1968), reprint of fifteen-part series in the *Christian Science Monitor,* May 1–Aug. 7, 1968.

30. Ibid., pp. 43–44.

31. Ibid., p. 49.

32. Ibid., p. 53.

33. Ibid.

11. GREATER YELLOWSTONE

1. The Craigheads produced many technical and popular publications based on their study, the most comprehensive being Craighead et al., *The Grizzly Bears of Yellowstone* (Washington: Island Press, 1995).

2. John J. Craighead and Frank C. Craighead, "Management of Bears in Yellowstone National Park," administrative report, Yellowstone Park Research Library, July 1967.

3. For books about bears with extended discussions of the Yellowstone controversy, besides Craighead et al., *Grizzly Bears of Yellowstone,* and Schullery, *Bears of Yellowstone,* see Bill Schneider, *Where the Grizzly Walks* (Missoula, Mont.: Mountain Press, 1977); Frank Craighead, *Track of the Grizzly* (San Francisco: Sierra Club Books, 1979); and Thomas McNamee, *The Grizzly Bear* (New York: Alfred A. Knopf, 1984). See also Pritchard, "Preserving Natural Conditions," pp. 366–398, for more on evolving attitudes toward wildlife management in Yellowstone, and the personality conflicts among the Craigheads, Glen Cole, and Jack Anderson.

4. U.S. Senate, "Hearings on Elk Population, Yellowstone National Park, before a Subcommittee of the Committee on Appropriations," 19th Cong., 1st Sess. (Washington: U.S. Government Printing Office, 1967).

5. The extent to which Leopold backed away from the immediate need to control the elk population is evident in a letter from him to Boyd Evison, superintendent of Sequoia and Kings Canyon National Park, June 9, 1983 (copy in author's

collection; copies were sent to Yellowstone's superintendent, Robert Barbee, and were then widely distributed). In part the letter discussed Yellowstone's aspen situation:

> In Yellowstone I am distressed with the progressive disappearance of aspen. It is clear that this once abundant plant is on the way out as a result of nonburning coupled with continuous gnawing by elk. With the loss of aspen you lose a whole array of woodpeckers, tree swallows, deer, beaver, and fall color. I would suggest that experimental management be initiated to find out how to restore this component of the landscape. Hopefully fire would reverse the trend without manipulating the elk. Failing that, the elk might be excluded from some aspen nurseries by temporary, unobtrusive fencing. Surely there must be some reasonable way to bring back aspen patches.

Leopold, like many people, regarded the aspen as an essential aesthetic element of the Yellowstone scene. Writing in 1983, he did not know that even the fires of 1988 would not allow the aspen seedlings to reach tree height, nor that the aspen were merely the result of a short period of growth in the late 1800s and not necessarily a permanent part of the Yellowstone landscape. It would be interesting to hear Leopold's views if he were alive today — yet another in the long list of reasons that he is missed.

It would probably be fairly easy to construct barriers around a number of aspen groves to protect them from elk and other ungulates and to ensure the continuation of this pretty element of the setting. Considering the sorrow and anger many people feel about the disappearance of aspen, if such a minor artificiality worked, it might be worth trying.

6. See, for example, Steve Herrero, *Bear Attacks: Their Causes and Avoidance* (New York: Nick Lyons Books, 1985), and Gary Brown, *Safe Travel in Bear Country* (New York: Nick Lyons Books, 1996).
7. Robert H. Mac Arthur and Edward O. Wilson, *The Theory of Island Biogeography* (Princeton: Princeton University Press, 1967).
8. The literature of biodiversity and ecosystem management is already immense. A few very helpful recent publications on the modern dilemmas of protecting ecosystems and the effects of isolation are Christensen, "Succession and Natural Disturbance," pp. 62–86; R. Edward Grumbine, *Ghost Bears: Exploring the Biodiversity Crisis* (Washington: Island Press, 1992); and United States General Accounting Office, "Ecosystem Management: Additional Actions Needed to Adequately Test a Promising Approach" (Washington: U.S. Government Printing Office, 1994). In addition to Christensen's paper, cited above, the entire volume edited by Agee and Johnson is extremely useful.
9. Bartlett, *Yellowstone: A Wilderness Besieged,* p. 226. The origin of the twentieth-century "Greater Yellowstone" movement is best chronicled in Haines, *Yellowstone Story,* 2:219–236.

10. Philip G. Terrie, *Forever Wild: Environmental Aesthetics and the Adirondack Forest Preserve* (Philadelphia: Temple University Press, 1985), p. 95.

11. George Bird Grinnell, "The Care of the National Park," *Forest and Stream,* Jan. 29, 1885, p. 1. I am especially grateful to graduate student Sarah Broadbent of the Montana State University History Department on this point. I had noticed that early park defenders mentioned watershed protection, but Broadbent's recent study of the role of sportsmen in the protection of the park in the 1880s made me better aware of the extent to which watershed protection became an important rallying cry among conservationists defending Yellowstone. The earliest reference I have seen to watershed protection as a justification for the park is Theodore B. Comstock, "The Yellowstone National Park," *American Naturalist,* March 1874, p. 164, in which Comstock fully expressed this justification.

12. Bartlett, *Yellowstone: A Wilderness Besieged,* pp. 347–361; Haines, *Yellowstone Story,* 2:336–346; Horace Albright and Robert Cahn, *The Birth of the National Park Service: The Founding Years, 1913–1933: The Yellowstone Era Begins* (Salt Lake City: Howe Brothers, 1985), pp. 10–13. This booklet describes Albright's efforts to stall surveys and otherwise block development plans for the park.

13. Haines, *Yellowstone Story,* 2:95–99. This book is the source for the following discussion. The eventual boundary adjustments described below are from pp. 330–332. See also John F. Reiger, "Wildlife, Conservation, and the First Forest Reserve," in *Origins of the National Forests: A Centennial Symposium,* ed. Harold K. Steen (Durham, N.C.: Forest History Society, 1992), pp. 106–122, and Mary S. Culpin, "Yellowstone and Its Borders: A Significant Influence Toward the Creation of the First Forest Reserve," in Steen, *Origins of the National Forests,* pp. 276–283.

14. Horace Albright, letter to Thomas Elwood Hofer, Jan. 6, 1926. Hofer Collection, manuscript files, Yellowstone Research Library.

15. Greater Yellowstone Coordinating Committee, "Vision for the Future: A Framework for Coordination in the Greater Yellowstone Area" (Billings, Mont.: Greater Yellowstone Coordinating Committee), pp. 1.1–1.5.

16. Hough quote, ibid., p. 320.

17. Haines, *Yellowstone Story,* p. 320.

18. For the development of the ecological concepts involved in ecosystem thinking, see Worster, *Nature's Economy,* and Joel B. Hagen, *An Entangled Bank: The Origins of Ecosystem Ecology* (New Brunswick, N.J.: Rutgers University Press, 1992).

19. The best reason I can think of for preferring "Greater Yellowstone Area" to "Greater Yellowstone Ecosystem" is that the acronym for the former can be pronounced like "Gaia," the Greek word for earth-mother, a term popularized by James Lovelock and others as a scientifically defensible way of perceiving the entire planet as a superorganism; we could do a lot worse than so naming this

region symbolically. See James E. Lovelock, *Gaia: A New Look at Life on Earth* (New York: Oxford University Press, 1979).

20. I reviewed this growth in the perceived size of the ecosystem in Paul Schullery, "The Greater Yellowstone Ecosystem," in *Our Living Resources,* ed. Edward T. LaRoe (Washington: National Biological Service, U.S. Department of the Interior, 1995), pp. 312–314. For more detailed recent attempts to define the Greater Yellowstone Ecosystem or to analyze definition processes, see Duncan Patten, "Defining the Greater Yellowstone Ecosystem," in *The Greater Yellowstone Ecosystem: Redefining America's Wilderness Heritage,* ed. Robert B. Keiter and Mark S. Boyce (New Haven: Yale University Press, 1991), pp. 19–26; Richard A. Marston and J. E. Anderson, "Watersheds and Vegetation of the Greater Yellowstone Ecosystem," *Conservation Biology* 5, no. 3 (September 1991):338–346; and Tim W. Clark and Steven C. Minta, *Greater Yellowstone's Future: Prospects for Ecosystem Science, Management, and Policy* (Moose, Wyo.: Homestead Publishing, 1994), pp. 10–23. The first book on the Greater Yellowstone Ecosystem, and still an excellent introduction to the issues and resources of the area, is Rick Reese, *Greater Yellowstone: The National Park and Adjacent Wildlands* (Helena: Montana Magazine, 1984).

21. U.S. House of Representatives, Committee on Interior and Insular Affairs, Subcommittee on National Parks and Recreation, "Greater Yellowstone Ecosystem," oversight hearing, 99th Cong., 1st Sess., Oct. 24, 1985 (Washington: U.S. Government Printing Office, 1986).

22. Congressional Research Service, *Greater Yellowstone Ecosystem,* pp. 177–179.

23. Ibid., p. 167. In their conclusions, however (p. 179), the CRS criticized the structuring of these committees for redundancy and duplication of effort; I think they did not fully understand the roles of the committees, some of which were not strictly GYE-focused and thus had overlapping, rather than duplicative, roles.

24. For a general overview of the laws, see Michael Bean, *The Evolution of National Wildlife Law* (Washington: U.S. Government Printing Office, 1978). For some specific applications to Yellowstone, see Robert Keiter, "Taking Account of the Ecosystem on the Public Domain: Law and Ecology in the Greater Yellowstone Region," *University of Colorado Law Review* 60 (1989):923–1007; and William J. Lockhart, "'Faithful execution' of the Laws Governing Greater Yellowstone: Whose Law? Whose Priorities?" in Keiter and Boyce, *Greater Yellowstone Ecosystem,* pp. 49–64.

25. Robert Keiter, "Greater Yellowstone: Managing a Charismatic Ecosystem," *Natural Resources and Environmental Issues* 3 (1994):1–9.

26. In 1987 the Greater Yellowstone Coordinating Committee produced a large volume, *The Greater Yellowstone Area: An Aggregation of National Park and National Forest Management Plans* (Washington: U.S. Forest Service and Na-

tional Park Service, 1987). The *Aggregation* provided, for the first time in one place (no little achievement), a concise summary of many kinds of resources in the federal lands of the Greater Yellowstone Area (defined as "about 11.7 million acres"). By implication, at least, it defined the Greater Yellowstone Area as only the federal lands administered by the two agencies; private lands were beyond the scope of the agencies' analysis.

27. Robert D. Barbee, "A Vote for Posterity," *Courier,* January 1990, pp. 13–14.

28. Grumbine, *Ghost Bears,* pp. 164–165.

29. Ibid., p. 165.

30. Greater Yellowstone Coordinating Committee, *A Framework for Coordination of National Parks and National Forests in the Greater Yellowstone Area* (Billings, Mont.: Greater Yellowstone Coordinating Committee, 1991). Many post-mortems have been performed on the "Vision" document. These include Robert D. Barbee, Paul Schullery, and John D. Varley, "The Yellowstone Vision: An Experiment That Failed or a Vote for Posterity?" in *Partnerships in Parks & Preservation,* proceedings of a conference at Albany, N.Y., Sept. 9–12, 1991; Rocky Barker, *Saving All the Parts: Reconciling Economics and the Endangered Species Act* (Washington: Island Press, 1993), pp. 235–237; Clark and Minta, *Greater Yellowstone's Future,* pp. 96–102; Jim Robbins, *Last Refuge: The Environmental Showdown in Yellowstone and the American West* (New York: Morrow, 1993), pp. 262–265; Mary Ann Grasser, "The Greater Yellowstone Vision," in *Partners in Stewardship,* Proceedings of the Seventh Conference on Research and Resource Management in Parks and on Public Lands, Jacksonville, Fla., Nov. 16–20, 1993, pp. 201–206; Bruce Goldstein, "Can Ecosystem Management Turn an Administrative Patchwork into a Greater Yellowstone Ecosystem?" *Northwest Environmental Journal* 8 (1992):285–324; and Pritchard, "Preserving Natural Conditions," pp. 459–463.

31. Albert Harting and Dennis Glick, *Sustaining Greater Yellowstone: A Blueprint for the Future* (Bozeman, Mont.: Greater Yellowstone Coalition, 1994).

32. Dennis Glick, Mary Carr, and Bert Harting, eds., *An Environmental Profile of the Greater Yellowstone Ecosystem: Executive Summary* (Bozeman, Mont.: Greater Yellowstone Coalition, 1991), p. 7. For more on the GYE as "a rapidly evolving complex social system," see Patrick C. Jobes, "The Greater Yellowstone Social System," *Conservation Biology* 5, no. 3 (September 1991):393.

33. Samuel P. Hays, "The New Environmental West," *Journal of Policy History* 3, no. 3 (1991):237.

34. Thomas Michael Power, "Ecosystem Preservation and the Economy in the Greater Yellowstone Area," *Conservation Biology* 5, no. 3 (1991):397.

35. These economic changes are summarized in Clark and Minta, *Greater Yellowstone's Future,* pp. 24–31. Besides Power, "Ecosystem Preservation and the Economy," see especially Ray Rasker, Norma Tirrell, and Deanne Kloepfer, *The*

Wealth of Nature: New Economic Realities in the Yellowstone Region (Bozeman, Mont.: Northern Rockies and Intermountain Regional Offices, Wilderness Society, 1991), which is a thorough overview of GYE economics.

36. "Surely one of the greatest of all facts of life about this vast region is that no state of the Far West (the Montana–New Mexico tier westward) is less than 29 percent federally owned — Nevada is 87 percent, Alaska an incredible 96 percent — whereas no state to the east is more than 12 percent federal land." Michael P. Malone, "Beyond the Last Frontier, Toward a New Approach to Western American History," in Limerick, Milner, and Rankin, *Trails*, p. 149.

37. Charles F. Wilkinson, *The Eagle Bird: Mapping a New West* (New York: Pantheon Books, 1992), p. 185.

38. John W. Duffield, "An Economic Analysis of Wolf Recovery in Yellowstone: Park Visitor Attitudes and Values," in *Wolves for Yellowstone?* p. 2.81.

39. "World Heritage Committee Calls Yellowstone 'Endangered,'" *Yellowstone Science* 4, no. 2 (Spring 1996):18.

40. See, for example, Greater Yellowstone Coalition, "'Mine from Hell' Threatens Yellowstone," brochure, 1995, which quotes Superintendent Mike Finley as saying, "I'm stunned this could be taking place. How could the logical mind approve this?" During President Bill Clinton's August 1995 visit to Yellowstone National Park, he and Superintendent Finley flew over the mine site, and the president became an outspoken opponent of the mine's development.

41. The World Heritage Site designation, which Yellowstone received in 1978, does not provide for any formal or legal oversight of Yellowstone's management by any foreign nation, but there was a remarkable amount of what can only be called paranoia in the region upon the announcement that the designation had been changed to "endangered." For example, in a press release entitled "Burns Pans Park Designation," Dec. 5, 1995, Montana Senator Conrad Burns stated, "The designation would also seek to put a halt to activities in the park such as travel by motor vehicles as well as to create a buffer zone around the park that would run roughshod over private property rights. That's just ridiculous. This is a thinly veiled attempt to push a radical environmental agenda upon Westerners and all Americans who enjoy Yellowstone National Park. We cannot allow public access to the crown jewel of the national park system to be denied, nor can we allow a body of outsiders to make our decisions for us. This is not the American way, nor is it in line with the traditions we have proudly upheld for decades in the American west."

The communications from the World Heritage Committee make no statement about restricting use or automobile traffic in any way or about anything that could be misinterpreted as a threat to property rights or public access.

42. Clinton quoted in Bob Ekey, "Victory for Yellowstone," *Greater Yellowstone Report* 13, no. 3 (Summer 1996):1.

43. William Romme and Monica Turner, "Implications of Global Climate Change for Biogeographic Patterns in the Greater Yellowstone Ecosystem," *Conservation Biology* 5, no. 3 (1991):373–386.

44. Terry McEneaney, "Neotropical Migrant Birds and the Yellowstone-Mexico Connection," paper presented at seminar at Mammoth Hot Springs, May 8, 1996.

45. Barbee, "Vote for Posterity," p. 13.

46. Dan Flores, "Spirit of Place and the Value of Nature in the American West," *Yellowstone Science* 1, no. 3 (Spring 1993):10.

12. HOLOCENE PARK

1. *Federal Register* 52, no. 148 (Aug. 3, 1987), p. 28795. For competing views and a reasonable overview of the issues concerning geothermal energy development in Greater Yellowstone (with special emphasis on the Corwin Springs Known Geothermal Resource Area), see Bruce F. Molnia, "Effects of Potential Geothermal Development on the Thermal Features of Yellowstone National Park," *GSA Today,* December 1994, pp. 291, 296–299.

2. T. Scott Bryan, *The Geysers of Yellowstone* (Boulder: Colorado Associated University Press, 1986), pp. 257–288.

3. Grumbine, *Ghost Bears,* p. 29. An excellent essay on the changing values of American wildlife management is Frederic H. Wagner, "American Wildlife Management at the Crossroads," *Wildlife Society Bulletin* 17 (1989):354–360.

4. Pritchard, "Preserving Natural Conditions," pp. 319–377.

5. National Research Council et al., *Science in the National Parks* (Washington: National Academy Press, 1992). This book is essential reading for those interested in how science has, does, and might play a role in resource management in national parks. It reviews the previous studies of science in the parks and reinforces numerous earlier reports on the inadequacy of the National Park Service science program. For an important new study of science in Yellowstone, see Pritchard, "Preserving Natural Conditions."

It takes only a brief involvement in Greater Yellowstone's issues to notice that virtually all advocates of serious positions in the management debates not only insist upon the need for the best science but also are convinced that science is on their side. Then, if the scientific studies they have insisted upon are funded and completed but do not support their position, they denounce them as bad science. No doubt some of the studies are poor science, but the denouncements are rarely trustworthy proof of that. For example, as new scientific evidence on the northern range suggests that old interpretations of the range as badly overgrazed were incomplete, naive, or erroneous, the denouncements of this new research, published in the foremost scientific journals, become progressively more hollow.

John Varley, chief of research in Yellowstone National Park for ten years and more recently director of the Yellowstone Center for Resources, has commented on the equivocal nature of science in management decisions:

> From the perspective of scientists we might point out that research, however much of it there may be, cannot always be expected to provide a simple and clear guiding light for managers. Research is necessary, but not sufficient, in the political realm of management.
>
> For example, the researchers often disagree among themselves (about methodology, findings, interpretations of each other's findings, and so on), [so] that interested advocacy groups in any issue are free to shop among the various scientific opinions for those most suitable to their needs. And, with so much research under way, understanding of these systems is growing at an accelerating pace, making at least the more savvy managers uneasy about decisions that may reach too far with too little information. Most of the administrators we know who deal with Greater Yellowstone issues will agree that the root obstacles to greater coordination are not scientific; they are social, based on fundamental differences of beliefs among agencies and constituency groups over how much public lands should be used.

John D. Varley, "Research in Yellowstone," *BioScience* 43, no. 3 (March 1993):131–132.

6. Houston, *Northern Yellowstone Elk,* lists Houston's other important papers on the northern range. Houston's book probably had little or no direct effect on public opinion. As the scientific disciplines related to park management have become more sophisticated and technical, and as books produced by these disciplines have become ever more expensive, the public has ceased to be an audience for the real research findings, depending more and more on the media and on the occasional scientist who bothers to "translate" findings for public consumption.

7. Houston, *Northern Yellowstone Elk,* pp. 114–118. See also Douglas B. Houston and Mary Meagher, *The Biology of Time* (Norman: University of Oklahoma Press, forthcoming), which contains 100 sets of historical photographic comparisons.

8. Ibid., p. 126.

9. Ibid., p. 128.

10. A detailed consideration by critics of natural regulation of the problems of defining "nature" and "natural" appears in Wagner et al., *Wildlife Policies,* pp. 22–28, 141–152. Among the weaknesses and errors in their argument, however, is their mistaken impression (p. 141) that population modelers now estimate the pre-1492 Indian population of North America at 100 million, a number they give without citation.

11. Douglas B. Houston, "Research on Ungulates in Northern Yellowstone National

Park," in *Research in the Parks: Transactions of the National Park Centennial Symposium* (Washington: National Park Service, 1976), pp. 11–25.

12. Kay, "Yellowstone's Northern Elk Herd," and Wagner et al., *Wildlife Policies,* pp. 152–155, and 165–166, take a dim view of the experiment; a recent and reliable short overview of how research has tested Houston's findings and hypotheses is Michael B. Coughenour and Francis J. Singer, "Elk Population Processes in Yellowstone National Park under the Policy of Natural Regulation," *Ecological Applications* 6, no. 2 (1996):573–593.

13. Houston, *Northern Yellowstone Elk,* p. 25; Francis J. Singer, "The Ungulate Prey Base for Wolves in Yellowstone National Park," in Keiter and Boyce, *Greater Yellowstone Ecosystem,* pp. 323–348. However, all these population estimates are subject to interpretations almost as far-reaching as were the earliest attempts to count the herds because of the "sightability" factor. That is, depending upon conditions during the census flights, some percentage (at times as high as 50 percent) of the animals may be in cover and thus missed by the counters. See John A. Mack and Francis Singer, "Population Models for Elk, Mule Deer, and Moose on Yellowstone's Northern Winter Range," in *Wolves for Yellowstone?* pp. 4.3–4.32.

14. Schullery, *Bears of Yellowstone,* pp. 45–56, summarizes recent research on the food habits of grizzly bears. For more on ungulates and trout as grizzly bear food, see Christopher Servheen et al., "Report to the IGBC on the Availability of Foods for Grizzly Bears in the Yellowstone Ecosystem," Interagency Grizzly Bear Study Team report, 1986, manuscript file, Yellowstone Research Library; and Daniel P. Rinehart and David J. Mattson, "Bear Use of Cutthroat Trout in Spawning Streams in Yellowstone National Park," *Bears — Their Biology and Management* 8 (1990):343–350.

15. David Mattson, Bonnie Blanchard, and Richard Knight, "Food Habits of the Yellowstone Grizzly Bear," paper presented at the Seventh International Conference on Bear Research and Management, Williamsburg, Va., February 1986.

16. "Interim Report on Northern Range Research," National Park Service, Research Division, Yellowstone National Park, p. 1.

17. Elizabeth Hadly, "Evolution, Ecology, and Taphonomy of Late-Holocene Mammals from Lamar Cave, Yellowstone National Park, Wyoming" (Ph.D. dissertation, University of California, Berkeley, 1995).

18. Kay, "Aboriginal Overkill and Native Burning."

19. See Chapter 1, nn. 8 and 11.

20. Schullery and Whittlesey, "Documentary Record of Wolves."

21. Douglas A. Frank and Samuel J. McNaughton, "Evidence for the Promotion of Aboveground Grassland Production by Native Large Herbivores in Yellowstone National Park," *Oecologia* 96 (1993):157–161; Francis J. Singer, "Effects of Grazing by Ungulates on Upland Bunchgrass Communities of the Northern Winter Range of Yellowstone National Park," *Northwest Science* 69 (1995):191–203.

22. Linda L. Wallace and S. A. Macko, "Nutrient Acquisition by Clipped Plants as a Measure of Competitive Success: The Effects of Compensation," *Functional Ecology* 7 (1993):326–331. The exclosures, visible at several points along the road from Mammoth to the Northeast Entrance, have often been the subject of misunderstanding. Naive critics have seen their tall, seemingly healthy growth as proof of how the range "should" look, when in fact it shows us only what the range would look like if it had no grazing animals on it. Of course the growth is taller inside the fence; it is artificially protected from use by native grazers. This isn't to say that the growth outside the exclosure is perfectly "natural," only that the heavy growth inside proves that we can keep the animals from eating their native foods.

Grassland studies are opening fascinating windows on the nutrient systems of wildland ranges. Researchers are, for example, exploring the complex energy paths involved in the elk's use of the vegetation. Large groups of ungulates do not merely stomp across the landscape eating everything and then leaving. They consume and process tons of plant matter, cycling it back into the soil (as feces and urine), which they unintentionally till with their hooves. Then (unlike domestic livestock) they die there, and the carcasses remain in the system, either decomposing on site or being consumed by predators and scavengers. See, for example, Douglas Frank, "Interactive Ecology of Plants, Large Mammalian Herbivores, and Drought in Yellowstone National Park" (Ph.D. thesis, Syracuse University, 1990).

23. To some extent this new research just echoed a sentiment expressed by an iconoclastic (and almost sarcastic) park naturalist fifty years earlier as he watched the annual hand-wringing over the condition of the range: "The climatic conditions vary greatly from year to year and with these varying climatic conditions not only the amount of forage produced but the total acreage of range utilized varied greatly. Indeed, climate seems to be a much more important factor in the fortunes of the range than the numbers of elk, except that number of elk is a controllable factor and the climate is not." Quoted in Despain et al., *Wildlife in Transition*, pp. 83–84.

For an overview of the competing and conflicting definitions of "overgrazing," see Michael B. Coughenour and Francis J. Singer, "The Concept of Overgrazing and Its Application to Yellowstone's Northern Range," in Keiter and Boyce, *Greater Yellowstone Ecosystem*, pp. 209–230. A sampling of other important recent publications on northern range ecology not yet mentioned in these notes must include Elizabeth Barnosky, "Ecosystem Dynamics through the past 2000 Years as Revealed by Fossil Mammals from Lamar Cave in Yellowstone National Park, U.S.A.," *Historical Biology* 8 (1994):71–90; Evelyn H. Merrill and Mark S. Boyce, "Grassland Phytomass, Climatic Variation and Ungulate Population Dynamics in Yellowstone National Park," in Keiter and Boyce, *Greater Yellowstone Ecosystem*, pp. 263–274; Evelyn Merrill, N. L. Stanton, and J. C. Hak,

"Responses of Bluebunch Wheatgrass, Idaho Fescue, and Nematodes to Ungulate Grazing in Yellowstone National Park," *Oikos* 69 (1994):231–240; Francis J. Singer and Roy A. Renkin, "Effects of Browsing by Native Ungulates on the Shrubs in Big Sagebrush Communities in Yellowstone National Park," *Great Basin Naturalist* 55, no. 3 (1995):201–212; Michael B. Coughenour, "Biomass and Nitrogen Responses to Grazing of Upland Steppe on Yellowstone's Northern Winter Range," *Journal of Applied Ecology* 28 (1991):71–82; and Monica G. Turner et al., "Simulating Winter Interactions among Ungulates, Vegetation, and Fire in Northern Yellowstone Park," *Ecological Applications* 4, no. 3 (1994):472–496.

24. Henry Shovic, Jana Mohrman, and Roy Ewing, *Major Erosive Lands in the Upper Yellowstone River Drainage from Livingston, Montana, to Yellowstone Lake Outlet, Yellowstone National Park* (Yellowstone National Park: Yellowstone Fisheries Project Office, U.S. Fish and Wildlife Service, 1988). See also John R. Lane, "Characterization and Comparison of Soils Inside and Outside Grazing Enclosures on Yellowstone National Park's Northern Winter Range" (M.S. thesis, Montana State University, 1990), for an evaluation of the supposed erosion on grassland sites.

25. D. R. Engstrom, C. Whitlock, S. C. Fritz, and H. E. Wright, "Recent Environmental Changes Inferred from the Sediments of Small Lakes in Yellowstone's Northern Range," *Journal of Paleolimnology* 5 (1991):139–174. The validity of this analysis is challenged and defended in W. L. Hamilton, "Comment: Recent Environmental Changes Inferred from the Sediments of Small Lakes in Yellowstone's Northern Range (Engstrom et al., 1991)," *Journal of Paleolimnology* 10 (1994):156–158; and D. R. Engstrom, C. Whitlock, S. C. Fritz, and H. E. Wright, "Reinventing Erosion in Yellowstone's Northern Range," *Journal of Paleolimnology* 10 (1994):159–161.

26. This unpublished report's results have entered the public scientific literature through description and citation in Wagner et al., *Wildlife Policies*, p. 53. The results of erosion studies, in fact, are rather typical of those of many other studies. On the one hand, the studies disagreed strongly with traditional beliefs (all erosion was incorrectly assumed to be the result of the large numbers of elk, when in fact most of the sediment seems to be the result of non-grazing-related geological processes), but on the other hand, the studies did not resolve important questions, such as how much sediment the ungulates *are* contributing and how we determine whether or not *that* sediment is somehow excessive.

27. Whitlock et al., "A Prehistoric Perspective on the Northern Range," in *The Greater Yellowstone Ecosystem*, ed. Robert Keiter and Mark Boyce (New Haven: Yale University Press, 1991), pp. 298–308. Houston, *Northern Yellowstone Elk*, p. 87.

28. Charles E. Kay and Frederic H. Wagner, "Historical Condition of Woody Vegetation on Yellowstone's Northern Range: A Critical Evaluation of the 'Natural Regulation' Paradigm," in *Plants and Their Environments: Proceedings of the*

First Biennial Scientific Conference on the Greater Yellowstone Ecosystem, ed. Don Despain (Yellowstone National Park: National Park Service, 1994), pp. 160–162.

29. Warren, "Study of the Beaver," p. 179. Romme et al., "Aspen, Elk, and Fire in Northern Yellowstone."

30. Steve W. Chadde and Charles E. Kay, "Tall-Willow Communities on Yellowstone's Northern Range: A Test of the 'Natural Regulation' Paradigm," in Keiter and Boyce, *Greater Yellowstone Ecosystem,* pp. 231–262, take the former view, while Francis J. Singer, Lauryl Mack, and Rex Cates, "Ungulate Herbivory of Willows on Yellowstone's Northern Range," *Journal of Range Management* 47 (1994):435–443, suspect that the situation is more complicated.

31. See also the exchange in F. H. Wagner, R. B. Keigley, and C. L. Wambolt, "Ungulate Herbivory of Willows on Yellowstone's Northern Winter Range: Comment to Singer et al. (1994)," *Journal of Range Management* 48 (1995):475–477; and Francis J. Singer and Rex G. Cates, "Response to Comment: Ungulate Herbivory on Willows on Yellowstone's Northern Winter Range," *Journal of Range Management* 48 (1995):563–565.

32. For the effects of ungulate browsing on birds' use of willows on the northern range, see Sally Jackson, "Relationships between Birds, Willows, and Native Ungulates in and around Northern Yellowstone National Park" (M.S. thesis, Utah State University, 1992). For the effects of ungulate carcasses on beetle abundance and diversity on the northern range, see Derek Scott Sikes, "Influences of Ungulate Carcasses on Coleopteran Communities in Yellowstone National Park" (M.S. thesis, Montana State University, 1994). For an example of the complexity of ecological processes in the dung of ungulates, see K. Michael Foos, "*Pilobolus* Ecology," *Yellowstone Science* 1, no. 3 (1993):2–5.

33. Warren, "Study of the Beaver."

34. A further complication in the beaver story has been selective use of questionable sources. For example, Wagner, Keigley, and Wambolt, "Ungulate Herbivory of Willows," cite Milton Skinner's mid-1920s estimate of 10,000 beaver in the park, though Skinner gave no specifics or data to show how he had arrived at this remarkable number. To give Wagner et al. the benefit of the doubt, I will assume that they were unaware that at the same time park naturalist Edmund Sawyer was estimating the park's beaver population at about 800. The larger number works better for Wagner et al.'s arguments, but they and others appear a little too eager to trust its reliability in the face of a competing number and the question "Where would 10,000 beaver *live* in Yellowstone, when the northern winter range, with the park's best beaver habitat at the time (and only major aspen concentrations), was supporting only a few hundred even at the peak of the population eruption?"

35. Price and Schullery, "Bison of Yellowstone"; *Yellowstone Bison: Background and Issues* (Montana Department of Fish, Wildlife and Parks, National Park Service, U.S. Forest Service, May 1990).

36. Lee Whittlesey, "Cows All Over the Place: The Historic Setting for the Transmission of Brucellosis to Yellowstone Bison by Domestic Cattle," *Wyoming Annals* (Winter 1994–1995):42–57.

37. Mary Meagher, "Evaluation of Boundary Control for Bison of Yellowstone National Park," *Wildlife Society Bulletin* 17 (1989):15–19.

38. There are a hundred interesting aspects to this story. For one thing, the bison hunt was a fascinating study in sport and its evolving ethics. An animal that had been exempted from the mainstream American sporting tradition for almost a century was suddenly made available again; in the intervening hundred years the tradition had evolved so much that it was almost impossible to place the animal in a reasonable context as a sporting target.

39. Two recent analyses of density dependence and population regulation in the northern Yellowstone elk herd are Brian Dennis and Mark L. Taper, "Density Dependence in Time Series Observations of Natural Populations: Estimation and Testing," *Ecological Monographs* 64, no. 2 (1994):205–224, and Coughenour and Singer, "Elk Population Processes." For background on population regulation, see Charles J. Krebs, "Two Paradigms of Population Regulation," *Wildlife Research* 22 (1992):1–10. Merrill et al., "Grassland Phytomass, Climatic Variation and Ungulate Population Dynamics," discusses the sufficiency of the summer range.

40. Francis J. Singer, Kate K. Symonds, and Bill Berger, "Predation of Yellowstone Elk Calves," *Park Science* 13, no. 3 (Summer 1993):18.

41. Ibid. See also Kerry Gunther and Roy Renkin, "Grizzly Bear Predation on Elk Calves and Other Fauna of Yellowstone National Park," *Bears — Their Biology and Management* 8 (1990):329–334; and Steve French and Marilynn French, "Predatory Behavior of Grizzly Bears Feeding on Elk Calves in Yellowstone National Park," *Bears — Their Biology and Management* 8 (1990):335–342.

42. William H. Romme and Don G. Despain, "Historical Perspective on the Yellowstone Fires of 1988," *BioScience* 39, no. 10 (1989):695–706; Paul Schullery, "The Fires and Fire Policy," *BioScience* 39, no. 10 (1989):686–694.

43. Romme and Despain, "Historical Perspective."

44. Ibid.

45. Ibid.

46. John D. Varley and Paul Schullery, "The Yellowstone Fires," *Encyclopedia Britannica Yearbook of Science and the Future 1991* (Chicago: Encyclopedia Britannica, 1990), pp. 130–144.

47. Quoted in Paul Schullery, *Pregnant Bears and Crawdad Eyes: Excursions and Encounters in Animal Worlds* (Seattle: Mountaineers, 1991), p. 166.

48. Romme and Despain, "Historical Perspective"; Norman L. Christensen et al., "Interpreting the Yellowstone Fires of 1988," *BioScience* 39, no. 10 (1989):678–685. The single most authoritative source of research findings on the Yellowstone fires of 1988 is Greenlee, *Ecological Implications of Fire*.

49. I am grateful to Ron Des Jardins of the U.S. Forest Service, Gallatin National Forest, for illuminating conversations on this subject.

50. Some people took comfort in thinking that we wouldn't have to worry about a big fire for a long time because 1988 took care of the big episode and that however ugly the politics, the ecosystem got the episodic jolt it was due for. However, even if global warming doesn't soon increase the likelihood of more large fires, another big episode could happen anytime. Yellowstone's plant ecologist, Don Despain, who had watched and helped create the Yellowstone fire program since its beginning, pointed out in conversations with journalists that hundred-year fires are like hundred-year floods; there's nothing that says you can't have another one the next year.

51. Lee Metzgar, "Comments on Grizzly Bear Recovery Plan, Revised Draft," undated memorandum to conservation organizations concerned with grizzly bear recovery, author's files. Grizzly bear recovery in the northern Rockies is one of the most visible tests of the Endangered Species Act, as is wolf recovery. The leader of Yellowstone's wolf project has repeatedly stated that wolf restoration, because it can be accomplished ahead of schedule and under budget, may prove that the act can work. For more on the state of the Endangered Species Act, see Charles C. Mann and Mark L. Plummer, *Noah's Choice: The Future of Endangered Species* (New York: Alfred A. Knopf, 1995); and Timothy H. Tear, J. Michael Scott, Patricia H. Hayward, and Brad Griffith, "Status and Prospects for Success of the Endangered Species Act: A Look at Recovery Plans," *Science* 262 (November 12, 1993):976–977.

52. Barker, *Saving All the Parts*, pp. 212–218, reviews the recent discussions of corridors and interecosystem connections that may be necessary to keep grizzly bears from being permanently isolated. For the complexities of determining if the Yellowstone grizzly bear population is in any danger from genetic isolation, I relied on several papers and manuscripts provided by Lisette Waits: Lisette P. Waits et al., "Phylogeography of North American Brown Bear and Implications for Conservation," submitted to *Conservation Biology*, 1996; Lisette Waits, David Paetkau, and Curtis Strobek, "The Genetics of the Bears of the World" (Gland, Switzerland: International Union for the Conservation of Nature, Conservation Plan, in press); Lisette Waits et al., "Mitochondrial DNA Phylogeography of the Brown Bear and Implications for Management," submitted to the proceedings of the Tenth International Conference on Bear Research and Management; and Lisette Waits et al., "A Comparison of Genetic Diversity in North American Brown Bear Populations," submitted to the proceedings of the Tenth International Conference on Bear Research and Management.

Among the most ambitious proposals for protecting grizzly bear ecosystems is one for an interecosystem and international management plan for the entire Rocky Mountain area from Yellowstone to the Yukon. See Gary M. Tabor,

Yellowstone-to-Yukon: Canadian Conservation Efforts and Continental Land-scape/Biodiversity Strategy (Henry P. Kendall Foundation, 1996).

53. Quoted in Clark and Minta, *Greater Yellowstone's Future*, p. 138.
54. U.S. Fish and Wildlife Service, *1995 Annual Report of the Rocky Mountain Inter-agency Wolf Recovery Program* (Helena, Mont., and Yellowstone National Park: U.S. Fish and Wildlife Service, 1996), p. 8. For more on wolf restoration, see Hank Fischer, *The Wolf Wars* (Helena, Mont.: Falcon Press, 1995); and Paul Schullery, *The Yellowstone Wolf: A Guide and Sourcebook* (Worland, Wyo.: High Plains Publishing, 1996).
55. D. A. McNaught, "Park Visitor Attitudes toward Wolf Recovery in Yellowstone National Park" (M.S. thesis, University of Montana, 1985).
56. U.S. Fish and Wildlife Service, "Appendix 3. Public Attitudes about Wolves: A Review of Recent Investigations," in *The Reintroduction of Gray Wolves to Yellowstone National Park and Central Idaho, Final Environmental Impact Statement* (Helena, Mont.: U.S. Fish and Wildlife Service, 1994), pp. 6.32–6.35.
57. Mark Boyce, "Natural Regulation or the Control of Nature?" in Keiter and Boyce, *Greater Yellowstone Ecosystem*, pp. 182–208.
58. Wagner et al., *Wildlife Policies*, pp. 142–143, discuss "criterion for naturalness." A thoughtful and entertaining response to that book is Sam McNaughton, book review, *Journal of Wildlife Management* 60, no. 3 (1996):685–687. Thomas Bonnicksen, "Fire Gods and Federal Policy," *American Forests* (July/August 1989):14–16, 66–68, proposed "standards of naturalness" that were transparently intended to restrict the variability of fire regimes in national parks to ensure "safe and attractive forests," an aggressive sort of husbandry that is out of favor with most wilderness advocates and many park managers. Responses to Bonnicksen appeared in Robert D. Barbee et al., "Replies from the Fire Gods," *American Forests* (March/April, 1990):34–35, 70.

The recent flurry of scholarly attention to the nature of wilderness and to questions about how "wild" North American landscapes were when millions of Indians were actively manipulating them or are now when hundreds of millions of modern humans are creating much greater pressures has quite logically led to a reconsideration of parks and similar reserves. A number of scholars and other commentators have proposed that the entire concept of wilderness is something of a delusion we practice on ourselves and that for thousands of years there has been little real wilderness in the modern sense of the term, of humans having no effect on the landscape. See, for example, Kay, "Aboriginal Overkill"; Arturo Gómez-Pompa and Andrea Kaus, "Taming the Wilderness Myth," *Bio-Science* 42, no. 4 (1992):271–279. This discussion has been valuable because it has compelled land managers and public-land users to recognize the important role played by humans in the pre-Columbian landscape. But it has also been used rather like a weapon in land-management debates. What began as an important corrective in our understanding of wild landscapes has become a blanket criticism of all wildland management. It is now apparently presumed that because Indians had many influences on many North American places, they had all those influences in all those places.

59. Boyce, "Natural Regulation or the Control of Nature?" p. 202. One of the most important reasons that the parks are worthy of perpetuation is their role as ecological baselines against which we can measure our effects on other landscapes. Most ecological research projects last only a few years, far too short a time to take account of the great variations in natural systems. Parks like Yellowstone give us the opportunity to monitor changing systems over decades or for as long as we wish. For an overview of long-term ecological research, see D. Tilman, "Ecological Experimentation: Strengths and Conceptual Problems," in *Long-term Studies in Ecology — Approaches and Alternatives,* ed. G. Likens (New York: Springer-Verlag, 1989), pp. 136–157. For applications of long-term research to national parks, see William L. Halverson and Gary E. Davis, *Science and Ecosystem Management in the National Parks* (Tucson: University of Arizona Press, 1996), especially John D. Varley and Paul Schullery, "Yellowstone Lake and Its Cutthroat Trout," pp. 49–73, which discusses the many values of long-term monitoring of the trout population and its various ecosystem neighbors and dependents.

60. Holmes Rolston, "Biology and Philosophy in Yellowstone," *Biology and Philosophy* 5 (1990):241–258.

Conservation biologist Michael Soule, "Natives Versus Exotics," *Yellowstone Science* 4, no. 4 (1996):8–12 (interview), recently summed up the great value of Yellowstone in the modern conservation movement in terms of its completeness, even recognizing that it is not a "perfect" native ecosystem: "One thing that distinguishes Yellowstone is that it contains virtually a complete array of its native carnivores and herbivores. The completeness of this system, and its scale, can't be found in any other place in the lower 48 states. The sense of wilderness and wildness here is incomparable" (p. 12).

13. IMAGINING YELLOWSTONE

1. Lee Whittlesey, personal communication, 1996.
2. Lee Whittlesey, personal communication, 1995.
3. White, *"It's Your Misfortune and None of My Own,"* p. 613.
4. Notable recent surveys of visitors and the public include: Alistair J. Bath, "Attitudes toward Fire and Fire Management Issues in Yellowstone National Park" (Ph.D. dissertation, University of Calgary, 1993); Alistair J. Bath, "Who Visits Yellowstone?" *Yellowstone Science* 2, no. 2 (Winter 1994):15–18; Kenneth R. Schultz, University of Arizona, visitor survey report in letter to Superintendent Robert D. Barbee, April 8, 1985, Yellowstone National Park files; Branch of Transportation, Denver Service Center, *Alternative Transportation Modes, Feasi-*

bility Study, vol. 3: *Executive Summary* (Denver: National Park Service, 1994); Margaret Littlejohn, *Visitor Services Project, Yellowstone National Park, Visitor Study* (Moscow, Idaho: University of Idaho, 1996); Gail W. Compton, "Visitors and Wildlife, Yellowstone National Park," report of the Eastern Michigan University Research Team in cooperation with the Center for Wildlife Information (Ypsilanti, Mich.: 1992); Gail W. Compton, "Visitors and Wildlife, New Information on Attitudes, Risk, and Responsibility," *Yellowstone Science* 2, no. 2 (Winter 1994):5–8; Scott E. Atkinson, et al., *Socioeconomic Impact Analysis of the Proposed Relocation of Fishing Bridge Facilities in Yellowstone National Park* (Laramie: Institute for Policy Research and Department of Economics, University of Wyoming, and Western Research Corp., 1986); and Gary E. Machlis and Dana E. Dolsen, *Visitor Services Project Report 15, Yellowstone National Park* (Moscow, Idaho: Cooperative Park Studies Unit, University of Idaho, 1988).

5. T. W. Recreational Services, "Yellowstone National Park Statistics and Fun Facts," three-page handout, undated, provided by T. W. Services, Inc.

6. National Park Service, Ranger Division, "Yellowstone National Park, Wyoming, 82190, Law Enforcement Status Report," Public Affairs Office, Yellowstone National Park, undated, inclusive of 1994.

7. John D. Varley and Paul Schullery, eds., *Yellowstone Center for Resources 1994 Annual Report* (Yellowstone National Park: National Park Service, Yellowstone Center for Resources, 1996), p. 70.

8. Bath, "Who Visits Yellowstone?" p. 18. Personal observations suggest to me that just as there are two kinds of fishermen in Yellowstone — serious enthusiasts and casual opportunists who throw some tackle in the car just in case — there are two types of wildlife watchers. Although there is a continuum of skills from one group to the other, they can be characterized as either expert or casual. The masses of casual visitors who want to see a bear are not aware that the experts see them regularly, just as the expert fishermen catch fish regularly from waters where the average visitor is sure to get skunked. Perhaps one reason that the complaint "I didn't see any bears" is not viewed more sympathetically is that some people are seeing lots of bears. The wildlife watching of the old days, when bears were handy for viewing along roads and in dumps, has been replaced by a whole new game that requires the development of skills and the dedication of time and energy. Park bears have reverted to a broader and less readily accessible distribution, and in response, serious watchers have had to learn the bear's world far better than the crowds at the dumps had to. The addition of wolves to the scene has only heightened the excitement for these new recreationists.

But wildlife watching in this new, less artificial Yellowstone wildlife scene offers perplexing challenges. While managers and predator enthusiasts proudly point to the thousands of people who have sighted bears and wolves, they must also face the reality that millions of other visitors have not. Grizzly bears and black bears are no longer an industrial-scale recreational resource, with sightings guaranteed to visitors no matter how brief their stay. Bears, like the trophy trout, the high peak, the long ski trail, or the rare bird, are now a recreational achievement. Though innovative interpretive approaches could certainly increase the number of people who see the park's large predators, most visitors have to appreciate them indirectly.

The increase in expert wildlife viewing is already straining facilities. For example, roadside vegetation and soils at key viewing areas (virtually all of this new wildlife watching is done from the roadside; one need not be a toughened hiker) at key seasons are damaged as too many vehicles try to jam into too small a space. If the spaces are enlarged and the activity is tacitly or overtly encouraged (the almost invariable direction once a new activity has been endorsed as appropriate), what effect will the growing crowds have on the animals being watched?

This new set of issues is yet another product of the National Park Service's direction away from a manipulated landscape and toward natural regulation. The bears, like the trout, are still there to be appreciated and are ecologically better off for the new arrangement, but appreciation is won on harder terms than before. Aesthetic leaps like these are logical consequences of the changes in policy, but not everybody will willingly adjust.

9. Bath, "Who Visits Yellowstone?" One postfire study did, however, suggest that visitation to Yellowstone would have been higher had the fires not occurred. See M. S. Yuan, P. E. Polzin, and E. G. Schuster, "Economic Impacts of the 1988 Yellowstone National Park Fires on Adjacent Portal Communities," in *Ecological Implications of Fire in Greater Yellowstone, Second Biennial Scientific Conference on the Greater Yellowstone Ecosystem: Agenda and Abstracts,* September 19–21, 1993, Mammoth Hot Springs, Yellowstone National Park (Yellowstone National Park: Yellowstone Center for Resources, 1993). These findings, presented to suggest the true effects of the fires on the regional economy, led a number of people, grateful for smaller crowds, to say, "Thank God for the fires!"

10. Paul Schullery and John D. Varley, "Fires and Fish," *Trout* (Spring 1994):17.

11. National Park Service, "Alternative Transportation Modes," p. ES-4.

12. Machlis and Dolsen, *Visitor Services Project,* p. 23.

13. Ibid., p. 54.

14. Ibid., p. 14.

15. Compton, "Visitors and Wildlife," pp. 5–8.

16. Joseph L. Sax, *Mountains without Handrails: Reflections on the National Parks* (Ann Arbor: University of Michigan Press, 1980).

17. Ibid., pp. 89–90.

18. Quoted from Paul Schullery, "A Reasonable Illusion," *Rod and Reel,* November/December 1979, p. 48. This article appears to be the most thorough examination made of the issue of sport fishing in national parks. The portions of it

relevant to Yellowstone were reprinted in revised form in Schullery, *Mountain Time*, pp. 96–108.

The damage to Yellowstone's aquatic ecosystems by thoughtless human actions to "improve" the fishing is not merely a thing of the past. The 1994 discovery that someone had illegally introduced lake trout to Yellowstone Lake, where they pose a serious threat to the native cutthroat trout, exemplifies the continued problems of a public that does not really understand, or perhaps even care about, the long-term consequences of their actions in wildland ecosystems. The lake trout threaten to depopulate the lake of cutthroat trout, a species that dozens of other animals depend on, either in part or entirely, for food. See John D. Varley and Paul Schullery, eds., "The Yellowstone Lake Crisis: Confronting a Lake Trout Invasion, a Report to the Director of the National Park Service" (Yellowstone National Park: Yellowstone Center for Resources, National Park Service, 1995).

Invasions of nonnative species are viewed by many as among the most serious of Yellowstone's problems. See Soule, "Natives Versus Exotics."

19. Robert D. Barbee, "A Bee in Every Bouquet: The Administration of Science in Yellowstone," *Yellowstone Science* 3, no. 1 (Winter 1995):13.

20. My familiarity with the kayaking issue is the result of an assignment from *Newsweek* in the mid-1980s, when I interviewed several kayakers and researched the issue at Yellowstone.

21. Clark and Minta, *Greater Yellowstone's Future*, p. 138.

22. Lynne Bama, "Yellowstone: A Park Boss Goes to Bat for the Land," *High Country News*, April 29, 1996, pp. 1, 8–12, is a profile of Finley with a summary of his outspoken comments on visitor use and other issues. Daniel L. Dustin and Leo H. McAvoy, "Hardining National Parks," *Environmental Ethics* 2 (Spring 1980):41, analyzes the decline in the quality of another national park attraction, Yosemite Valley in Yosemite National Park. This is an especially important example for today's Yellowstone because the current superintendent, Mike Finley, was previously superintendent of Yosemite, where he took bold and controversial steps to limit the number of people in Yosemite Valley.

For more on the carrying capacities of recreational lands, see, for example, J. S. Wagar, *The Carrying Capacity of Wild Lands for Recreation*, Forest Science Monograph 7 (Washington: Society of American Foresters, 1964); David Lime, ed., *Managing America's Enduring Wilderness Resource* (St. Paul: University of Minnesota, 1990); F. R. Kuss, A. R. Graefe, and J. J. Vaske, *Visitor Impact Management: A Review of Research* (Washington: National Parks and Conservation Association, 1990); and Robert E. Manning, David W. Lime, Marilyn Hof, and Wayne Friemund, "The Carrying Capacity of National Parks: Theory and Application," manuscript, 1993.

23. National Park Service, *Winter Use Plan, Environmental Assessment* (Yellowstone National Park: National Park Service, 1990), pp. iii–v.

Winter puts the greatest stress on the park's ecological systems and thereby serves as the greatest agent in ecological process: for wildlife, winter is a predator on the weak, a selector of the fit, a conditioner of the herd, and a builder of barriers beyond which animals may not move. There has long been uneasiness about the added stress on wildlife from winter recreation. It has been demonstrated, for example, that cross-country skiers can very easily put large mammals through tremendous exertions merely by moving through their territory (E. Frances Cassirer, David J. Freddy, and Ernest D. Ables, "Elk Responses to Disturbance by Cross-Country Skiers in Yellowstone National Park," *Wildlife Society Bulletin* 20 [1992]:375–381). But animals can become habituated to trail and road travel by humans in winter just as they learn to adjust to car traffic in summer; if the people move in predictable patterns, as snowmobiles do on the park roads or as walkers and skiers do on the geyser basin boardwalks, the animals may not even be displaced from their preferred areas. Moreover, it is now argued that by grooming all the park's roads for the convenience of motorized over-snow traffic, we have given these animals a new winter travel network and have greatly increased their access to resources that were before available only by laborious movement through deep snow. It is further argued that opening these winter travel avenues has begun to affect the animals' use of the park in other seasons (Robert B. Keiter and Peter H. Froelicher, "Bison, Brucellosis, and Law in the Greater Yellowstone Ecosystem," *University of Wyoming College of Law Land and Water Law Review* 29, no. 1 [1993]:14–16). Groomed roads, according to this view, short-circuit some of winter's most powerful and essential effects.

24. James Hilton, *Lost Horizon* (New York: Pocket Books, 1939), p. 196.
25. Edward O. Wilson, *Biophilia* (Cambridge: Harvard University Press, 1984), p. 1.
26. Ibid., p. 2.
27. Judith Meyer, "The Spirit of Yellowstone" (Ph.D. dissertation, University of Wisconsin, 1994), p. 148. One interesting example of the way in which the arts redefine the experience of Yellowstone has emerged in the years since the fires of 1988. Artists and photographers accepted the challenge of stretching old aesthetics to include burned landscapes. I suspect that over time these images will probably do more to publicly legitimize landscape disturbance than all the interpretive brochures produced by federal agencies. A century ago it took a long time for a few visionary geographer-philosophers to awaken people to the glorious beauty of the arid Southwest, which seemed, and still seems to the uninitiated, to be a stark wasteland — and it will take time for the rawness of catastrophic landscape processes, whether fire or debris flow or freshet, to enter our artistic and aesthetic language and become tolerated, if not admired. Indeed, it will be harder for these processes to be seen differently because in so many places fire and mudslides and floods are necessarily viewed as evil. Just as the national parks compelled us to reconsider what is "good" in an animal and

to stop shooting those that failed our definition, they are now compelling us to reconsider the whole notion of beauty. We enjoy the Grand Canyon of the Yellowstone River as a great spectacle of nature without considering the geological violence that created it; our short lives incline us to be shocked by dramatic changes in settings we know, even though such changes are routine in the longer scale of time in which those settings evolved.

28. Wilson, *Biophilia,* p. 140.

EPILOGUE

1. John Muir, *Our National Parks* (New York: Houghton Mifflin, 1901), pp. 74–75.

ACKNOWLEDGMENTS

The notes amount to acknowledgment of the work of dozens of other scholars and writers, among whom I am most especially grateful to the historians who have worked on Yellowstone subjects in recent years: Aubrey Haines, Richard Bartlett, H. Duane Hampton, Susan Rhoades Neel, John Reiger, and Lee Whittlesey. We do not always agree on specifics, but we are all on the same search, and I could not ask for better company.

Among the park's ecological researchers, I have benefited frequently from the work of and conversations with Bonnie Blanchard, Mark Boyce, Robert Crabtree, Don Despain, Douglas Frank, Marilynn French, Steve French, Douglas Houston, Richard Knight, Mary Meagher, William Romme, Frank Singer, Linda Wallace, and John Varley.

It has been my good fortune to work with a number of park administrators over the past twenty-four years. Former superintendent John Townsley took time on several occasions to explain the workings of Yellowstone's political sphere to me, and the extended working partnership I have enjoyed with former superintendent Robert Barbee and Yellowstone Center for Resources director John Varley has been one of the most educational and entertaining professional experiences of my life.

The staff of Yellowstone's research library has changed several times over the past two decades, but the quality of service and enthusiasm for Yellowstone have not. The librarians of the various collections at Montana State University have been a mainstay of my work as well. Several instructors and two directors of the Yellowstone Institute compelled me to think out various history topics by inviting me to speak to various classes, and my own classes in grizzly bear ecology and management were as instructive for me as for any of my students.

For readings of the manuscript, I thank Rick Balkin, Harry Foster, Douglas Houston, Marsha Karle, Susan Rhoades Neel, and Lee Whittlesey. Your comments and suggestions contributed hugely to this book. Peg Anderson of Houghton Mifflin copyedited the manuscript, to its vast benefit.

My agent and friend, Rick Balkin, provided his customary wise guidance.

This book is dedicated to three people who represented the best impulses behind the search for Yellowstone. The role of A. Starker Leopold (1913–1983) in Yellowstone history is documented at some length in this book, but it extended far beyond his leadership in the policy issues discussed here; I am also grateful for the friendship and occasional counsel he provided me during our all-too-infrequent visits. Graeme Caughley (1937–1994), a prominent and gifted ecological thinker from Australia, published several key papers beginning in the 1960s that helped shape and interpret the philosophy of modern park management; he also provided some of us with provocative and pungent commentary on issues relating to park management. Mollie Beattie (1947–1996) made heroic stands on behalf of wolf recovery and other important initiatives, earning her the gratitude and admiration of the conservation community; grace is not a quality normally expected in a director of the U.S. Fish and Wildlife Service, but it was only one of the qualities that made her an outstanding conservationist. I did not know any of these people well, but I feel the force of their achievements.

INDEX

Canyon Village, 181, 183, 185, 187, 190
Carpenter, Robert, 108
Carroll, Lewis, 287m
Carson, Kit, 35
Cavalry, U.S., 87, 107, 111, 112–13, 132
Chase, Alston, 44, 45, 225, 278n40
Chillicothe, Ohio, 14, 15
Chittenden, Hiram, 23, 24, 57–58, 115–16
Christian Science Monitor, 191, 243
Cinnabar rail terminus, 99, 101. *See also* Northern Pacific Railroad (NPRR)
Clagett, William, 60
Clark, Tim, 257
Clark, William, 33
Clark City (now Livingston), Mont., 92–93
Clarks Fork River, 40
Clemens, Samuel, 38
Clements, Frederic L., 155, 167, 202
climate, changes in, 9–10, 16, 48, 124, 155, 226
    in first twenty years of park, 83, 229
    human-caused, 214
    Little Ice Age, 10, 25, 43, 48, 83, 244
    See also ecology
Clinton, Bill, 213–14
Clovis points, 7. *See also* projectile points
Cody, Wyo., 34, 189
Coeur d'Alene Indians, 26
Cole, Glen, 195–96, 220
Colter, John, and "Colter's Hell," 33–34, 38
concessions in park, 91–92, 101, 114, 126, 251
    consolidated, 134, 179–80, 181, 182
    control of, 113

lease violations, 109, 110
    NPRR and, 94
Conger, Patrick, 77, 108
Congress, U.S.
    act of, creating park, 60–61, 64–65, 74, 110, 289n9
    appropriations by, 111, 116, 121, 174, 225
    and Greater Yellowstone Ecosystem, 203, 205
    and park police force, 108, 111
    and wildlife protection (Lacey) act, 121
Congressional Research Service (CRS), 205
conservation biology, 218–19
conservation movement
    "conservation" vs. "preservation," 200–201
    husbandry-oriented approach, 154, 314n58
    the military and, 110, 113
    and park policy, 75–76, 100, 108–11
    professionalized, 157
    rise of environmentalism, 17, 167
    sportsmen and, 75–76, 78, 110, 119, 159
    vs. tourism, 128–29, 182, 183
    value of Yellowstone in, 315n60
    and water resources, 197, 199
    and wildlife, 121 (*see also* wildlife management)
    See also ecology; historic preservation
Continental Divide, 32
Cook, Charles, 41, 51, 59, 63
Cooke, Jay, 59–60, 93
Cooke City, Mont., 40, 93, 95, 116
Cooper Ornithological Club, 159
Cottam, Clarence, 168
cougars (mountain lions), 82, 87, 236

vegetation consumed by, 47–48, 83, 152, 228–30
winterkill, 124, 154, 223
Elk River, 31
Emigrant, Mont., 41, 68, 69
Endangered Species Act (1973), 188, 206, 224, 241
England, and ownership of Yellowstone, 32
environmental impact statement (EIS), 189. *See also* conservation movement
epidemics. *See* disease
Euramericans
  arrival of, 6–7, 19, 20, 23
  exploration by, 33
  and ownership of Yellowstone, 32
Evanoff, Jim, *243*
Everts, Truman, 52, 283*n*7

Farnsworth, Frances Joyce, 132
Ferris, Warren Angus, 39
Finley, Mike, 214, *243*, 257
fire
  anthropogenic (human-caused), 28, 29
  ecological effect of, 82, 233, 240
  federal government involved in fighting, 127
  fire management policy, 196, 208, 237–41, 292*n*2
  fire-return intervals, 28, 228, 237, 278*n*40
  Indian use of, 11, 26–29, 240
  as land or wildlife management tool, 11, 26–27, 172, 237, 241
  1988, 2, 28, 104, 182, 223, 237–41, 250–51, 293*n*2
Firehole River, 39, 56, 63, 86–87, 146, *184*
"Firehole Village" proposed, 190

Fish and Wildlife Service, U.S., 189
Fish Commission, U.S., 146
fishing, 146–47, 253–54
  "barren" waters, 86–87
  fish hatcheries, 87, 146, 196
  nonnative species introduced, 166, 219, 253
  overfishing, 172
  restrictions on, 190, 253–54
  tourism and, 166–67, 251
Fishing Bridge, 11, 181, 187, *188*, 189–90
Fitzpatrick, Thomas, 37
Flathead Indians, 26
Flores, Dan, 215
Folsom, David, and Folsom-Cook-Peterson expedition, 41, 51, 59
Folsom points, 7. *See also* projectile points
forensic science, 8–9
Forest and Stream magazine, 75, 95, 111, 121, 198, 199, 202
Forest Service, U.S., 123, 202, 215, 292*n*2
  created, 200
  coordination of, with other agencies, 206, 208
Fort Ellis (Mont.), 68
Fort Yellowstone, 112, 113–14, 134, 139
Fountain Hotel, 142, 178, 181
France, annexation of Yellowstone by, 32
fur trade, 23, 33, 34, 39, 49–50. *See also* hunting and trapping

Gabrielson, Ira, 168
Gallatin Range, 21
Gallatin River, 37, 198
garbage dumps, 85–86, 145, 156, 164, 281*n*36
  closed, 220, 241
  debate over, 194–96